IMAGES
of America

CLEBURNE COUNTY

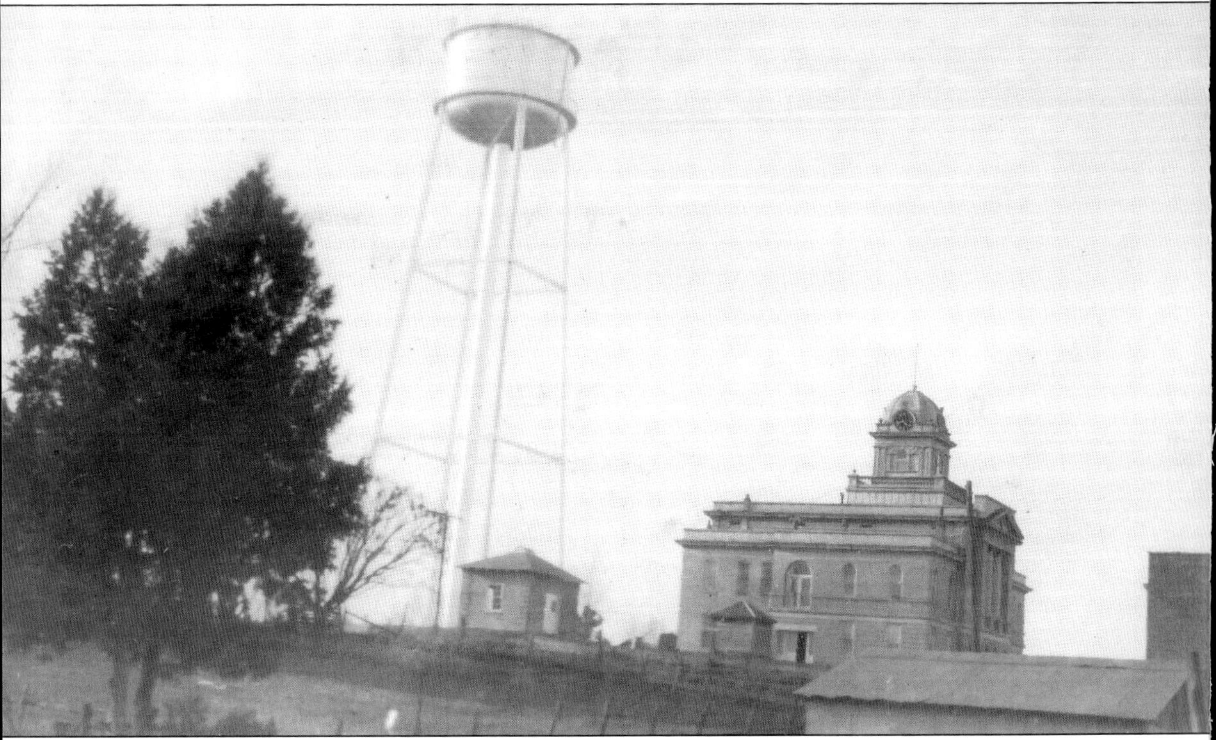

The Cleburne County Courthouse. The tall, domed structure in this photograph is the Cleburne County Courthouse in Heflin. To the left of the courthouse is a water tower and pump house. Judging by the clock on the dome, the photograph was taken about 3:45 in the afternoon in the mid-1930s. Vickery and Burns Streets intersect in the bottom right of the photograph behind the building in the foreground. (Courtesy Pete Wright.)

On the Cover: The Burgess Home in Edwardsville. The Burgess family was one of the founding families in Edwardsville and built this large three-story home. This photograph was taken during a family reunion. The home later burned. (Courtesy Charlotte Funderburk.)

IMAGES
of America

CLEBURNE COUNTY

Wayne Ruple

ARCADIA
PUBLISHING

ISBN 978-0-7385-8645-8

Published by Arcadia Publishing
Charleston, South Carolina

Printed in the United States of America

Library of Congress Control Number: 2010925043

For all general information, please contact Arcadia Publishing:
Telephone 843-853-2070
Fax 843-853-0044
E-mail sales@arcadiapublishing.com
For customer service and orders:
Toll-Free 1-888-313-2665

Visit us on the Internet at www.arcadiapublishing.com

Dedicated to the citizens of Cleburne County, who by living here have, in their own way, continued to make and write their own history.

Contents

ACKNOWLEDGMENTS

The author would like to thank the East Alabama History Museum, the Cleburne County Historical Society, and the Fruithurst Winery for their contributions and assistance along with that of Margaret Voss Pope, Pete Wright, Vertie Walker, Leesa Cheatwood, Charlotte Funderburk, Levis Boyd, Lorraine Watson, Jimmy Price, Johnny Laminack, Shannon Tucker, Patsy Smith, Mike Pollard, Carolyn Parker, Jane Beam, Suzanne Payne, Miriam Turner, Carol Sanders, Francis Whited, Linda Ayers, Lucile Jacobs, Christine Cantrell, the Lucile Morgan Public Library, and the Cleburne County Extension Office.

Introduction

Named for Irish-born Confederate general Patrick R. Cleburne, killed at the Battle of Franklin, Cleburne County was formally established in November 1866, when the state of Alabama carved it out of Benton County, which had included today's Cleburne, Calhoun, Talladega, and Randolph Counties. An 1855 census showed a population of 20,010 in Benton County.

Before white men came into Cleburne County from Georgia and the Carolinas, Native Americans lived in the territory, and the boundary for the Upper Creek and Cherokee Indians ran through a portion of the county. Oakfuskee, considered the largest community of the Creek Confederacy, was located on the Tallapoosa River in Cleburne County. Two other large Creek towns in Cleburne County were Niufaka and Atchinalgi along the Tallapoosa River. Atchinalgi was destroyed during the Creek War of 1813.

The oldest white settlement in the county was Ranburne. Early settler Thomas Blake came to the area in 1825 with a number of slaves and set about farming. Settlers traveling the McIntosh Trail established the communities of Muscadine, Palestine, Bordens Mill, Kemps Creek, and Arbacoochee. Families included Towsends, Bowlins, Parkers, Roberts, Steeds, Wheelers, and Bordens.

In 1832, a new treaty opened up much of the former Native American land for settlement, and efforts were made to remove the Native Americans from the area in 1838. Prior to the 1849 California Gold Rush, several eastern Alabama counties had yielded some 50,000 ounces of gold. From 1838 to 1860, coins were minted at the U.S. Mint in Dahlonega, Georgia, from Alabama gold. One of those early gold mining towns was Arbacoochee, located in Cleburne County and considered the gold center of the nation in 1840. It produced over $5 million in gold. Historian George Yarbrough described the Arbacoochee Mine as "probably the most profitable gold mine in Alabama's history," and it was here that Alabama gold was first discovered in 1832. In Cleburne County, gold was found from Muscadine on the northeastern side southward into Coosa County. Arbacoochee was among about 100 mining towns in Alabama located in or near the Upper Gold Belt, or Dahlonega Belt, which ran from northern Georgia down into Alabama.

Arbacoochee was by some accounts Alabama's biggest town in 1845, with a population of around 5,000, five saloons, a school, two churches, two hotels, two mining supply stores, a fire department, a race track, and over 100 homes and tents. But the rush to California's goldfields left Arbacoochee a ghost town by 1849. Some interest in gold-mining was reignited in 1853, when some Cornish miners from Ducktown, Tennessee, found gold while searching for copper. As late as the 1930s, gold-panning provided a livelihood for local residents. Overall, nearly 30,000 ounces of gold were uncovered in Cleburne County. Deposits of copper and mica also drew miners to the county's southern half.

But miners were not the only fortune seekers to Cleburne County. In the late 1800s, settlers were attracted to the north Cleburne County community of Zidonia, where they set about building a town and renamed it Fruithurst. The town became internationally known for its wines and as having one of the finest hotels in the South. Notable Fruithurst leaders included Ernest Rudolph

Carlson and George Washington Morris. Born in Sweden, Carlson was president and manager of the Fruithurst Winery, a councilman, and later the mayor of Fruithurst.

George Morris came from Michigan by way of Minnesota where he had run a lumber business before being named director of the Fruithurst Vineyard and Product Company. He also had interest in the Reliance Gold Mining Company of Washington, D.C., which operated in Cleburne County along the Tallapoosa River. Both Carlson and Morris served as councilmen, as Fruithurst's mayor, and as members of the Cleburne County Democratic Executive Committee.

Gradually, the market for wines and grapes soured, and a harsh winter and plant diseases killed the vines. There were also rumors of mismanagement, and in the end, in April 1898, the C. S. Curtiss Company of New York paid $15,455 for the town and all of the real estate (including the famous hotel) belonging to the Alabama Fruit Growing and Winery Association.

The county, like the nation, was split in its loyalties during the Civil War, with sharp divisions between those living in the northern end of the county and those in the southern end. Some historians estimate there were less than 100 slaves in the whole county, as there were few slave owners. The Stone Hill community suffered some Union raids, but most of the county saw no conflict.

In 1867, Cleburne County had its first election. The South Carolina–born Edwards brothers, who had arrived in Cane Creek in 1835, donated land on which to build a courthouse. The first court was held the following year in the rough log structure, which had a jail, four corner offices, and one large room. Meanwhile, Edwardsville was developing around it. In 1905, following efforts to move the county seat from Edwardsville to Heflin, a county-wide election was held, and Heflin won by a small majority. The residents of Edwardsville did not give up without a fight, and a long legal battle followed, with the Alabama Supreme Court ruling in 1906 to move the courthouse to Heflin. The following year, construction began on a new facility. The cornerstone was laid on July 4, 1907, with an estimated 3,000 attending the ceremony.

All across Cleburne County, a number of communities had sprung up, many with little one-room schools that sometimes served both as school and church. One of these locales was Borden Springs, situated at the far northern end of Cleburne County. Just before 1900, a group of 12 men from Atlanta, Newnan, and Carrollton, Georgia, had formed the Borden-Wheeler Company and purchased land from the Wheeler family on which a mineral spring was located. The group purchased the old Fruithurst Inn and employed the J. C. Bass Company of Carrollton, Georgia, to take it apart, piece by piece, and carry it 16 miles over a mountain with mules and wagons and reassemble it as the Borden-Wheeler Hotel.

The finished product consisted of 125 rooms with nine concert pianos, running hot and cold water, a large outdoor swimming pool, electricity, a dance pavilion, and a 14-hole golf course. Dotting this display of opulence were a number of guest cottages with maid service, running water, and electric lights. The Borden-Wheeler Hotel became a well-known resort; the properties of the mineral water were promoted as being "a close second to Ponce de Leon's famed Fountain of Youth." The facility offered every appointment possible and employed a staff of 40, but the rates of $15 per week or $50 per month (equivalent to $314 and $1,040 today) were not high enough to keep the operation profitable, and soon it was up for sale. In 1935, after numerous changes of ownership, a fire swept through the hotel and 20 of its cottages.

The following year, petitioned by local officials, Pres. Franklin D. Roosevelt established the Talladega National Forest, which included almost all the western half of the county. Before this, the farmers had suffered through the Depression, and farm and forest lands in the county were worn out and unproductive. The U.S. government purchased land from individuals and lumber companies for an appraised value. This was the beginning of the Talladega National Forest lands in Cleburne County.

In June 1933, employees of the Civilian Conservation Corps began working to build a road along the top of Cheaha Mountain and develop Mount Cheaha State Park. The CCC built roads, lodges, cottages, cabins, picnic shelters, hiking trails, swimming areas, lakes, and beaches that now form the basis of the present-day park. Cheaha State Park Observation Tower is now on the Alabama Register of Landmarks and Heritage.

Among the county's other small communities was Sugar Hill, just south of Heflin, and Belltown along the Tallapoosa River. Abernathy was settled in 1855. Macedonia Baptist Church, built in the 1880s and nearly 130 years old today, continues to be the center of life in the Macedonia community. Hopewell was a thriving place in the 1890s, as money was generated by timber harvesting and transport.

The beauty of Cleburne County drew national attention in January 1961, when Hollywood actress and Oscar winner Susan Hayward and her husband, F. Easton Chalkley of Carrollton, Georgia, purchased property along the Tallapoosa River. The couple bought the W. J. Cole home and 600 acres of land and called their new ranch Chalmar. They remodeled the house originally built in 1912 by W. O. Owen, built a new air-conditioned barn, renovated a small outbuilding for a studio, and brought in 200 to 300 cows and a prized $30,000 polled Hereford bull.

Not until the 1950s did the county and the city of Heflin began to really see economic growth. Originally the city was known as a cotton center; cotton farmers throughout the county brought their bales into town for shipment by train. In the 1950s and 1960s, however, industries began moving into Heflin, including the Heflin Chenille Manufacturing Corporation, Moore Business Forms, Inc., Dixie Mines, Inc., and Swell Manufacturing Company.

Once Interstate 20 was completed through the county, however, it diverted most of the interstate traffic off of U.S. Highway 78, and the cities of Heflin, Edwardsville, and Fruithurst saw business decline. The commercial development of nearby Oxford in Calhoun County also attracted shoppers, and many Cleburne County merchants were forced to shut their doors. Of the companies locating in Heflin in the 1950s and 1960s, only Swell Manufacturing Company remains in operation today. Most Cleburne County residents commute outside the county to work; the county's cities and towns are now commonly considered bedroom communities for Oxford and Anniston, Alabama, and west metropolitan Atlanta, Georgia.

One

Fruithurst
Wine Capital of the South

Just 30 years after the Civil War, a group of Northern investors calling themselves the Alabama Fruit Growers and Winery Association descended on the small Cleburne County community of Zidonia, now known as Fruithurst, and set about buying properties for what they dreamed would become the world's second-best vineyards. Garrett Ryckman of Brocton Wine Cellars in the New York state was among the investors. Clearing of the land for the vineyards began in 1895 under the direction of supervisor C. W. Farcist. "Promoters and investors began to arrive so fast during this time that homes could not be constructed rapidly enough to meet the demand, and many of these new arrivals had to be 'put up' as boarders," writes Virginia Voss Pope in *Fruithurst, Alabama's Vineyard Village*. The promoters planned the entire layout of the city down to the smallest detail, including the erection of the town's flagpole. And right behind the flagpole came the magnificent Fruithurst Inn, a showplace for the whole town and a masterpiece of Victorian architecture built in the 1890s at a cost of $40,000 that was said to be one of the finest in the South. International cuisine and gourmet delicacies were served in its dining rooms.

By 1898, Fruithurst was a real boomtown made up of 800 residents from around the nation and Europe. "It was meticulously laid out into gardens, parks, and an experiment station," writes Pope. Viticulturists included E. B. Hammitt, G. W. Morris, and numerous others, corporate and independent. Several packinghouses were built to handle the 3,000 acres of grapes. Pickers were paid 30¢ per day. Over 100 varieties of grapes were grown in Fruithurst, and yields were staggering; one vineyard produced 8,324 pounds of grapes in a single year. In 1898, a collective 23,000 gallons were produced by five wineries. A French winemaker called the product "the best wine [I have] seen in the South." However, the wine market slumped, native vine diseases attacked the more familiar northern varieties, and a severely cold winter and national Prohibition helped close the wineries by 1919.

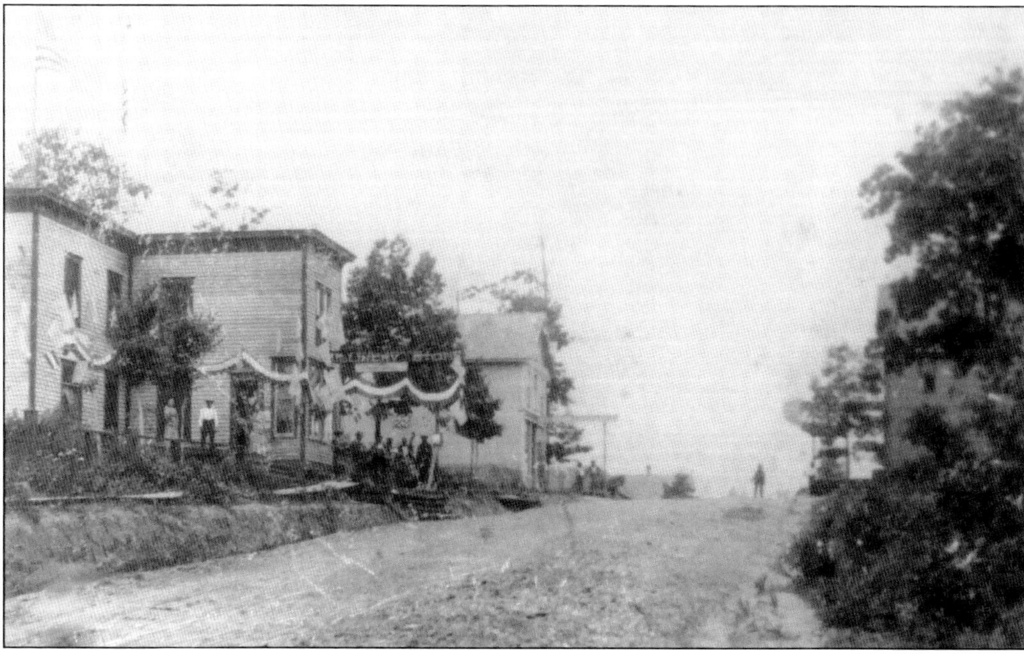

Fruithurst, Main Street, 1909. Here is Main Street (now U.S. Highway 78) looking eastward when it was the old public road from Talladega, Alabama, to Atlanta, Georgia. A majority of the businesses were located along this road, and as the years passed, more and more businesses located along the street. It would later become the main highway between Birmingham, Alabama, and Atlanta, Georgia. (Courtesy Virginia Pope.)

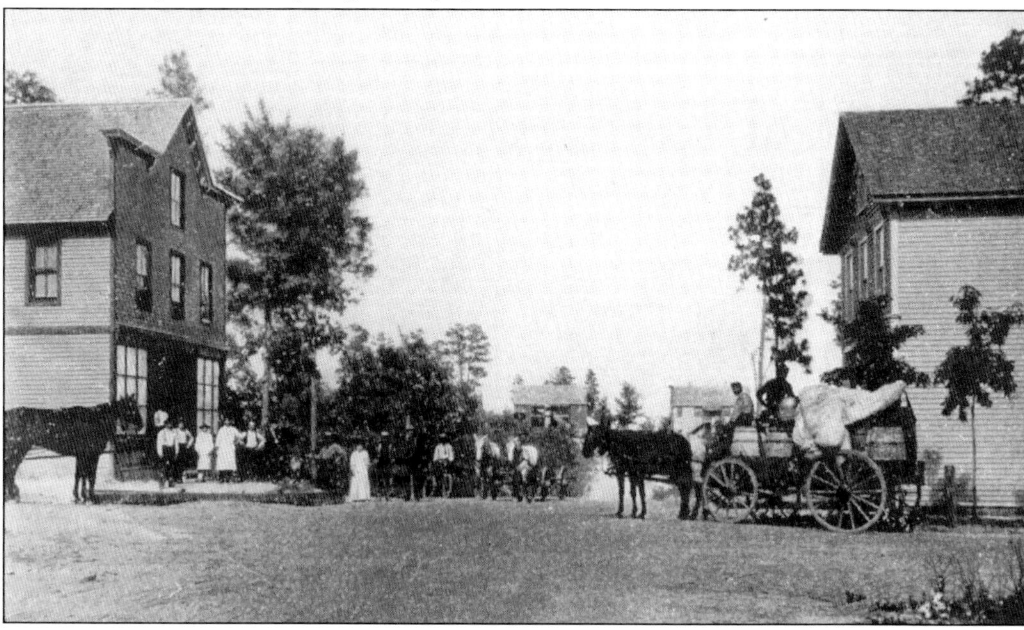

La Vinta Avenue, Fruithurst. This was the view of La Vinta Avenue looking east from Vinona Street. Most of the streets and avenues in Fruithurst have names suggestive of wine and wineries. The town itself was laid out in plots rather than blocks, and land purchasers received a warranty deed, perfect title, and abstract. (Courtesy Virginia Pope.)

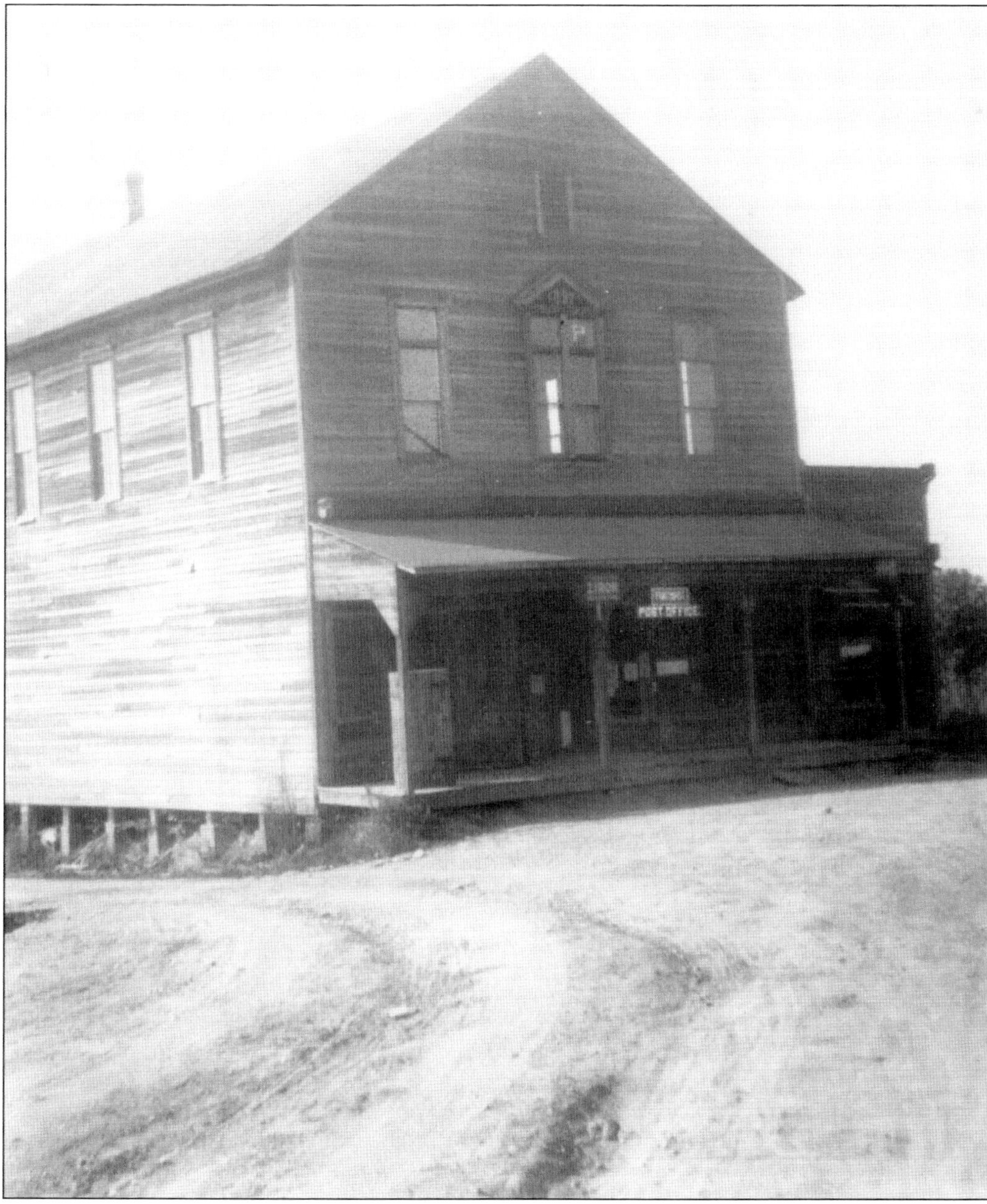

"K. P. HALL," FRUITHURST, 1897. Known locally as the "K. P. Hall," this was the meeting place for the Knights of Pythias, an international non-sectarian fraternal order established in 1864 in Washington, D.C. Several leading men of Fruithurst were members of Lodge No. 157, including Ernest Carlson, president and manager of the Fruithurst Winery Company, and George Morris, the director of Fruithurst Winery Company. The Order of Knights of Pythias was established by Justus H. Rathbone and was the first fraternal order to be chartered by an act of Congress. Today its members are dedicated to universal peace, and Pythians are pledged to the promotion of understanding among men of goodwill as the surest means of attaining this goal. According to their Web site, "The distinguishing principles of the Order of Knights of Pythias are Friendship, Charity, and Benevolence." (Courtesy Virginia Pope.)

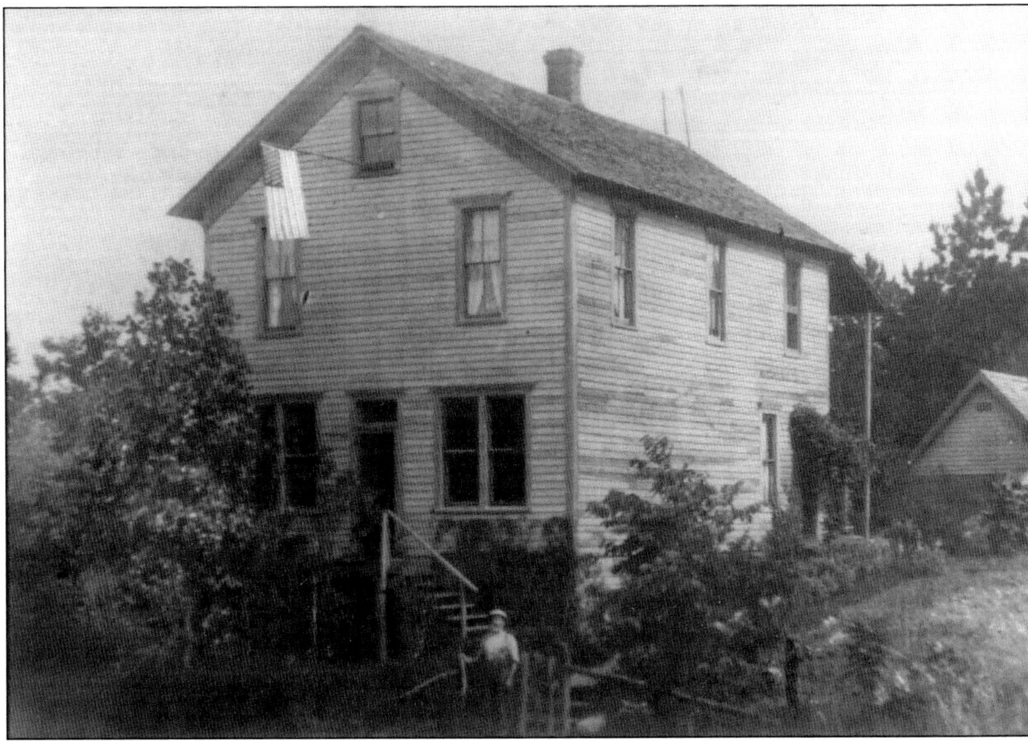

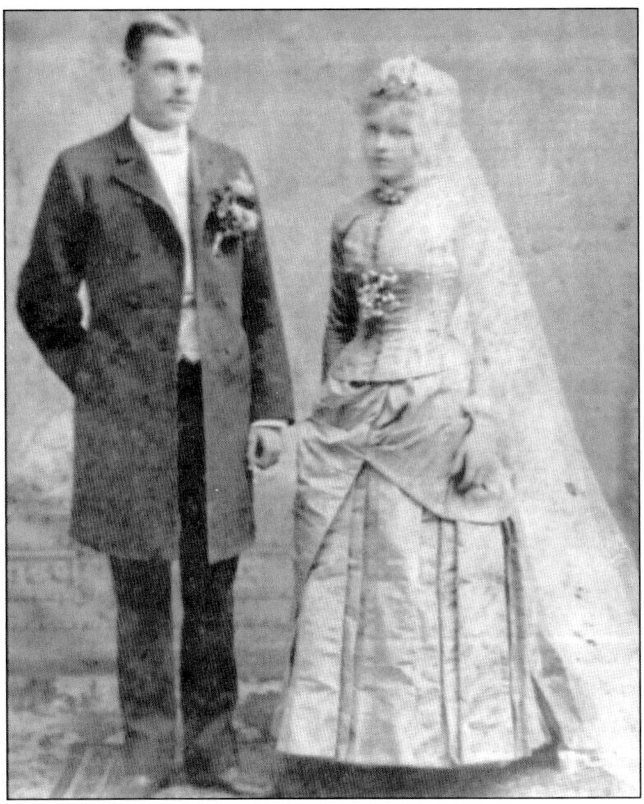

Olson's Bakery, Fruithurst, 1895. Olson's Bakery was one of about 20 businesses located in Fruithurst in 1895. On March 19, 1925, the *Cleburne News* reported the death of Gus Olson, a member of one of Fruithurst's pioneer families. He had come from Sweden 30 years earlier. He was survived by a sister and brother, both of whom had remained in Sweden. (Courtesy Virginia Pope.)

Prominent Residents. John Gustaf Granath was born in Vernamo, Sweden, in 1860. He married Sophia Johnson on September 27, 1885, in New York. The couple moved to Atlanta, Georgia, where Granath worked for a tailor. When his employer dissolved the business, the Granaths became one of the first couples to move to Fruithurst. (Courtesy Shannon Tucker.)

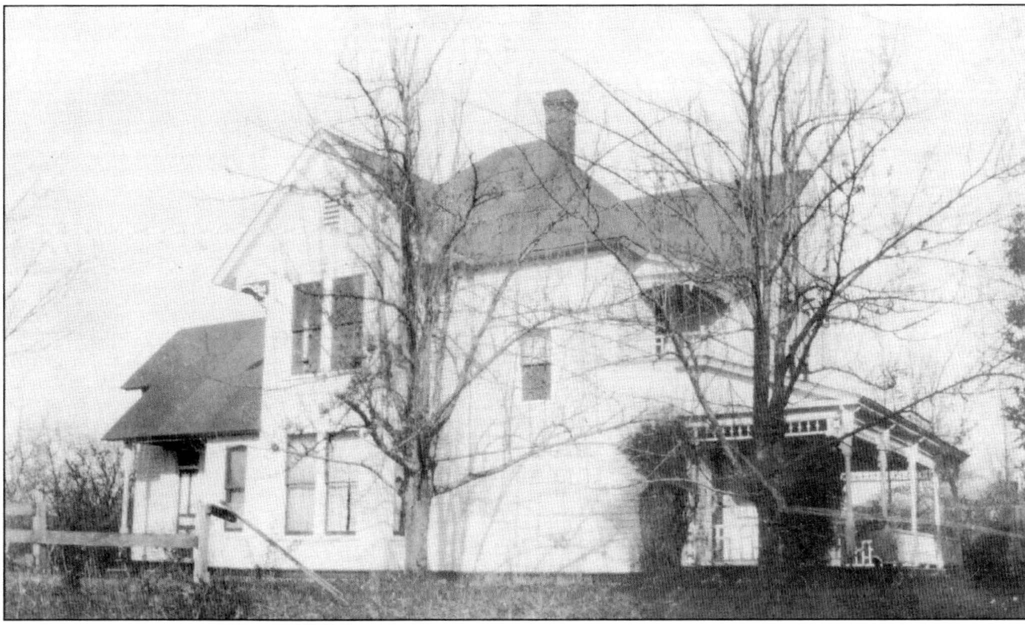

GRANVILLA, FRUITHURST. Located at 51 First Street West, Granvilla was the Granath family's home. John and Sophia raised four children here. The home later became a bed-and-breakfast inn featuring a pool and cozy rooms, but it is now a private home. (Courtesy Shannon Tucker.)

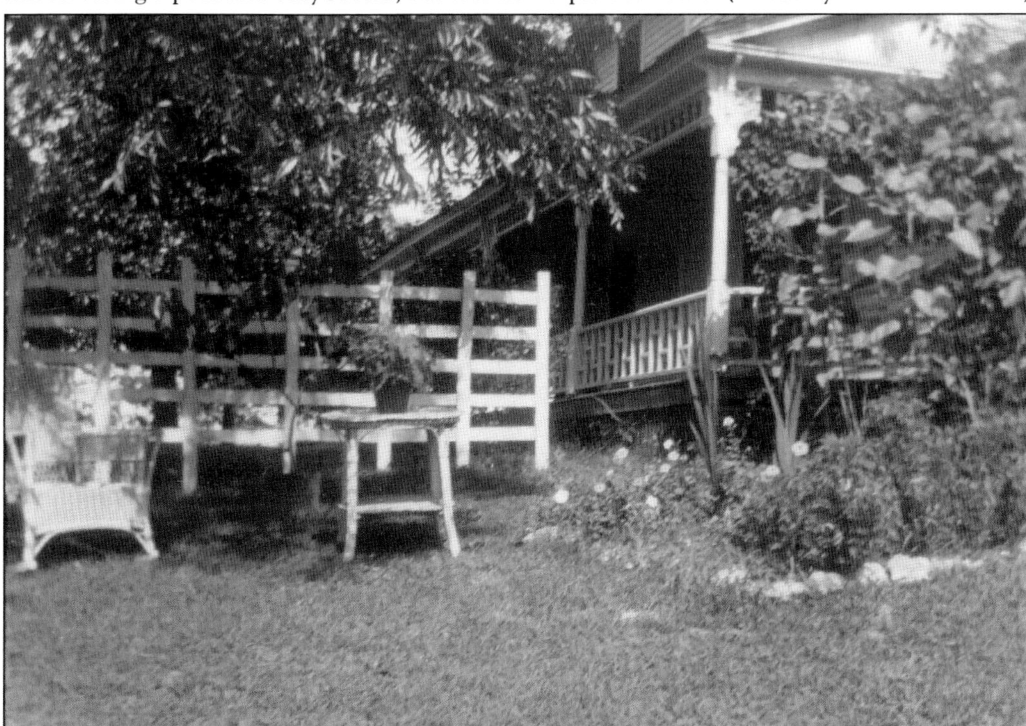

GARDEN SPOT. The backyard was Granvilla's relaxing garden spot. Many cool summer afternoons were spent here entertaining friends and enjoying what had been advertised as "The Healthiest Spot in the United States." (Courtesy Shannon Tucker.)

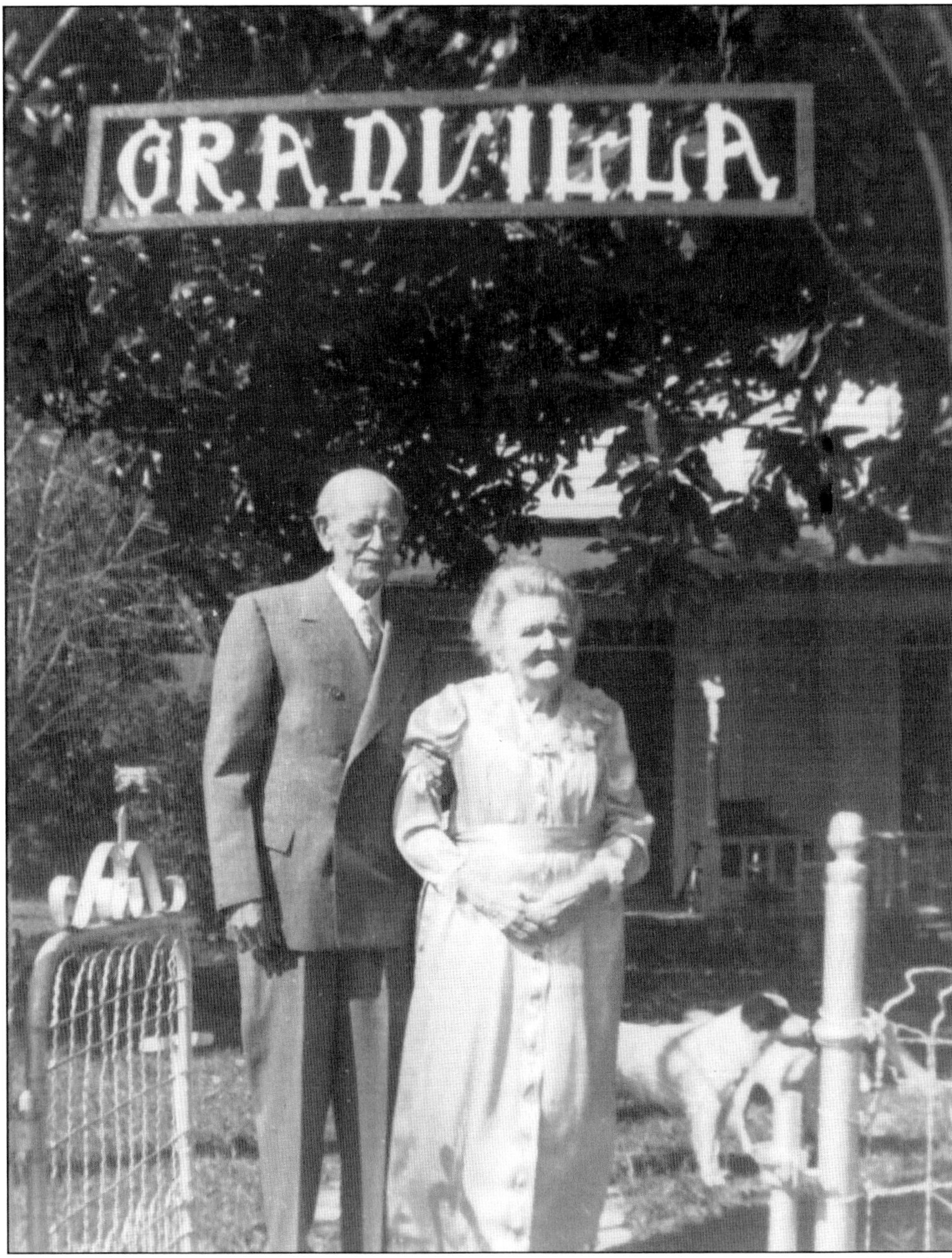

WEDDING ANNIVERSARY. The Granaths stand under the grand arch at their home, Granvilla, on their 68th wedding anniversary, September 27, 1953. The motto for their home was, "May it be gazed on by all for many, many moons. When you enter here, hope is revived and rest assured." The Granaths were among several Scandinavians who joined the colony and brought their talents and occupations to Fruithurst in hopes of brighter futures. The couple was well known throughout Cleburne County. Granath used his talents as a tailor to assist in outfitting local members of the Red Cross. In a March/April 1943 issue of the *Cleburne News*, the local Red Cross chapter thanked him for his work and saluted him as "one who embodies the spirit of the organization." (Courtesy Shannon Tucker.)

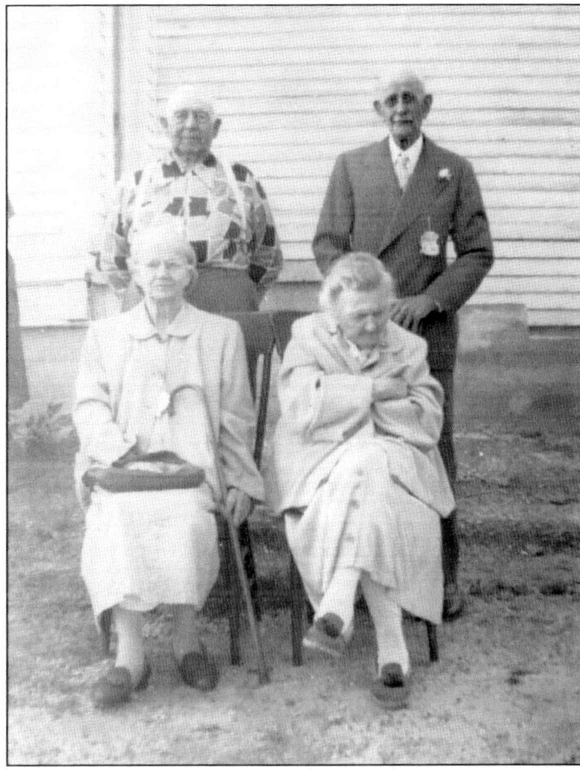

Oldest Couples in Fruithurst. The oldest couples in Fruithurst were recognized on May 6, 1954. They were (left) Mr. and Mrs. A. J. Kerr Sr. and (right) John and Sophia Granath. The Granaths were the older of the two couples. John Granath was 94 years old, and his wife, Sophia, was 91 years old. (Courtesy Shannon Tucker.)

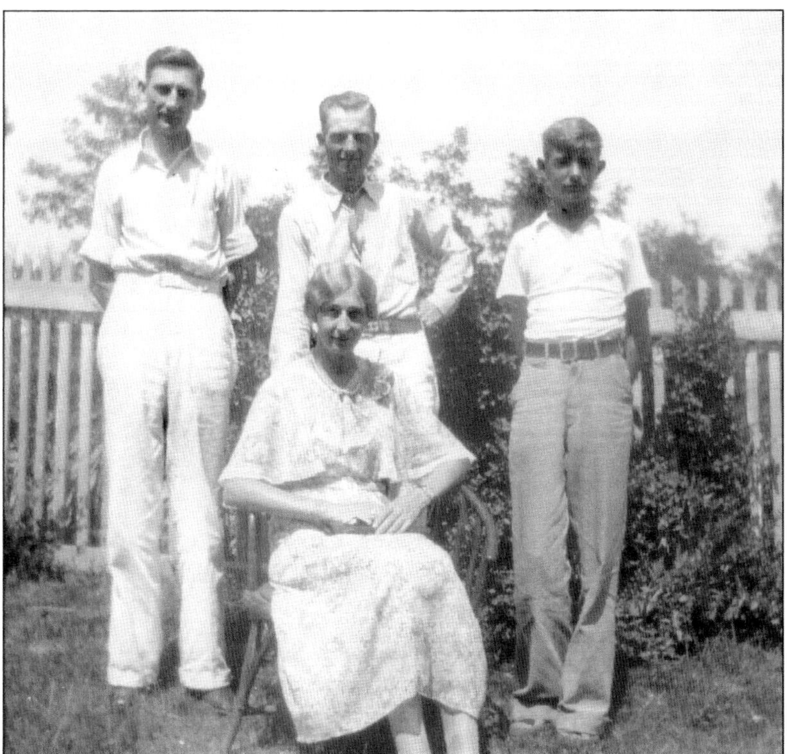

The Granath Children. Here are the four Granath children in September 1939. From left to right, the boys are Arvid, Conrad, and Iver. Their sister is Ethel. Arvid later moved to East Point, Georgia. Iver attended school in Georgia and was a member of the class of 1923 at Georgia Tech, where he cowrote the alma mater and several other famous Georgia Tech songs. (Courtesy Shannon Tucker.)

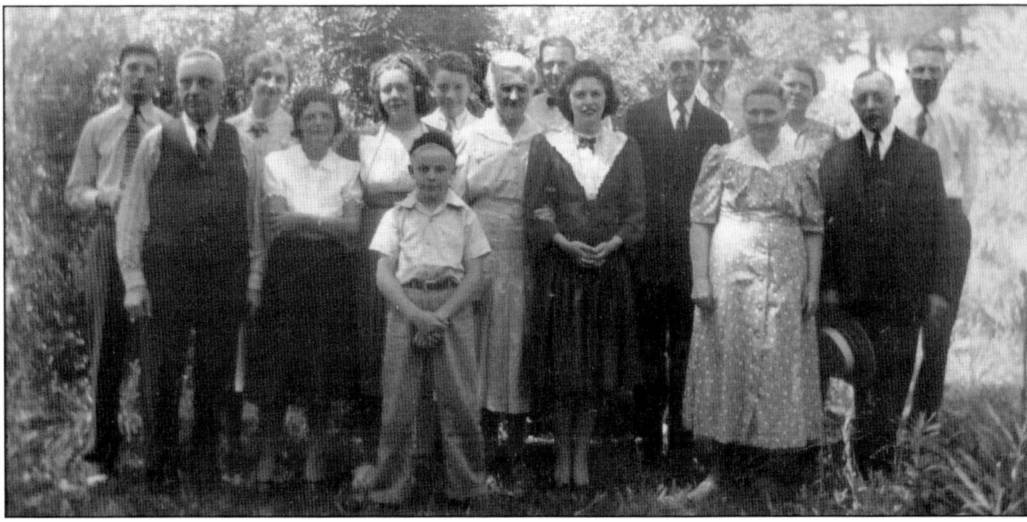

Granath Family Reunion. This photograph is of the Granath family reunion on May 19, 1941. The reunion included those family members who had lived in the Fruithurst colony as well as relatives from other regions of the country. (Courtesy Shannon Tucker.)

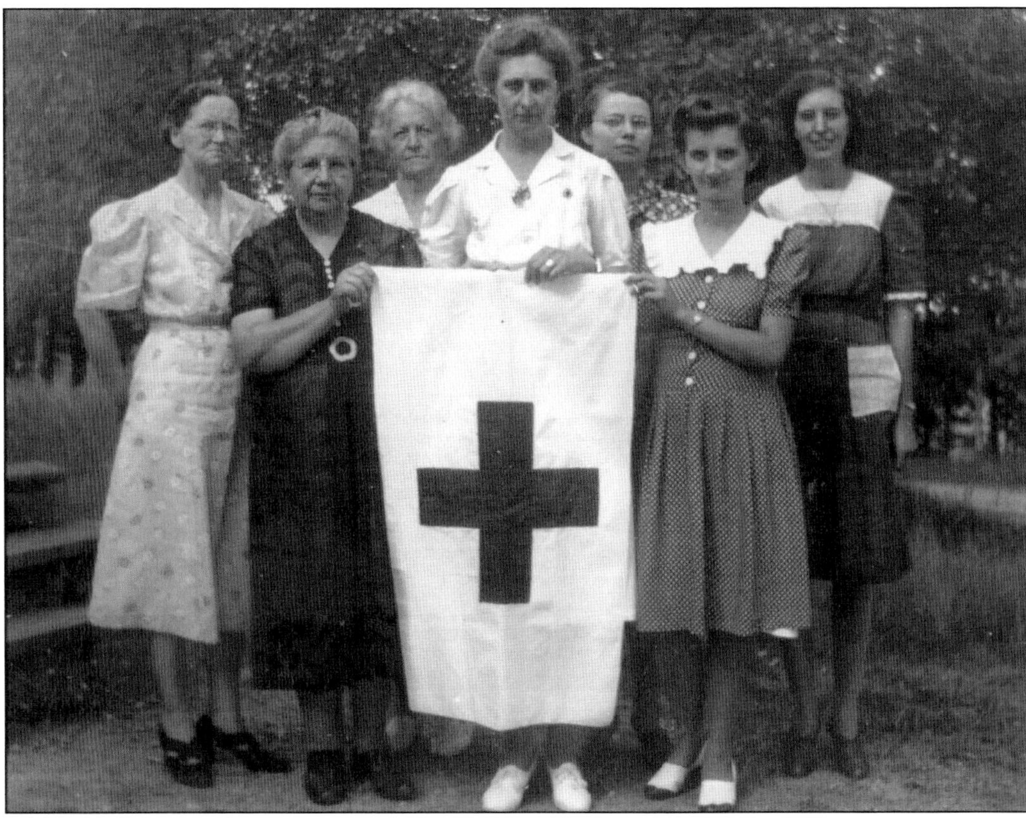

Home Nursing Class Graduates. The home-nursing class of Fruithurst graduated seven women in June 1942. From left to right, they are Mrs. A. B. Bennett, Mrs. Charles Simon, Mrs. E. R. Carlson, Ethel Granath, Mrs. D. Garner, Mrs. Loval Walker, and Mrs. Varrdy. (Courtesy Shannon Tucker.)

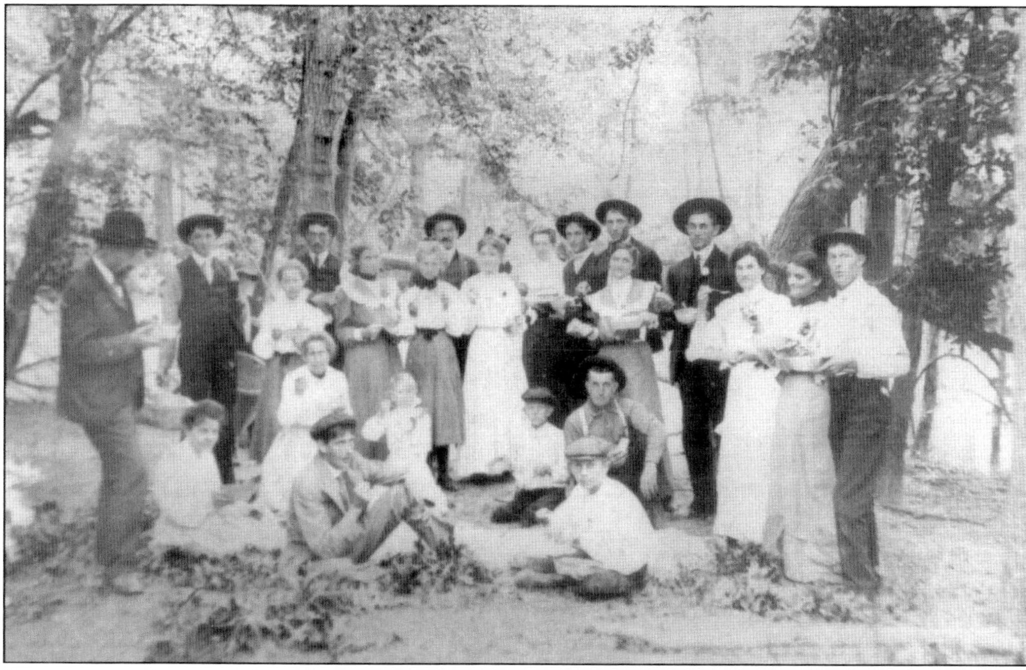

ENJOYING A PICNIC. This photograph shows a group of Fruithurst residents enjoying a picnic in the area. The climate of the region was very conducive to outdoor activities, and the nearby mountains, now part of the Talladega National Forest, were a popular place to gather. (Courtesy Virginia Pope.)

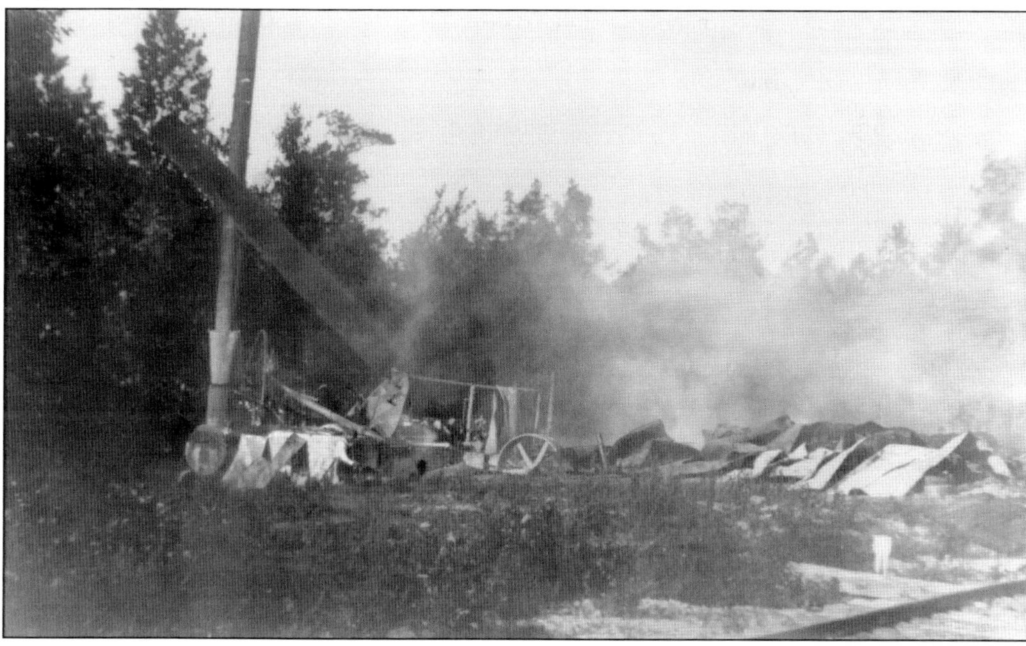

EXCELSIOR FACTORY FIRE. In June 1906, the excelsior factory in Fruithurst burned to the ground due to a fire. This photograph was taken after the fire and shows what little remained of the factory. Excelsior usually consisted of fine wood shavings used for stuffing and packing, particularly around wine bottles. (Courtesy Virginia Pope.)

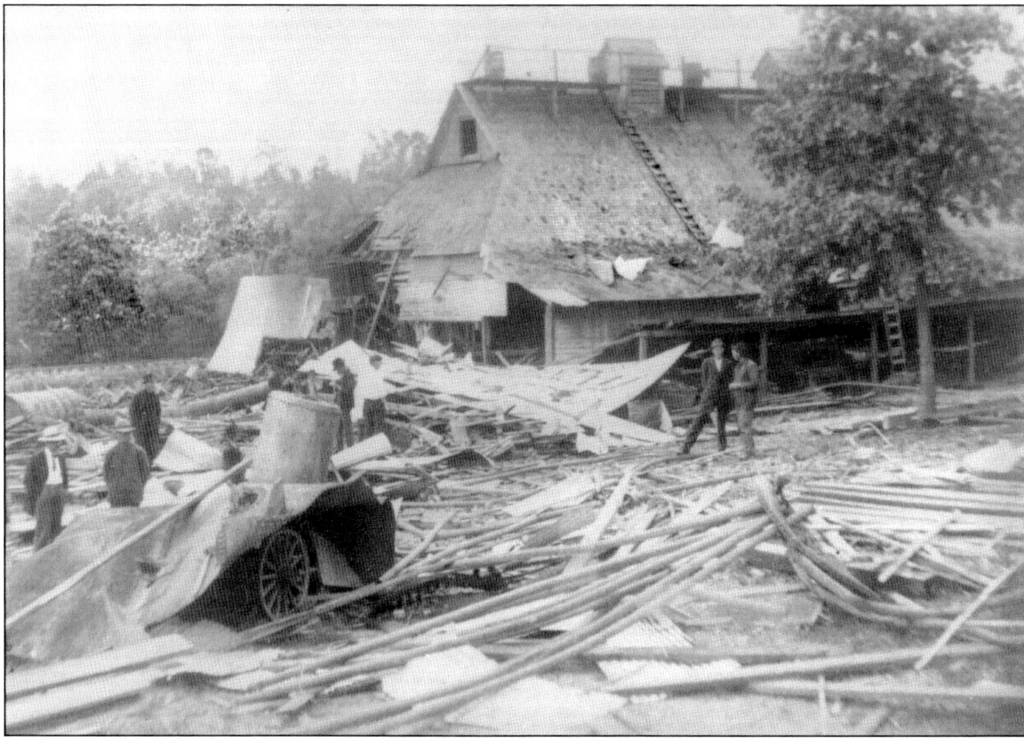

PLANING MILL EXPLOSION. This photograph shows the aftermath of an explosion at the I. J. Grant Planing Mill in Fruithurst. The mill, built in 1898, served as a final processing plant for lumber. No records have been found giving the cause of the explosion, but old newspaper reports across the country reported similar explosions due to the steam boilers used to power the machinery. (Courtesy Virginia Pope.)

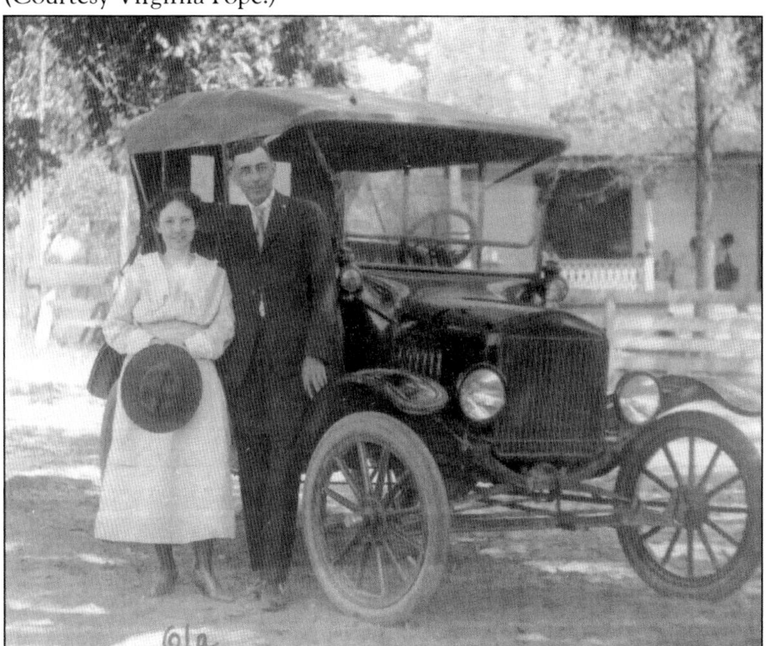

FIRST CAR. Warren Maust was the proud owner of the first car in Fruithurst. In this photograph taken on September 28, 1919, Maust and an unidentified woman stand beside his vehicle. The *Cleburne New Era*, on August 4, 1906, reported "Warren Maust, photographer of Fruithurst, was in town Friday taking scenes for postcards that will be on sale at Coggin's card stand in a few days." (Courtesy Virginia Pope.)

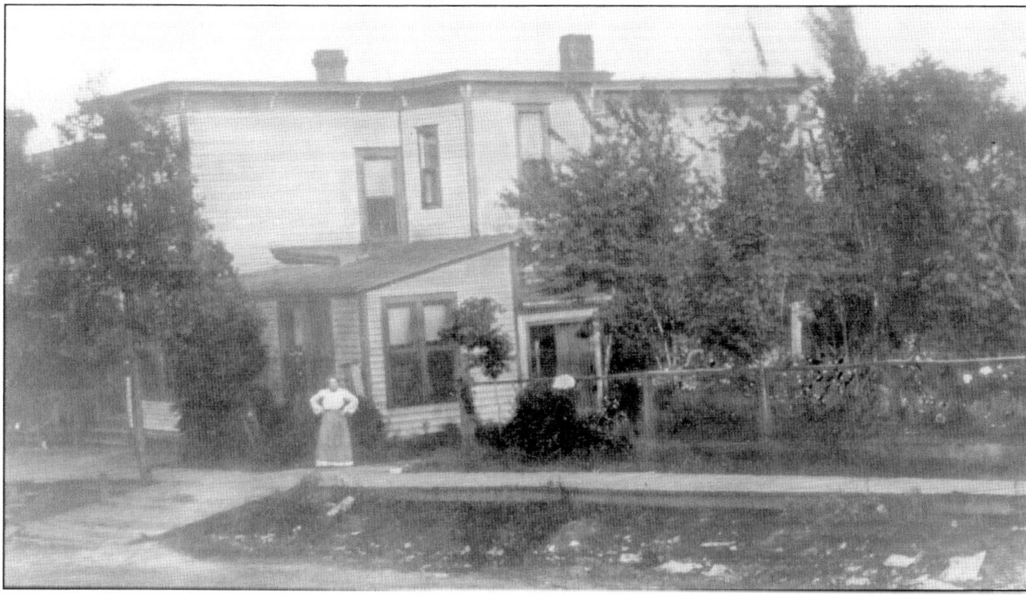

Fruithurst Post Office. Located on Main Street, Fruithurst's post office stood across from Voss Grocery. In this 1906 photograph, a woman stands outside the building. The post office was attached to a building belonging to the Grizzard family. Prior to being named Fruithurst, the small village and its post office were called Zidonia. (Courtesy Virginia Pope.)

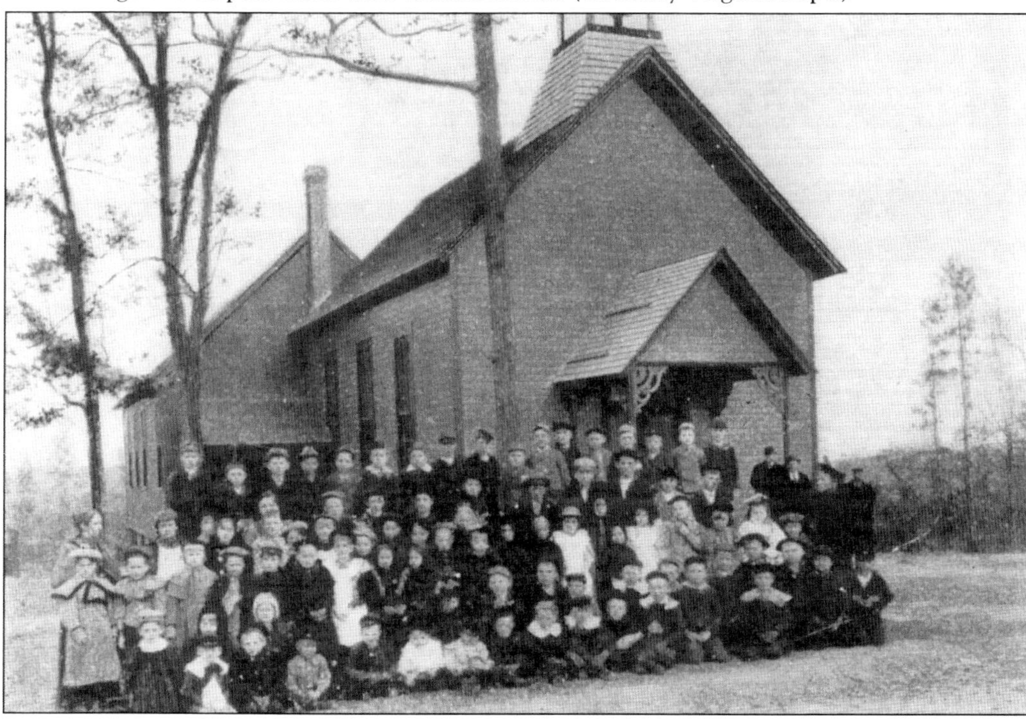

Fruithurst Public School. Fruithurst children were provided a free public school as part of the Cleburne County school system. The school had a total of 106 enrolled pupils. The first structure was a wood-frame building. One of the early principals was Margaret Voss. (Courtesy Fruithurst Winery.)

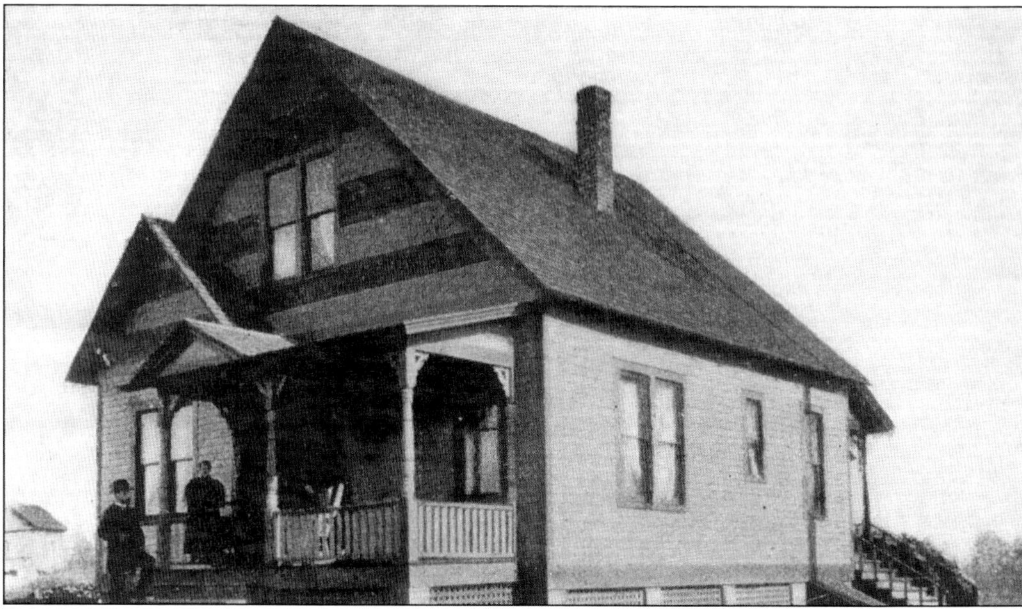

Neff Family Residence. This is a photograph of the Abram Neff family residence on Northeast Avenue. Since many of the settlers in Fruithurst were of Scandinavian descent, their homes reflected this type of architecture. (Courtesy Fruithurst Winery.)

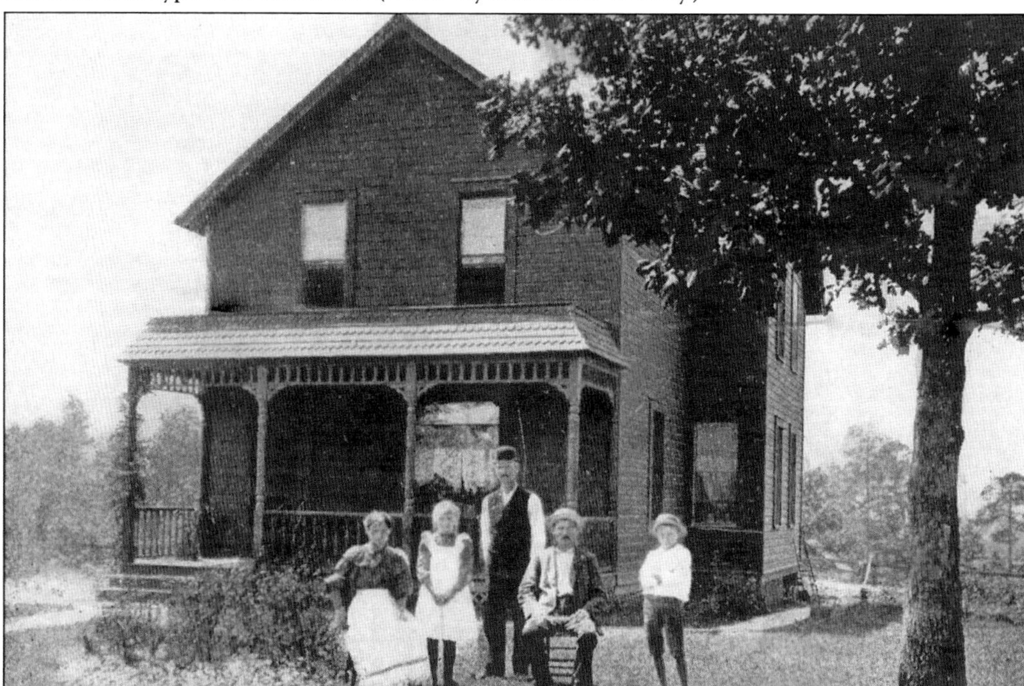

Johnson Family Home. The M. Johnson family lived in this nice two-story house on Vindemia Street. An aggressive advertising and promotional campaign brought individuals and families like the Johnsons to the booming town. At its peak, the town had a bank, barbershop, hardware store, planing mill, laundry, furniture store, pharmacy, livery barn, meat market, grocery, bakery, drugstore, watch repair, and telegraph office. (Courtesy Fruithurst Winery.)

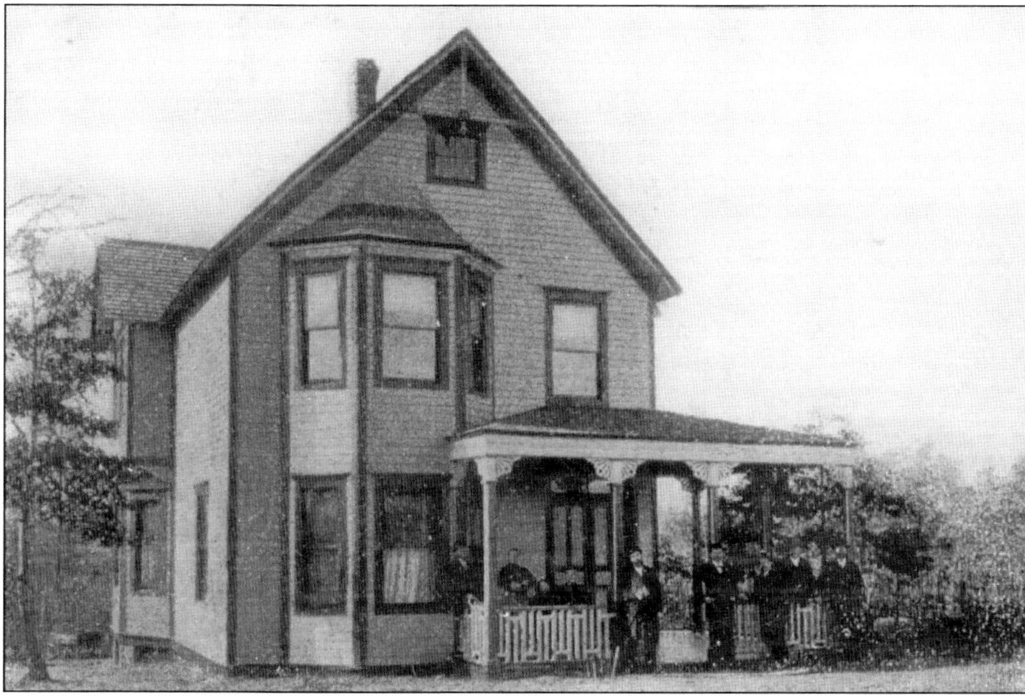

Johnson House. August Johnson's home stood on Villa Vinta Street and fronted West Park. Johnson was involved in an Alabama Supreme Court case in the late 1800s that sought the enforcement of a material man's lien upon his property, a two-story frame building on Lot Nine, Block Five in Fruithurst. The court found in Johnson's favor. (Courtesy Fruithurst Winery.)

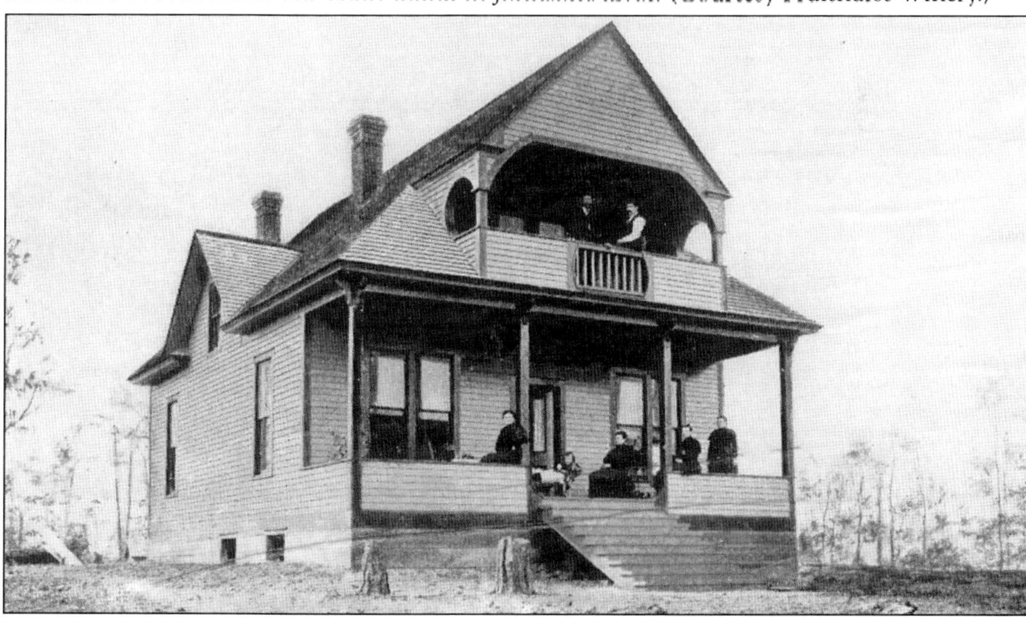

Alexander Residence. The home of L. T. Alexander on Vinegrove Street was among over 150 that made up the settlement. Many of the settlers included Swedes, Danes, and Norwegians as well as "Yankees" from several northern states. The New Yorkers who organized the colony dreamed of developing fruit growing through a cooperative effort. (Courtesy Fruithurst Winery.)

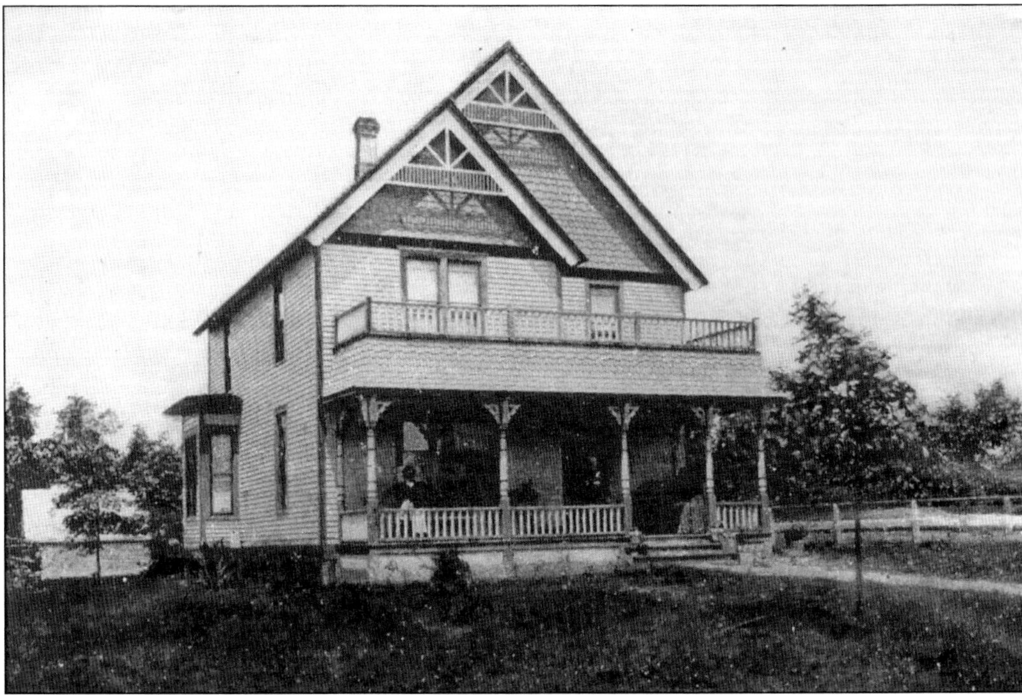

VIEW OF MODEL ORCHARDS. The residence of C. A. Crawford, on Villa Vinta Street, fronted the model orchards of the Fruithurst colony. Among early settlers were C. W. Fox, N. C. Matthews, R. L. Spencer, R. E. Pineo, J. B. Merrill, L. D. Phillips, and W. W. Summerlin, who were all stockholders in the Fruithurst Association. (Courtesy Fruithurst Winery.)

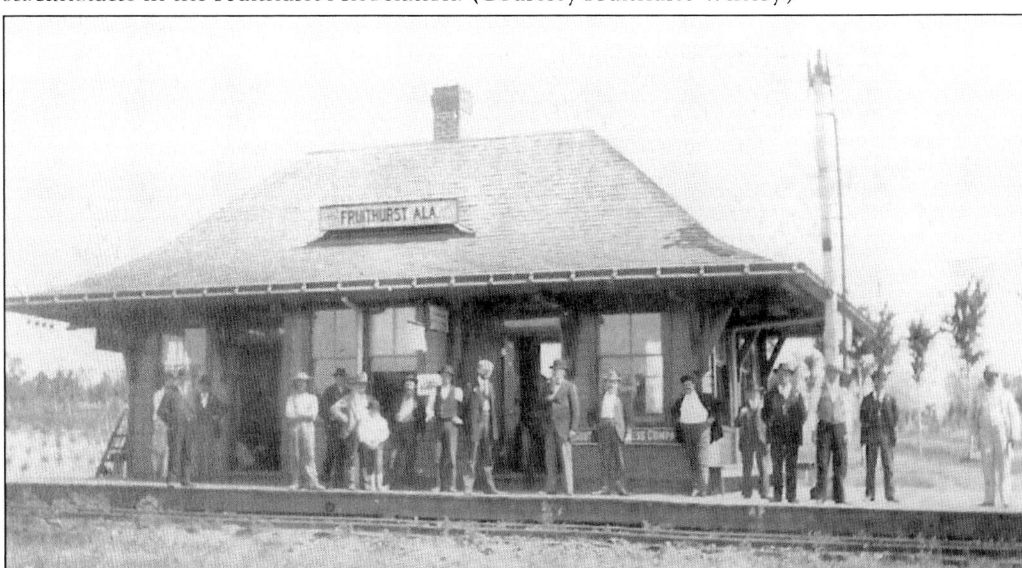

WAITING ON THE TRAIN. This group of men are waiting for the train at the depot in Fruithurst. In the *Annual Report of the Railroad Commission of Alabama* for 1913 and 1914, the Alabama Public Service Commission ordered, on April 8, 1914, that the Southern Railway Commission prepare plans for a passenger station "at the old site where the station was destroyed by fire" and when approved, start construction "without any unnecessary delay." (Courtesy Charlotte Funderburk.)

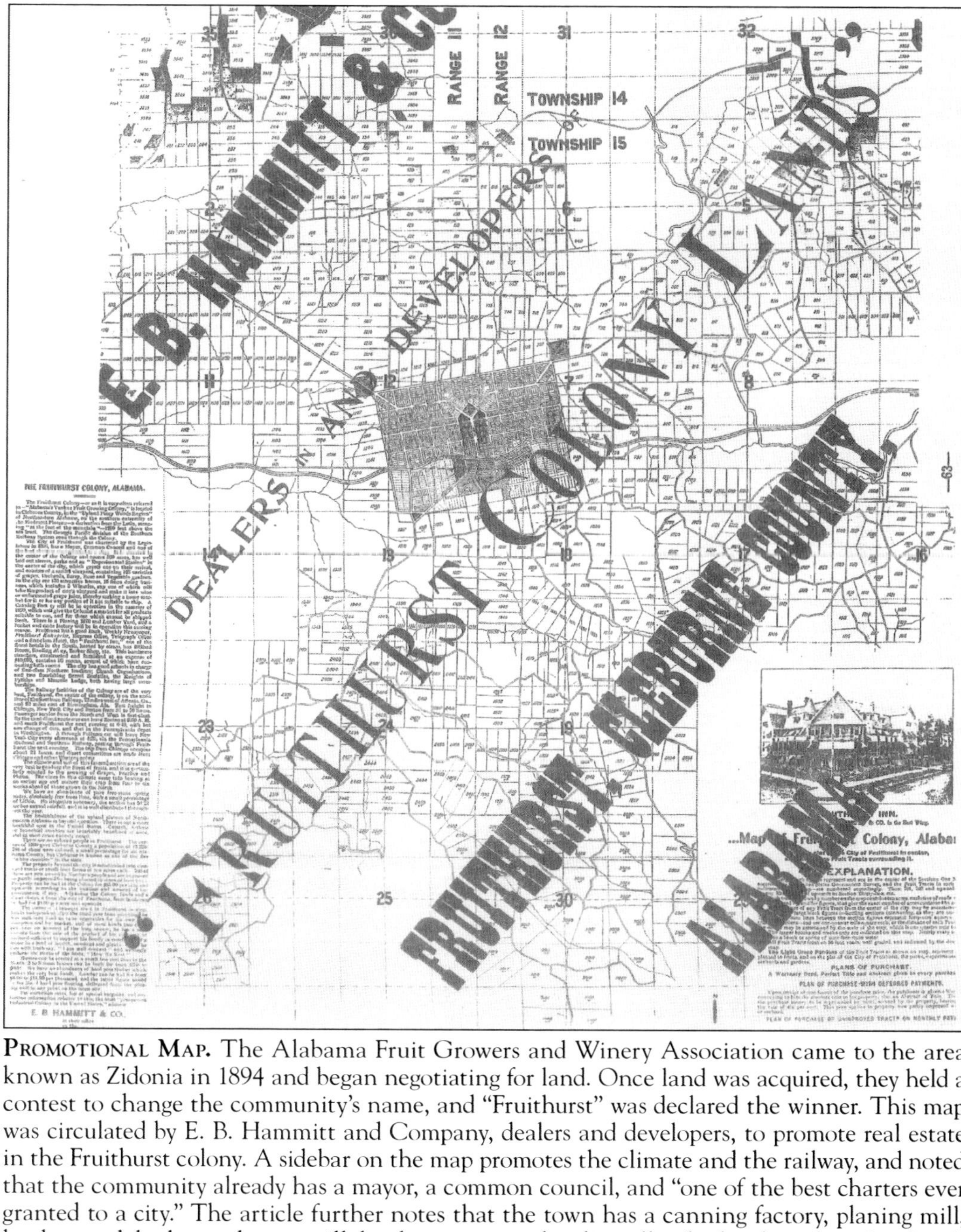

Promotional Map. The Alabama Fruit Growers and Winery Association came to the area known as Zidonia in 1894 and began negotiating for land. Once land was acquired, they held a contest to change the community's name, and "Fruithurst" was declared the winner. This map was circulated by E. B. Hammitt and Company, dealers and developers, to promote real estate in the Fruithurst colony. A sidebar on the map promotes the climate and the railway, and noted that the community already has a mayor, a common council, and "one of the best charters ever granted to a city." The article further notes that the town has a canning factory, planing mill, lumber yard, basket and crate mill, bank, newspaper, bowling alley, barbershop, first-class hotel, good schools, church organizations, billiard room, and two flourishing secret societies. (Courtesy Fruithurst Winery.)

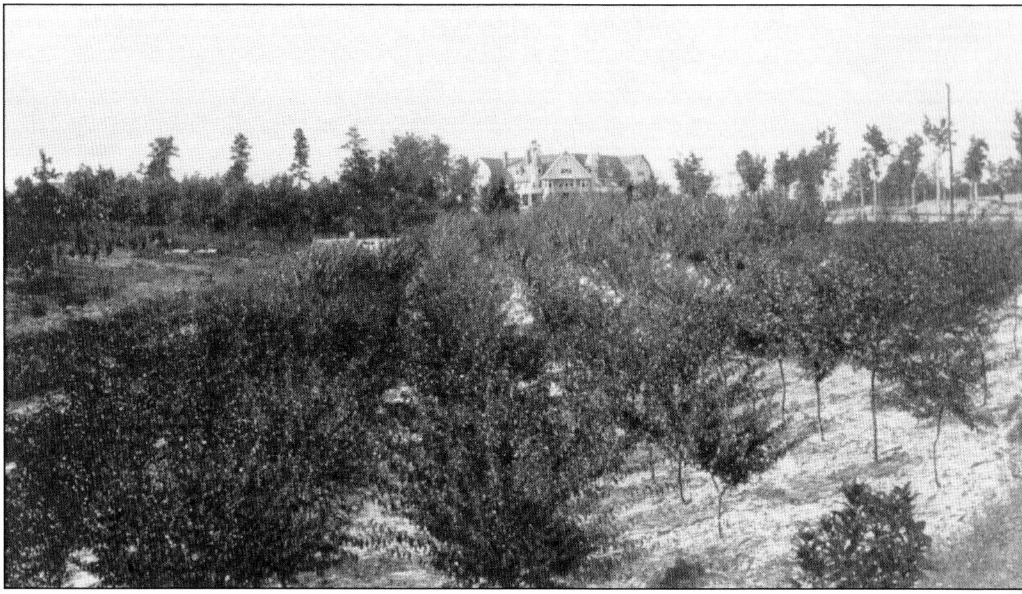

Cultivated Fruit Trees. In addition to grapevines, the colonists also grew botan and wild goose plum trees and other fruits in their experimental gardens. The Fruithurst Inn can be seen in the background. Orchards, parks, vineyards, and the experimental gardens covered a total of 3,000 acres. (Courtesy Fruithurst Winery.)

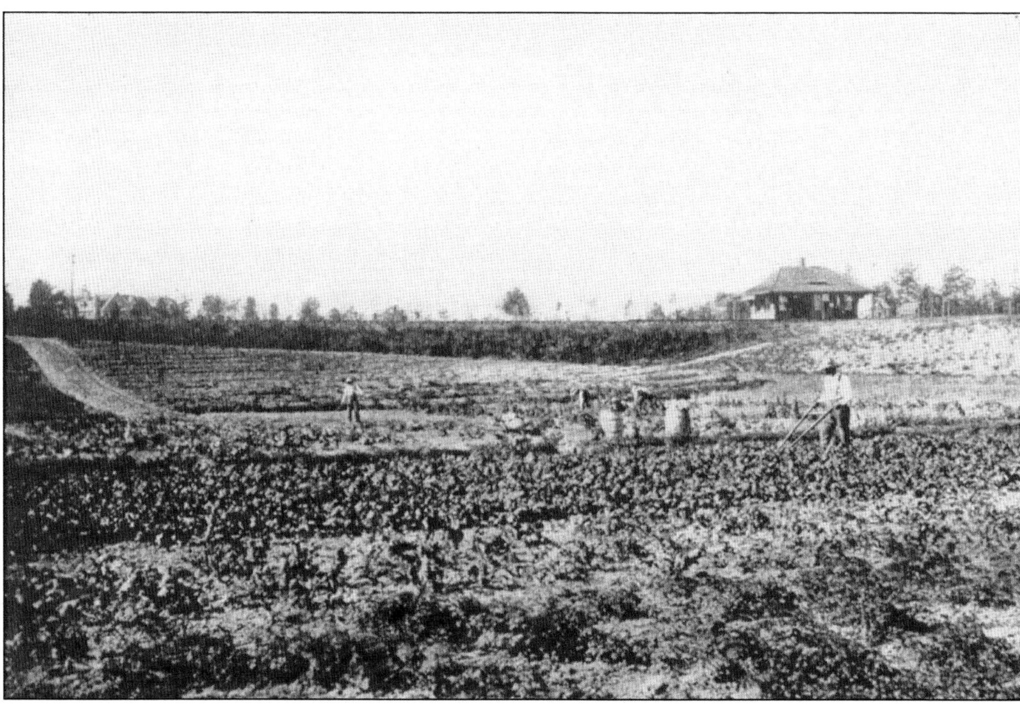

Experimental Vegetable Gardens. A wide variety of vegetables were grown in the experimental vegetable gardens within the colony. This is a view of the vegetable gardens looking northeast toward the train depot, which can be seen in the background. The colonists sought to determine what vegetables would grow best in the area. (Courtesy Fruithurst Winery.)

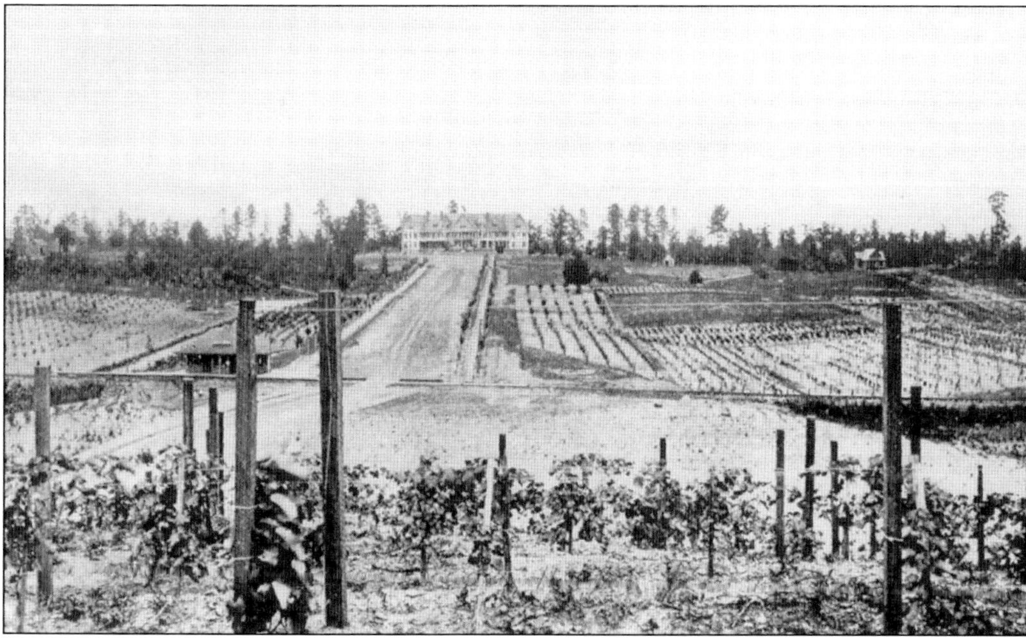

GARDENS, PARKS, AND INNS. This photograph gives a view of the experimental gardens, parks, train depot, and the Fruithurst Inn. The group thought it could develop new varieties in its experimental gardens, and its efforts have been compared to that of the later work of the Alabama Cooperative Extension Service. (Courtesy Fruithurst Winery.)

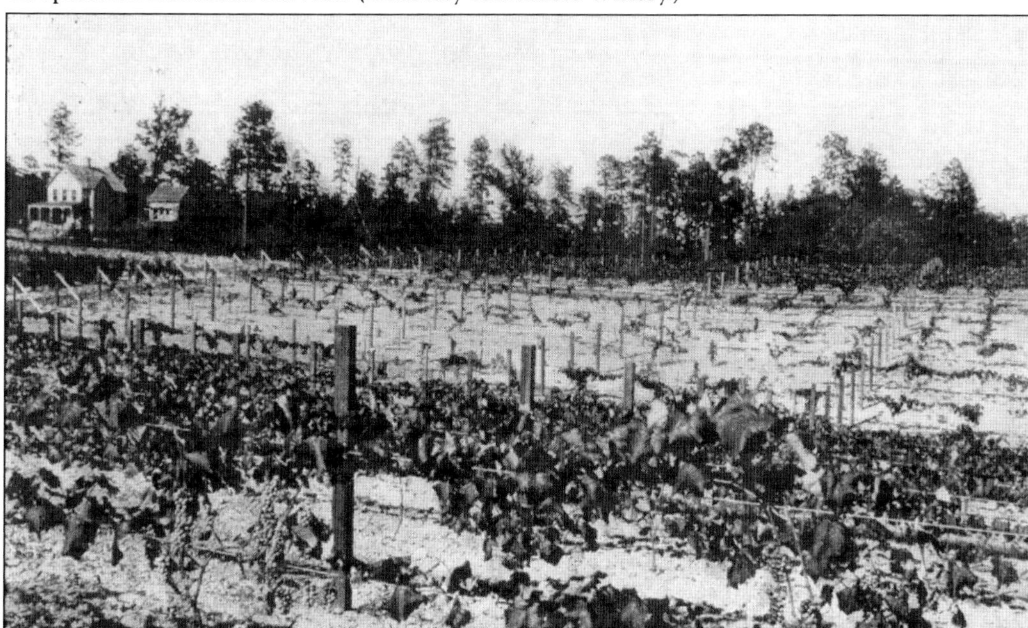

VINEYARDS IN THEIR SECOND YEAR. Within the second year, the vineyards showed much promise due to the mild climate and the composition of the earth. By 1898, production reached 23,000 gallons of wine. Later, a blight on the grapes and a few bad growing seasons helped start the colony's decline. (Courtesy Fruithurst Winery.)

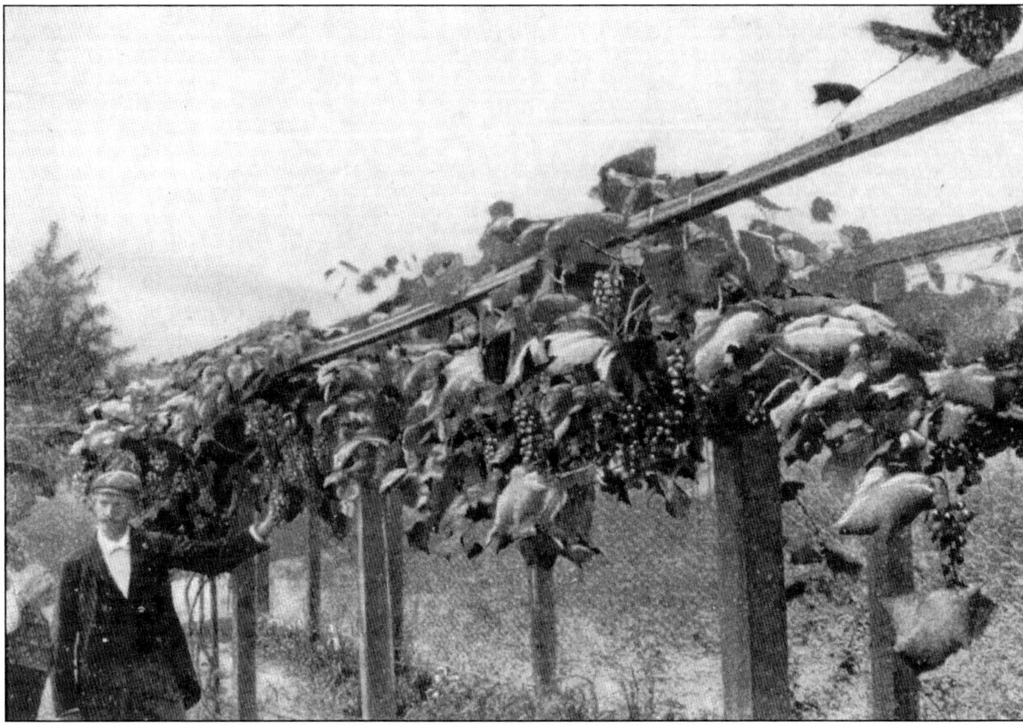

CONCORD GRAPEVINES. These gentlemen look at a six-year-old Concord grapevine, which, in 1896, produced 900 bunches that cumulatively weighed over 300 pounds. This photograph was taken on July 25, 1896. The experimental station had 105 varieties of grapes, orchards, berry patches, rose beds, and vegetable gardens. (Courtesy Fruithurst Winery.)

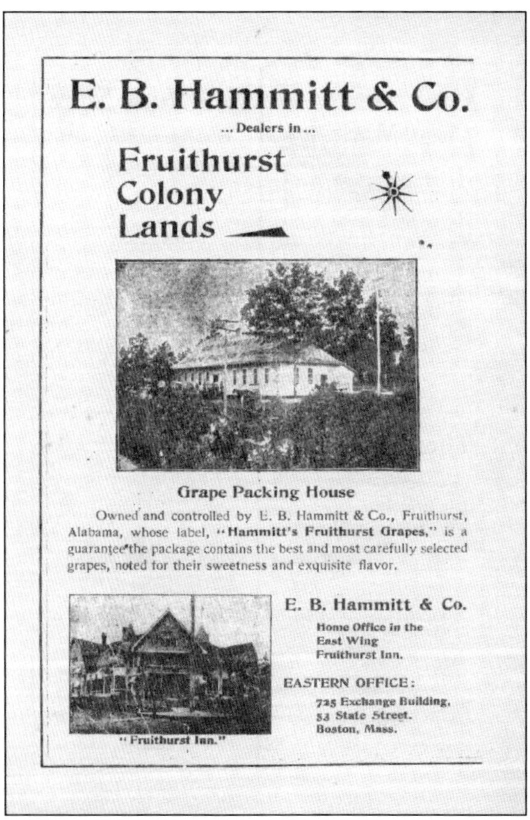

COLONY ADVERTISEMENT This E. B. Hammitt and Company advertisement promoted the Fruithurst colony lands. The two photographs show a grape packinghouse and the Fruithurst Inn. The E. B. Hammitt Company had an office in the Fruithurst Inn and also in Boston, Massachusetts. The company owned one of the major packinghouses in Fruithurst and advertised the grapes "for their sweetness and exquisite flavor." (Courtesy Charlotte Funderburk.)

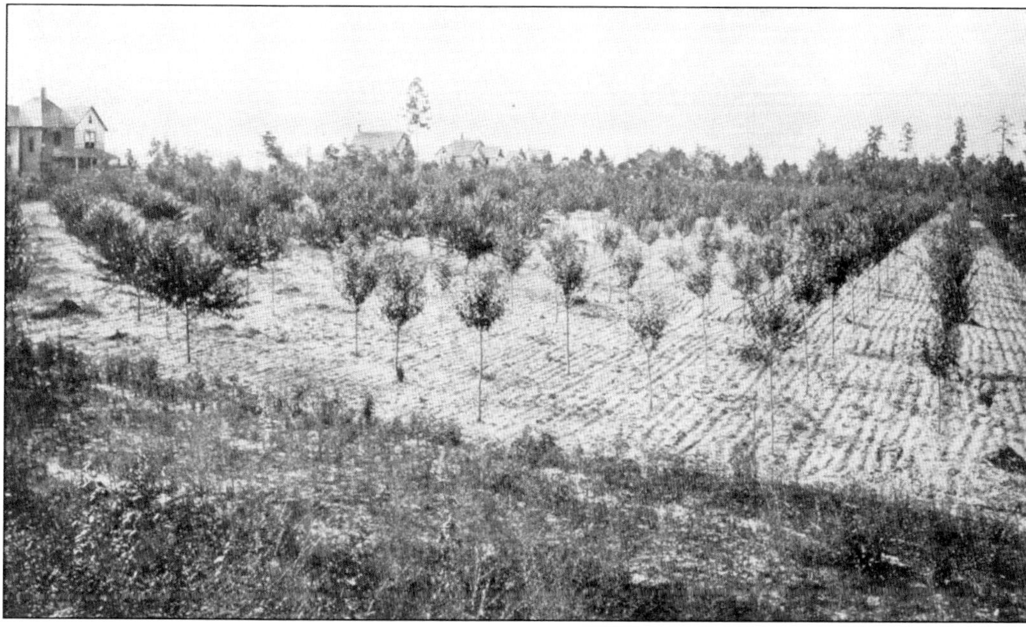

Residences Overlook Orchards. These houses along Second Street West overlooked a young apple and peach orchard. The town attracted residents from across the nation. It was incorporated in December 1896, and by the end of 1897, forty-six buildings had been built, and 18 more were under construction. By 1898, Fruithurst was a boomtown of 800 residents. (Courtesy Fruithurst Winery.)

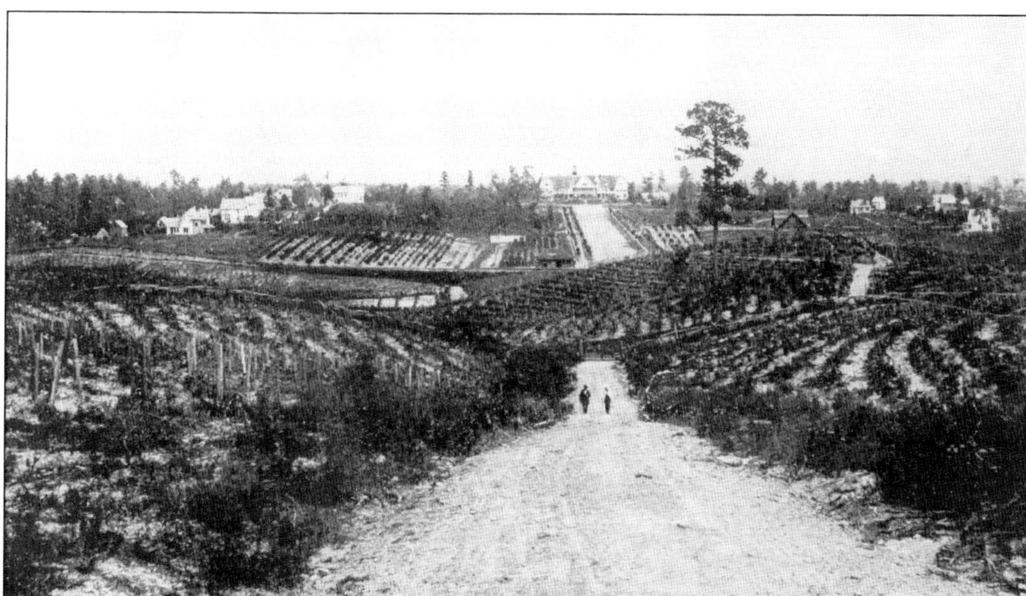

View Up Central Avenue. Two gentlemen can be seen walking down Central Avenue, while behind them, looking north from Ridge Road, can be seen the experimental vineyards, gardens, orchards, and the Fruithurst Inn. Central Avenue, the city's main street, was lined with two rows of maple trees and a single row of magnolia trees. (Courtesy Fruithurst Winery.)

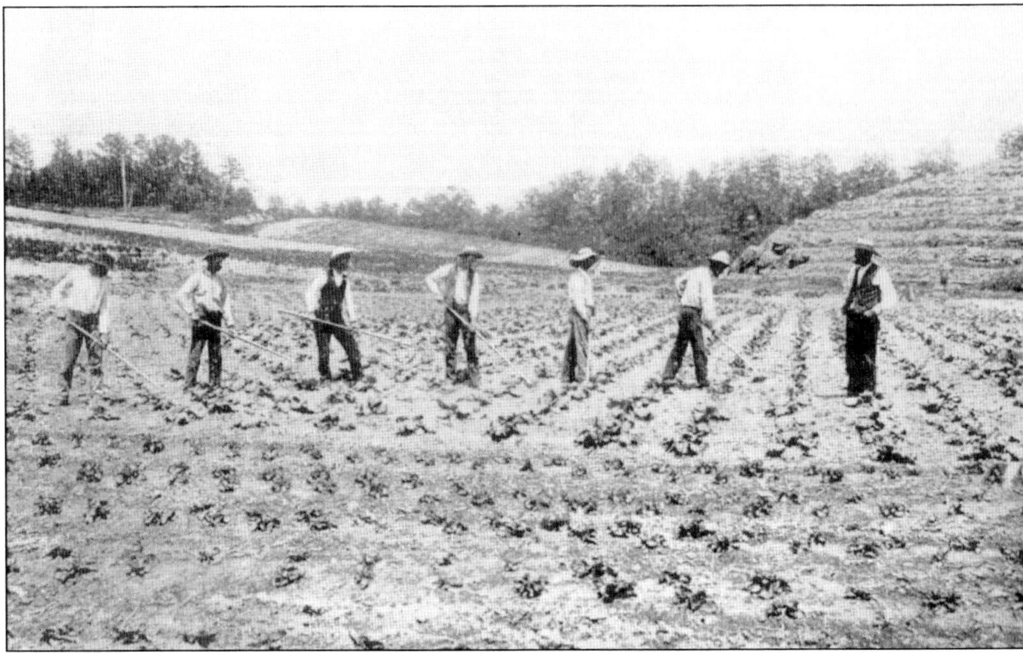

Men at Work. These men are tending the experimental garden, in which they grew a variety of vegetables. A year earlier, this site had been a canebrake and alder swamp. (Courtesy Fruithurst Winery.)

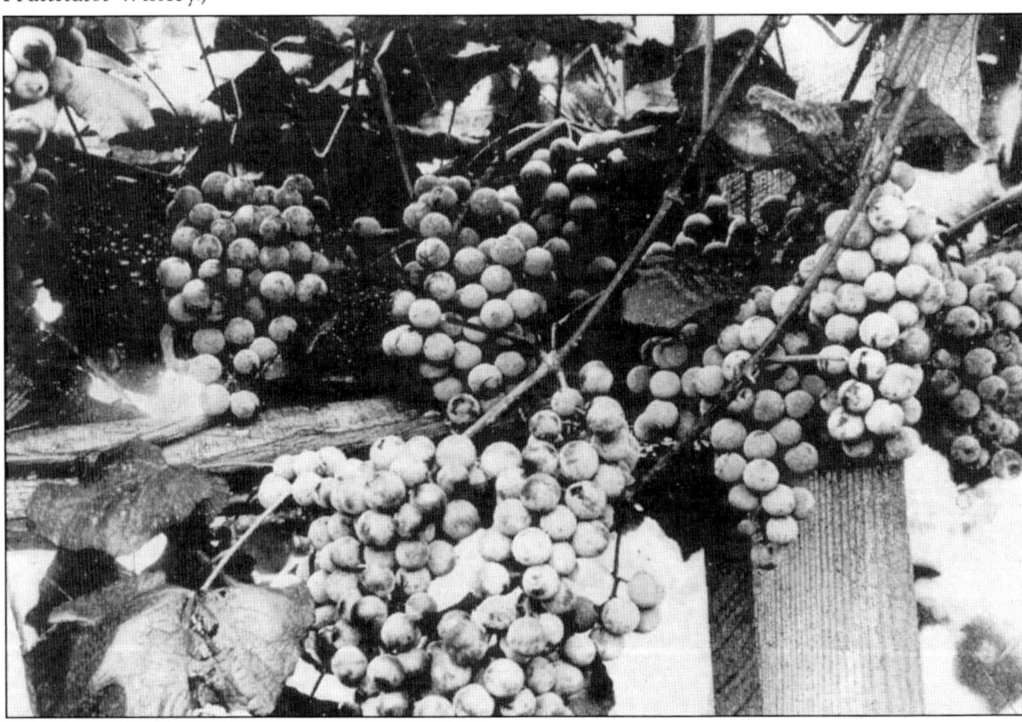

Grapes on the Vine. Here is a close-up view of grapes on the vines in the Fruithurst colony. Most of the wine produced in Fruithurst was shipped by train to Northern cities. In 1903, the colony shipped 2,885 crates, and in 1904, it shipped 3,574 crates. (Courtesy Fruithurst Winery.)

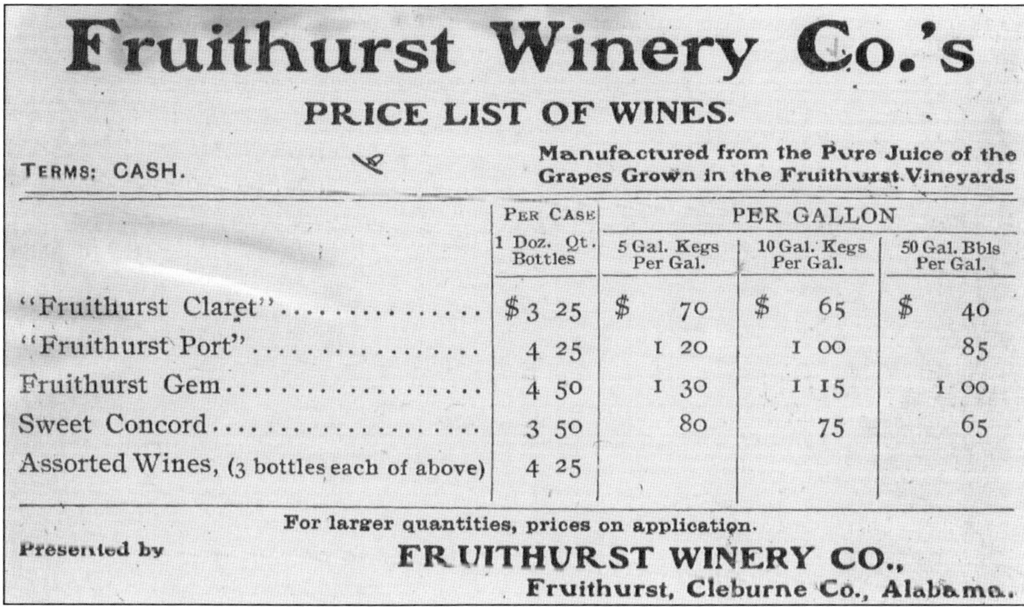

Fruithurst Winery Co.'s

PRICE LIST OF WINES.

TERMS: CASH.

Manufactured from the Pure Juice of the Grapes Grown in the Fruithurst Vineyards

	PER CASE 1 Doz. Qt. Bottles	PER GALLON 5 Gal. Kegs Per Gal.	10 Gal. Kegs Per Gal.	50 Gal. Bbls Per Gal.
"Fruithurst Claret"	$3 25	$ 70	$ 65	$ 40
"Fruithurst Port"	4 25	1 20	1 00	85
Fruithurst Gem	4 50	1 30	1 15	1 00
Sweet Concord	3 50	80	75	65
Assorted Wines, (3 bottles each of above)	4 25			

For larger quantities, prices on application.

Presented by

FRUITHURST WINERY CO.,
Fruithurst, Cleburne Co., Alabama.

PRICE LIST OF WINES. This Fruithurst Winery Company advertisement gave the price of their wines, including Fruithurst Claret, Fruithurst Port, Fruithurst Gem, Sweet Concord, and other assorted wines. In 1898, five wineries produced 23,000 gallons. A French winemaker said the product was the best wine he had tasted in the South. (Courtesy Fruithurst Winery.)

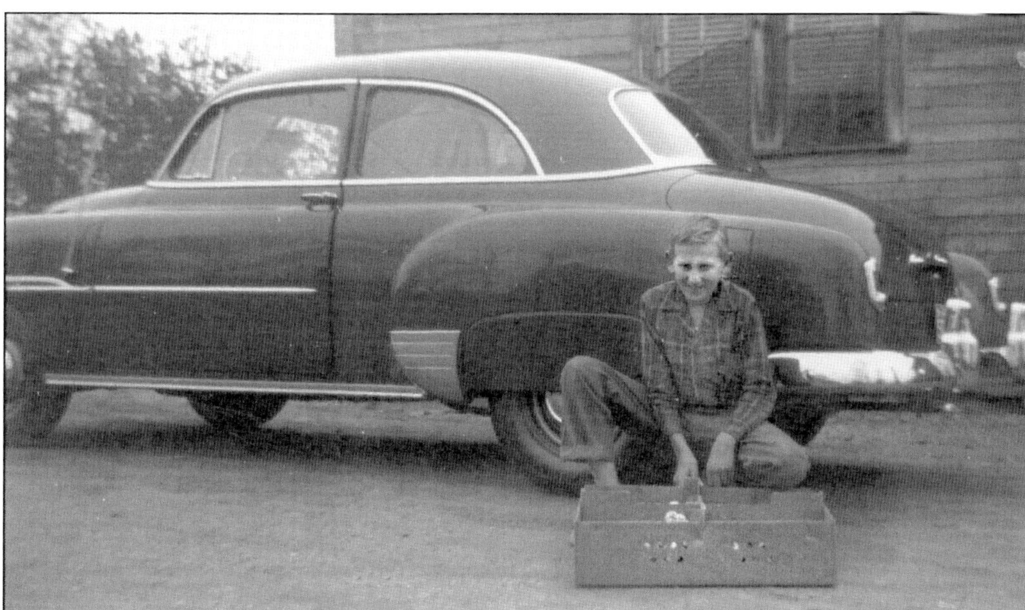

JERRY AND HIS CHICKS. Jerry Hollis of the Heflin area enjoyed growing chickens as part of his 4-H program. Here he is in 1950 displaying a batch of baby chicks. The Cleburne County Extension Office offered many young men like Hollis a variety of programs to teach them to be better farmers. (Courtesy Cleburne County Extension Office.)

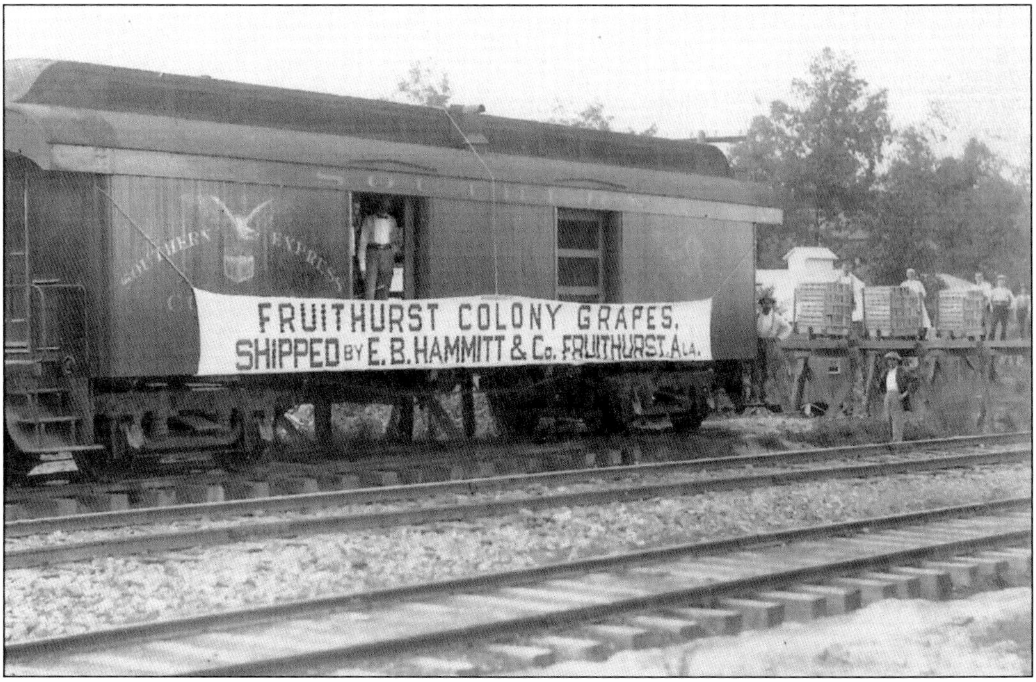

SHIPPED BY TRAIN. The Fruithurst colony shipped over 3,000 crates of grapes by rail each year to distribution points in Northern states. Wines included several varieties of clarets, ports, sherries, and muscatels. The grapes were of excellent quality. (Courtesy Charlotte Funderburk.)

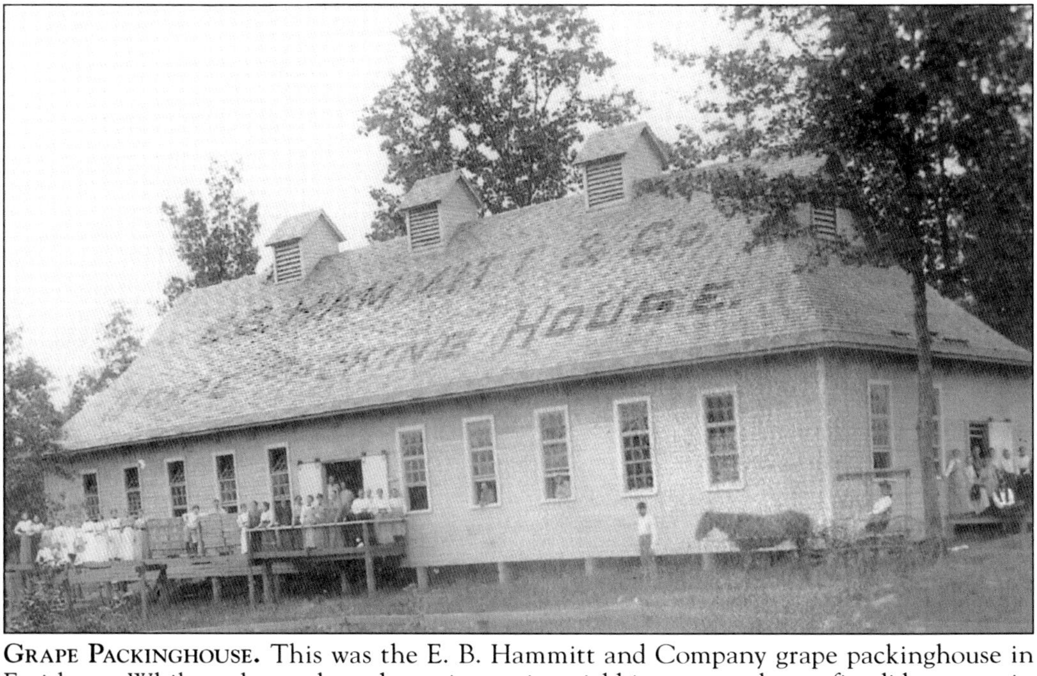

GRAPE PACKINGHOUSE. This was the E. B. Hammitt and Company grape packinghouse in Fruithurst. While each year brought an increasing yield in grapes, the profits did not run in proportion. There was no good market for the wines, and a 1903 freeze and Prohibition caused the last of the wineries to close in 1919. (Courtesy Charlotte Funderburk.)

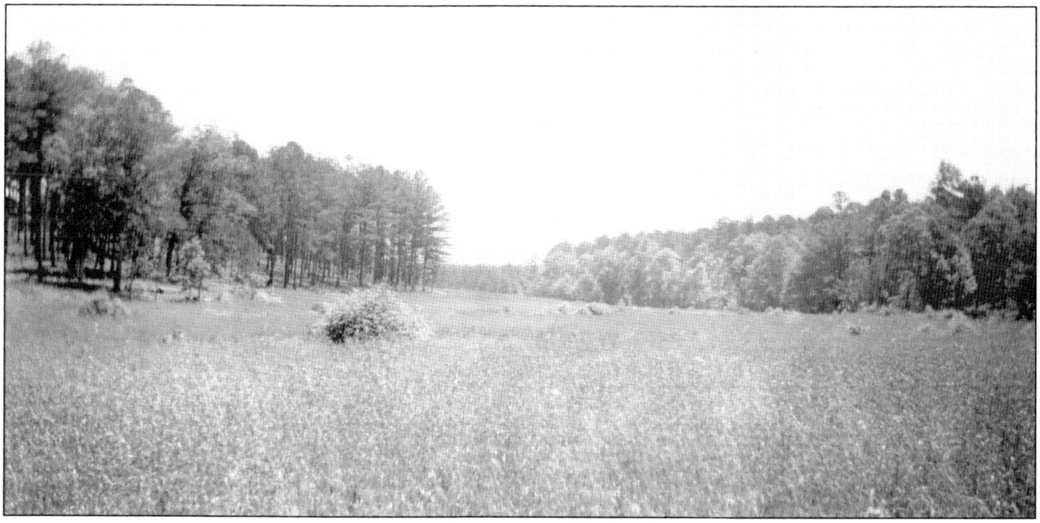

Rural Farmland. This photograph illustrates how much of Cleburne County's rural farmland appeared in the 1940s. At that time, there were more farms and more people working on farms than there are today. Cattle were grown for slaughter, and some row crops were planted. Heflin was once known as a hub for area farmers seeking to ship their cotton. By the 1940s, however, the acreage in cotton had fallen substantially. (Courtesy Cleburne County Extension Office.)

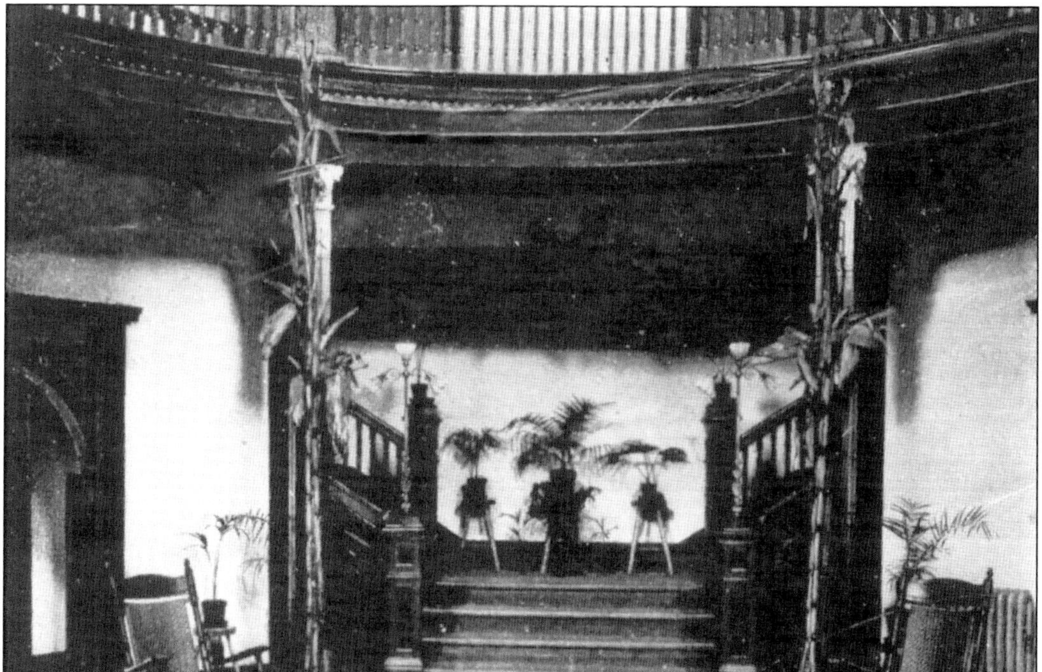

Inside the Fruithurst Inn. This is a view inside the rotunda of the Fruithurst Inn looking towards the grand staircase. The rotunda lobby was large enough to accommodate musicals or a full orchestra. The inn was built in the Victorian style and drew visitors from around the world. (Courtesy Fruithurst Winery.)

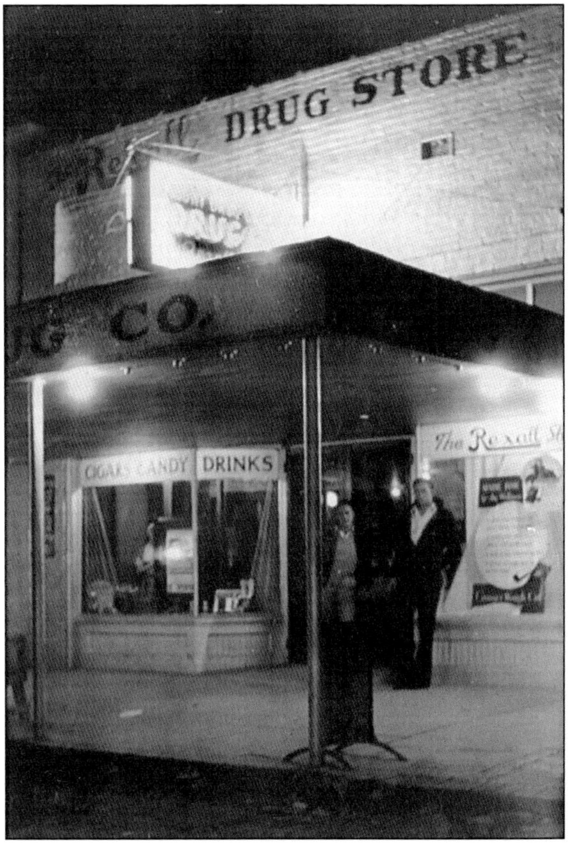

DRUGSTORE AT NIGHT. Two customers stand outside Wright's Rexall Drug Store in Heflin after nightfall some time in 1949. Wright Drug continues to do business today. In 2002, the store was recognized as an "exceptional pharmacy" in *Drug Topics* magazine. (Courtesy Pete Wright.)

HIGH SCHOOL BAND. The late-1940s photograph of the Cleburne County High School Band below was taken for the school annual. The band has always been very active, playing at school football games as well as at special school and town events. (Courtesy Pete Wright.)

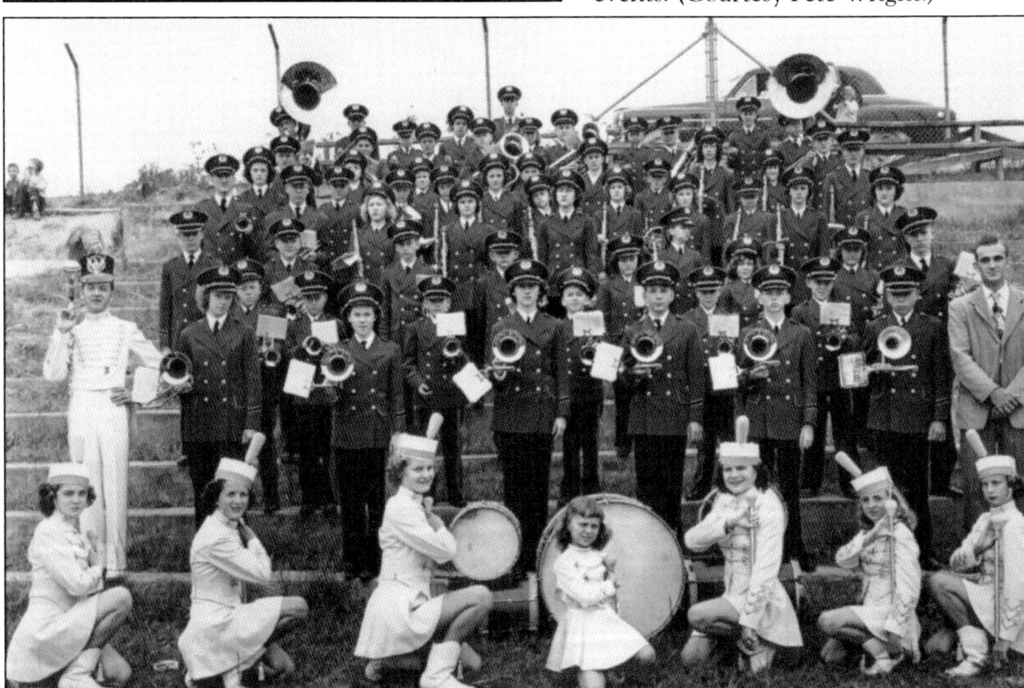

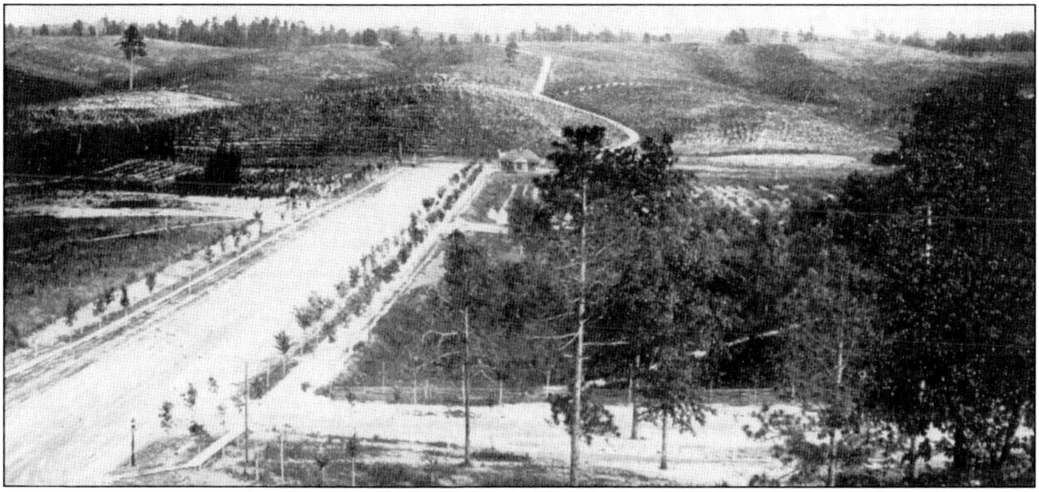

TOWER VIEW. This photograph taken from the water tower of the Fruithurst Inn looks southward down Central Avenue to the passenger depot of Southern Railway and vineyards in the distance. The railway served to transport vineyard production as well as to transport visitors to the inn. (Courtesy Fruithurst Winery.)

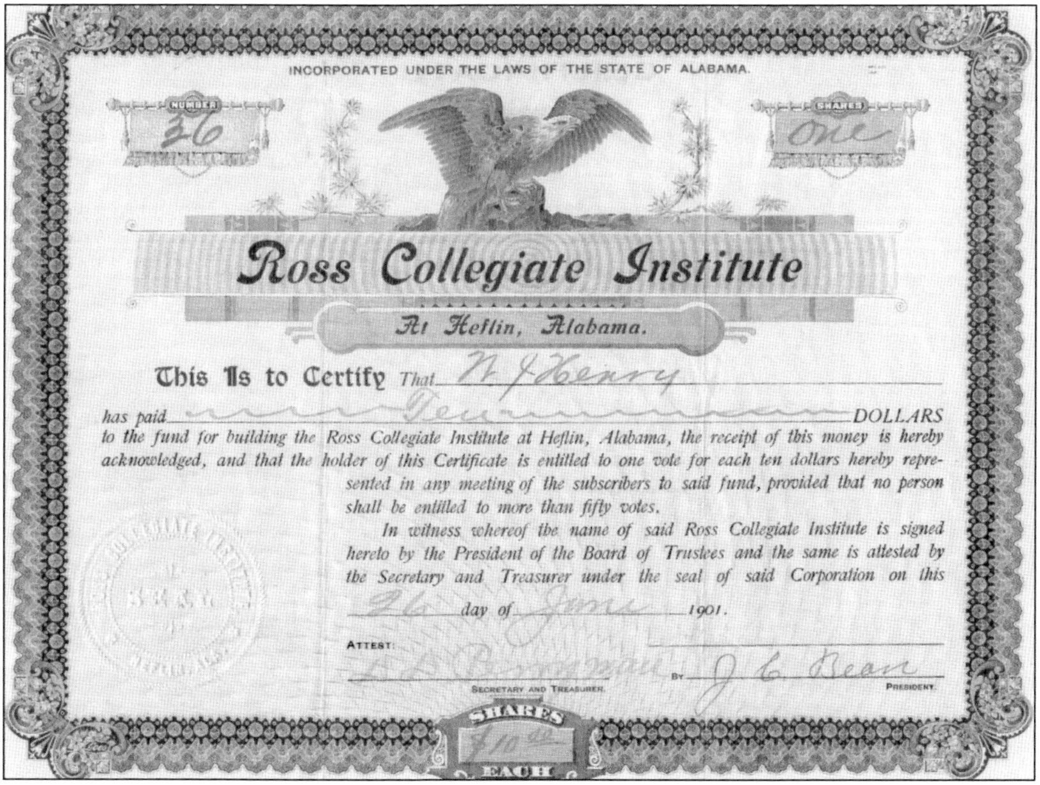

INCORPORATED UNDER THE LAWS OF THE STATE OF ALABAMA.

NUMBER 36

SHARES One

Ross Collegiate Institute

At Heflin, Alabama.

This Is to Certify *That* N J Henry

has paid Ten *DOLLARS to the fund for building the Ross Collegiate Institute at Heflin, Alabama, the receipt of this money is hereby acknowledged, and that the holder of this Certificate is entitled to one vote for each ten dollars hereby represented in any meeting of the subscribers to said fund, provided that no person shall be entitled to more than fifty votes.*

In witness whereof the name of said Ross Collegiate Institute is signed hereto by the President of the Board of Trustees and the same is attested by the Secretary and Treasurer under the seal of said Corporation on this 26 *day of* June *1901.*

ATTEST:

SECRETARY AND TREASURER. BY J C Bean PRESIDENT.

SHARES $10.00 EACH

SHARE. This certificate was given to N. J. Henry on June 26, 1901, after he had paid $10 to the fund for building the Ross Collegiate Institute in Heflin. The certificate served as a receipt as well as entitling the payee to one vote in any meeting of the fund's subscribers. The document, on file in the Lucile Morgan Public Library in Heflin, bears the signature of the Ross Collegiate Institute's president, J. C. Bean. (Courtesy Lucile Morgan Public Library.)

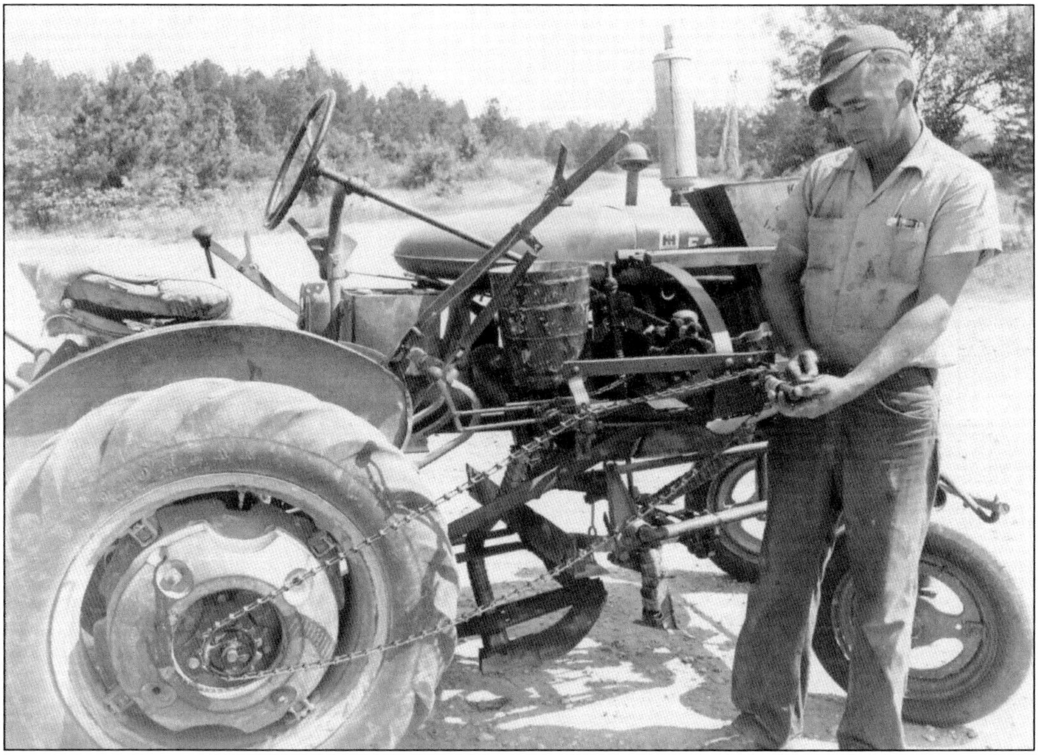

MAINTENANCE. Keeping farm tractors and equipment running and operating smoothly could be a challenge. This Cleburne County farmer works on his tractor and appears to be attaching chain-driven equipment to spread seed or fertilizer. The farmer is using a Farmall tractor, introduced in 1939. The Farmall A had the same engine as its predecessor, but the engine was to the left of the operator seat. (Courtesy Cleburne County Extension Office.)

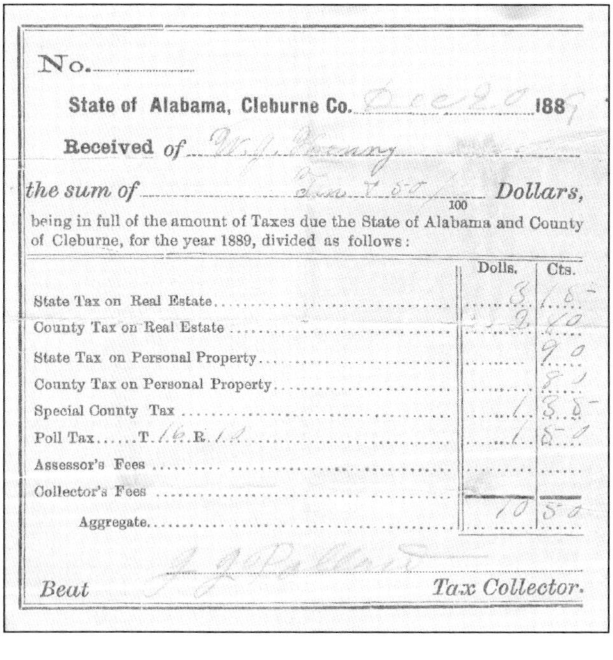

No.

State of Alabama, Cleburne Co. Dec 20 1889

Received of W. J. Hoenny

the sum of Ten 50/100 Dollars,

being in full of the amount of Taxes due the State of Alabama and County of Cleburne, for the year 1889, divided as follows:

	Dolls.	Cts.
State Tax on Real Estate	3	15
County Tax on Real Estate	2	80
State Tax on Personal Property		90
County Tax on Personal Property		80
Special County Tax	1	35
Poll Tax......T. 16 R. 10	1	50
Assessor's Fees		
Collector's Fees		
Aggregate	10	50

J. J. Pollard

Beat Tax Collector.

TAX RECEIPT. Cleburne County tax collector J. J. Pollard gave this receipt to W. J. Hoenny on December 20, 1889. In that year, Hoenny paid \$3.15 state tax on real estate, \$2.80 county tax on real estate, 90¢ on state personal property, 80¢ on county personal property, \$1.35 on a special county tax, and \$1.50 in poll taxes. Between 1889 and 1910, eleven Southern states adopted a poll tax of \$1.50. At the time of the passage of the 24th Amendment in 1964, Alabama was among five states still using poll taxes. (Courtesy Lucile Morgan Public Library.)

FRUITHURST INN.

C. H. ANDREWS, Prop'r.

CHRISTMAS MENU=1898.

Blue Points.

SOUP.

Bisque a la Prince

Olives | Salted Almonds | Celery.

Sweet Pickles | Chow Chow

FISH.

Snapper Cuttels, Tartar Sauce

Potatoes beignets

PORT WINE

Boiled Leg of Mutton, Caper Sauce

Roast Turkey Stuffed with Chestnuts

Roast Young Geese, Farmer Style

Small Fillet of Beef, Larded Mushroom Sauce

Fruithurst Sherry

Supreme of Veal aux pillis sois | Bartlett Pears a la Conde

UNFERMENTED GRAPE JUICE

FRUITHURST CLARET | **DRY CLARET**

COLD DISHES.

Roast Beef | Ham | Potato Salad | Chicken Salad

VEGETABLES.

Boiled Potatoes | Mashed Potatoes | Green Peas | Sweet Corn

Stewed Tomatoes | Fried Parsnips

PASTRY.

Steamed Raisin Pudding, Hard Sauce

Pumpkin Pie | Mince Pie

DESSERTS.

Vanilla Ice Cream, Assorted Cake

Oranges | Grapes | Bananas | Appı

Mixed Nuts | California Raisins

American Cream Cheese and Crackers

CHRISTMAS MENU, 1898. The Fruithurst Inn's Christmas menu for 1898 featured a wide selection of food and drinks including Bisque a la Prince soup, salted almonds, snapper cuttels, potatoes beignets, port wine, Fruithurst sherry, boiled leg of mutton, roast turkey, roasted young geese, and assorted cold dishes, vegetables, pastries, and desserts. In addition to the lodging, the food at the inn was considered some of the best in the South. Many guests were surprised to find such as extravagant menu in what was considered by many to be an out-of-the-way location. The inn was one of the focal points of the town and helped make a positive impression on visitors and potential residents of the colony. The sherry and wines produced locally were served, and much of the food was grown or purchased locally. (Courtesy Fruithurst Winery.)

FRUITHURST INN.

C. H. ANDREW, Proprietor.

MENU---Thanksgiving, 1898.

Puree of Tomatoes a la Riene.

Sweet Pickle   Chow Chow

Columbia River Salmon   Chutney Sauce   Saratoga Chips

Roast Sirloin of Beef,   Roast Leg of Lamb

Mashed Potatoes,   Green Peas

Young Turkey Stuffed   Cranberry Sauce

Baked Sweet Potatoes   Saiger Corn

Salt Pork and Turnip Salad

Pickled Beets   Celery   Shrimp Salad

UNFERMENTED GRAPE JUICE

FRUITHURST CLARET   **DRY CLARET**

Wild Goose a la Farmiere

Queen of Souffle   Sabayon

PASTRY.

Steam Plum Pudding, Hard Sauce

Mince Pie   Pumpkin Pie

Dewey's Assorted Cakes

DESERTS.

Vanila Ice Cream and Fancy Cake

Oranges   Apples   Grapes   Mixed Nuts   Raisins

Adam's Cream Cheese Crackers

Coffee   Tea   Milk

THANKSGIVING MENU, 1898. With C. H. Andrew as proprietor, the Fruithurst Inn in 1898 served a Thanksgiving lunch of Columbia River salmon, a variety of vegetables, roasted leg of lamb, roast sirloin, shrimp salad, unfermented grape juice, dry claret and Fruithurst claret, wild goose a la Farmiere, pastries, and desserts. The inn served as a major meeting place in Fruithurst, and entertainment was offered in the grand lobby during certain times. A lot of the meal selections could certainly not be found at any other establishment in Cleburne County, and even today there is no restaurant serving up the selections that can compare with the Fruithurst Inn in 1898. The meals served were always considered of the highest quality, so many were disappointed when the inn closed. (Courtesy Fruithurst Winery.)

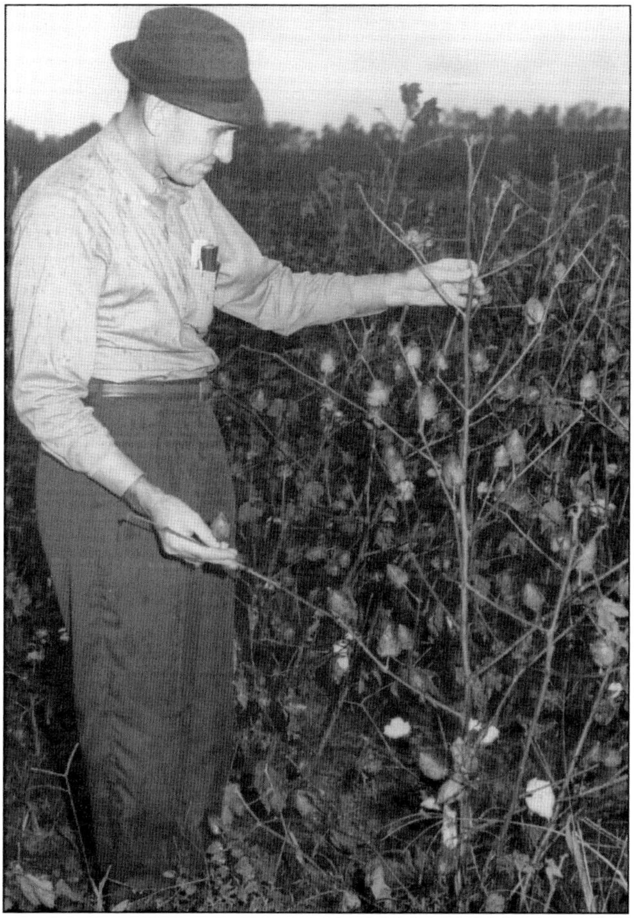

AGENT AT WORK. Heflin resident Emmett Farrington worked as a Cooperative Extension System agent in Cleburne County from 1946 to 1977, when he retired. Here he looks at a stalk of cotton in a Cleburne County field. In 2009, the City of Heflin, the Cleburne County Commission, and the Cleburne County Extension Office recognized Farrington for his 31 years of service. (Courtesy Cleburne County Extension Office.)

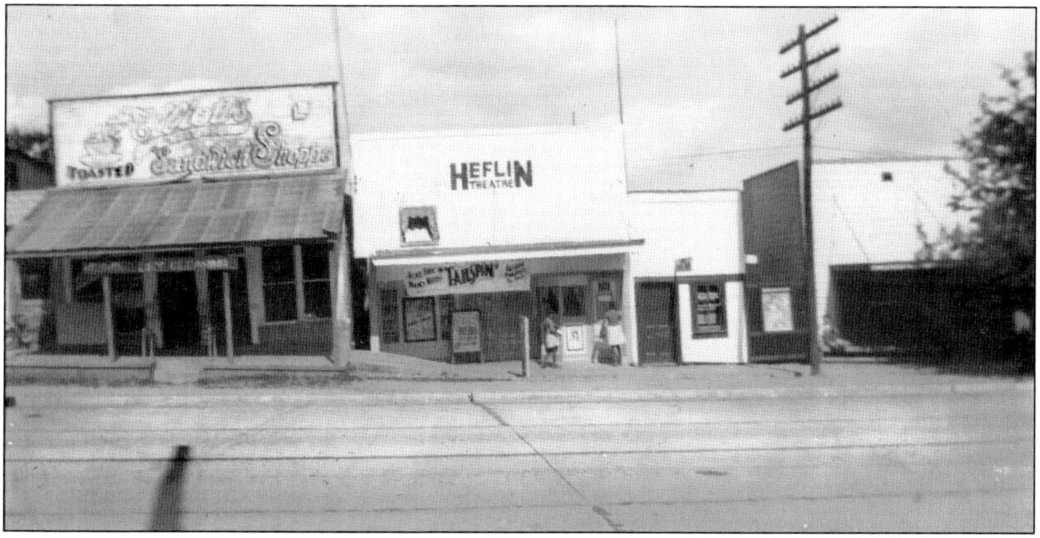

HEFLIN THEATRE. This photograph of downtown Heflin around 1950 gives a glimpse of the old theater (center) and a sandwich shop to the left. This area now is taken up by a cleaners, sewing shop, and newspaper office. (Courtesy Leesa Cheatwood.)

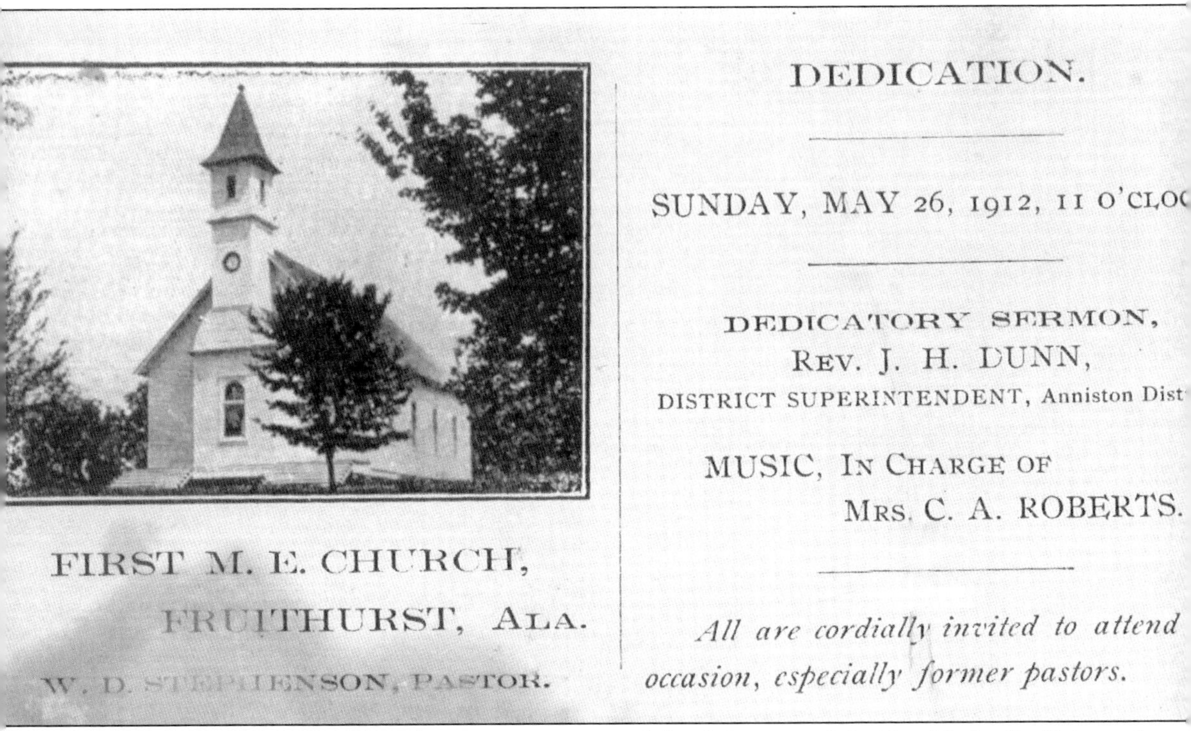

CHURCH DEDICATION. This advertisement promoted the dedication of the First Methodist Episcopal Church in Fruithurst on May 26, 1912. W. D. Stephenson was the pastor, and the Reverend J. H. Dunn delivered the dedicatory sermon with Mrs. C. A. Roberts in charge of music. The Methodist Episcopal church was the first expression of Methodism in the United States. Churches played vital roles in the communities of Cleburne County. At one time, there were at least 75 churches of various faiths in Cleburne County. Church events were usually expected to attract large crowds. As there were little or no other activities for people to get involved in, churches served both a religious and a social need. Many churches of the time had a typical bell tower or steeple, and some rang their bell to call worshipers to service. (Courtesy Fruithurst Winery.)

IF YOU WANT THE BEST AND SWEETEST FLAVORED GRAPES, ALWAYS ASK YOUR DEALER FOR THE

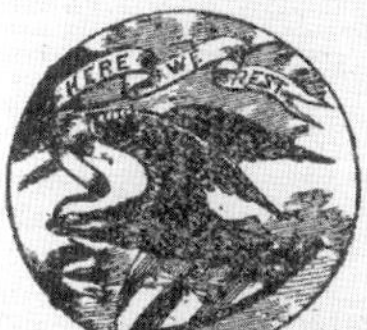

...Fruithurst Colony, Grapes

While you are eating and enjoying this delicious fruit, read this small circular and you will get a correct idea where and by whom these grapes are grown.

The Fruithurst Colony, or as it is commonly called, "The Vineyard City of the South," is located in CLEBURNE COUNTY, ALABAMA, in the northeastern part of the State, 73 miles west of Atlanta, Ga. and 93 miles east of Birmingham, Ala. The main line of the great Southern Railway System runs through the Colony, giving it the very best railroad accommodations. The model City of Fruithurst is located in the center of the Colony, has Mayor and Common Council, and one of the best Charters of any city in the South.

We have about 150 beautiful residences, seventeen business houses and three wineries, where all the grapes that are not shipped are made into wines.

The other enterprises are: One Bank, two Newspapers, a Planing Mill, Lumber Yards, a Basket and Crate Factory, a Canning Factory and a first-class Hotel, "The Fruithurst Inn," one of the most commodious hotels in the South, steam-heated, contains over eighty rooms, with several bath rooms. This beautiful hotel cost $40,000.

We have excellent FREE SCHOOLS. Four Church organizations and two secret societies. There is not a healthier spot in the United States than the uplands of Cleburne County, Alabama, located as we are 1,200 feet above the sea level. The lands through the Colony are well watered with pure free-stone spring water, absolutely free from lime and contains Lithia.

The Fruithurst Colony was started four years ago when the first acre of grapes was planted. To-day the Colony has over 3,000 acres planted to grapes and other fruits. The population of the Colony is about 1,000, nearly all from the northern States. They are industrious and prosperous, and have in this short time built up one of the prettiest towns in the South. The lands in the Colony are divided into ten acre tracts, which are partly or all planted to vines and fruit trees.

Lands are as yet cheap. Improved vineyards can be bought for $50.00 to $200.00 per acre, according to location and improvements made.

There are no colored people in Fruithurst, and less than five per cent. of the population in the County are of the colored race.

Come South and join us. Fruithurst extends to you a hearty welcome. Leave the frozen North with its cold and piercing winters and make your home here where the temperature hardly ever goes above ninety-five degrees and where zero weather is nearly unknown.

Any further information regarding our prosperous Colony and City will cheerfully be given by any member, mentioned below, of the FRUITHURST SHIPPING ASSOCIATION.

Dr. S. L. B. BLACKE, President.	J. E. HEFFERNAN, President Board of Education.
C. A. METZGER, Secretary.	A. W. NELSON, Contractor.
E. R. CARLSON, Treasurer.	A. L. SINCLAIR, Contractor.
E. M. CLEVELAND, Vineyardist.	J. A. WESTERLUND, Real Estate.
NEIL GREGORY, Contractor.	
J. A. JOHNSON, Contractor.	

Address, FRUITHURST, ALA.

"No better evidence of the fruitfulness of immigration work can be found than in the Colony planted at Fruithurst, in Cleburne County, where a large body of lands has multiplied more than six-fold in assessed values within about two years, and the influx of industrious citizens continues."—*From the Message of Gov. J. F. Johnston to the General Assembly of Alabama.*

Send for a sample copy of the FRUITHURST VINEYARDIST, Fruithurst, Ala. The largest Newspaper in the County.

DISPATCH PRINT, BIRMINGHAM.

PROMOTION FOR GRAPES AND THE FRUITHURST COLONY. This promotion, printed by Dispatch Print in Birmingham, Alabama, promoted the grapes and the positive attributes of the Fruithurst colony. At that time, members of the Fruithurst Shipping Association included Dr. S. L. B. Blacke, president; C. A. Metzger, secretary; E. R. Carlson, treasurer; E. M. Cleveland, viticulturist; Neil Gregory, J. A. Johnson, A. W. Nelson, and A. L. Sinclair, contractors; J. E. Heffernan, president of the board of education; and J. A. Westerlund, real estate. The population of Fruithurst was around 1,000, mostly from northern states, living in 150 residences, and land was selling between $50 and $200 and acre. Water was said to be "free-stone spring water, absolutely free from lime and contains Lithia." (Courtesy Fruithurst Winery.)

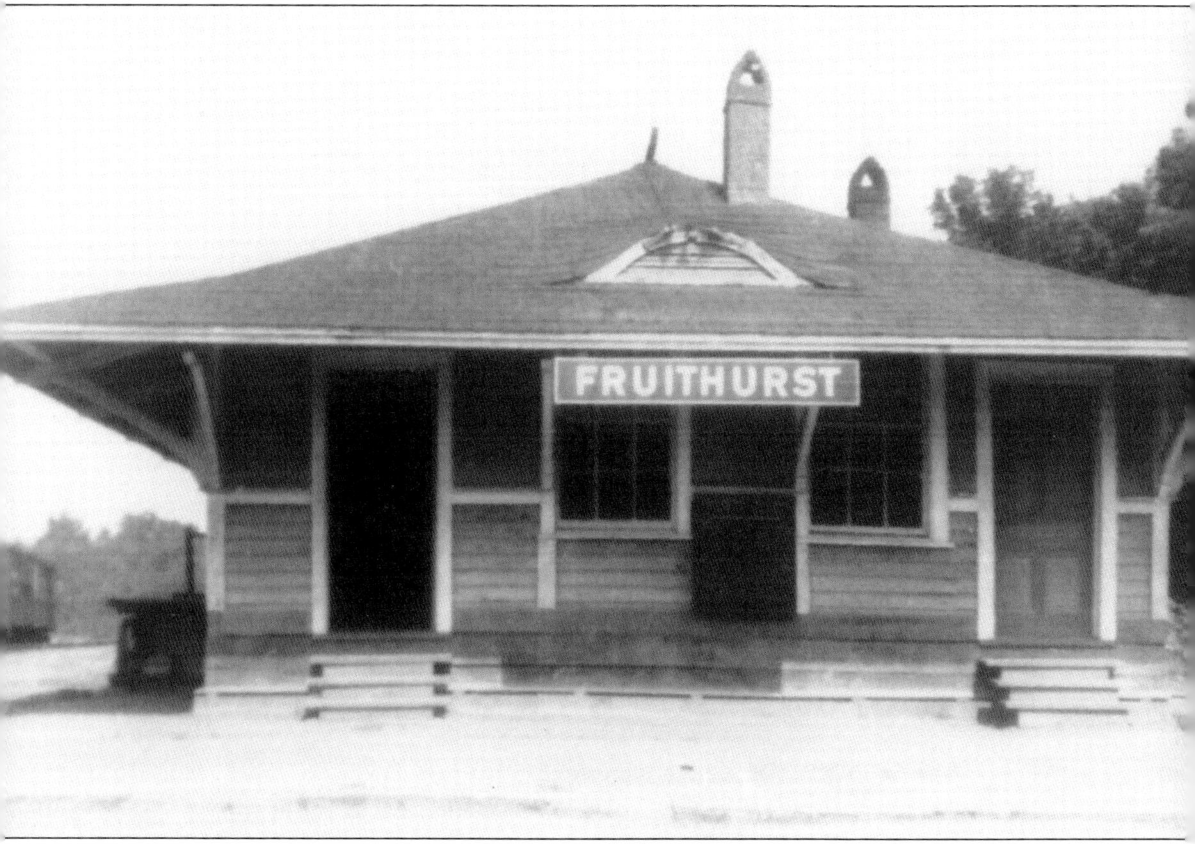

FRUITHURST TRAIN DEPOT, 1906. The Southern Railway train depot in Fruithurst is pictured as it appeared in 1906. The depot was vital to the economic success of the colony, but when Prohibition, a severe freeze, and other financial woes caused the colony to go defunct, the need for rail service in the town quickly declined. By 1914, no tickets were sold at this station, as it had become only a flag station—trains did not stop unless signaled to do so by a hanging flag or some other method of signal. In 1917, there was a court case in which C. J. Wade alleged he tried to board a train at this station, and the train got underway before he could get the car door open, so he grabbed outside handholds, but a few minutes later, he became fatigued, fell off the train, and was injured. (Courtesy Fruithurst Winery.)

Two

Heflin
A Great Place to Call Home

In 1830, a group of people left Edgefield, South Carolina, on a westward migration and settled to grow crops in the lowlands of what is now Cleburne County near the Tallapoosa River. Among them were John and Nancy Ross and their 13 children. As their family plantation prospered, John gave land for churches, schools, and cemeteries, which gradually became a settlement that was later named Heflin. The main street of Heflin was named in his honor. This street had a well in the middle, downtown, so that farmers delivering cotton could draw water to give their teams of horses. The well remained until the early 1920s. Heflin was named after local physician Dr. Wilson L. Heflin through an election. He played a large part in the civic, social, economic, and religious life of eastern Alabama and was a close friend of the Ross family. Heflin was founded in 1882 with one store and a population of 75 to 100. That same year, the Georgia Pacific Railroad was completed to Heflin from Atlanta. The town was incorporated by the legislature on December 10, 1892, and J. F. Morgan was the first mayor. Early settlers were J. C. Bean, M. D. Robinson, W. F. Stephenson, J. P. Morgan, J. C. Osborn, W. J. Henry, W. A. Porter, B. F. Owens, Dr. W. A. Neal, Dr. J. C. McClinlock, N. R. Hunnicutt, and M. L. Pinson. Heflin became a cotton center after the railroad was completed. People who brought bales of cotton to the railroad often camped overnight in the wagon yard and cooked in a camp house located behind Atkins and Owens' warehouse. In 1885, the Methodist Episcopal church, South, was organized, stemming from the Cahulga Church, established in 1840. The Baptists built the first church in Heflin in 1882. A Methodist Episcopal North building was erected in 1890. The first merchants were W. H. Hunnicutt and Son, C. A. Smith and Son, Charles Prescott, Mark Pinson, J. A. Morgan, Young and Bean, Atkins and Owens (who had the first brick building in town), and Wright Drug Company, established in 1902.

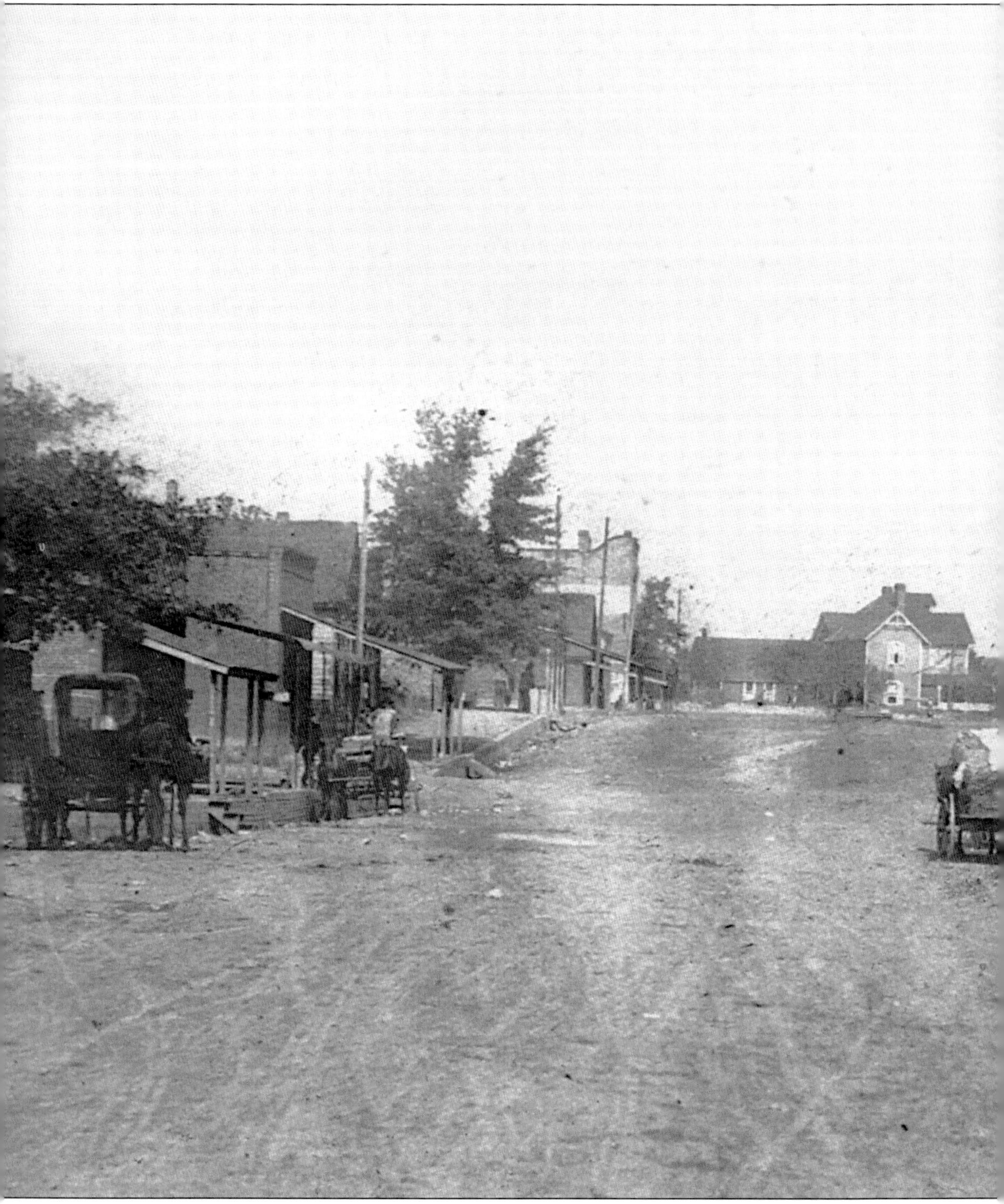

Looking East down Ross Street. Heflin's main street was named after John Ross, one of Heflin's early pioneers, who prospered and matched his prosperity with generosity, giving land for schools, churches, and cemeteries in the area now within the corporate limits of the city. In this early photograph looking eastward, the large two-story Alexander Hotel looms in the distance

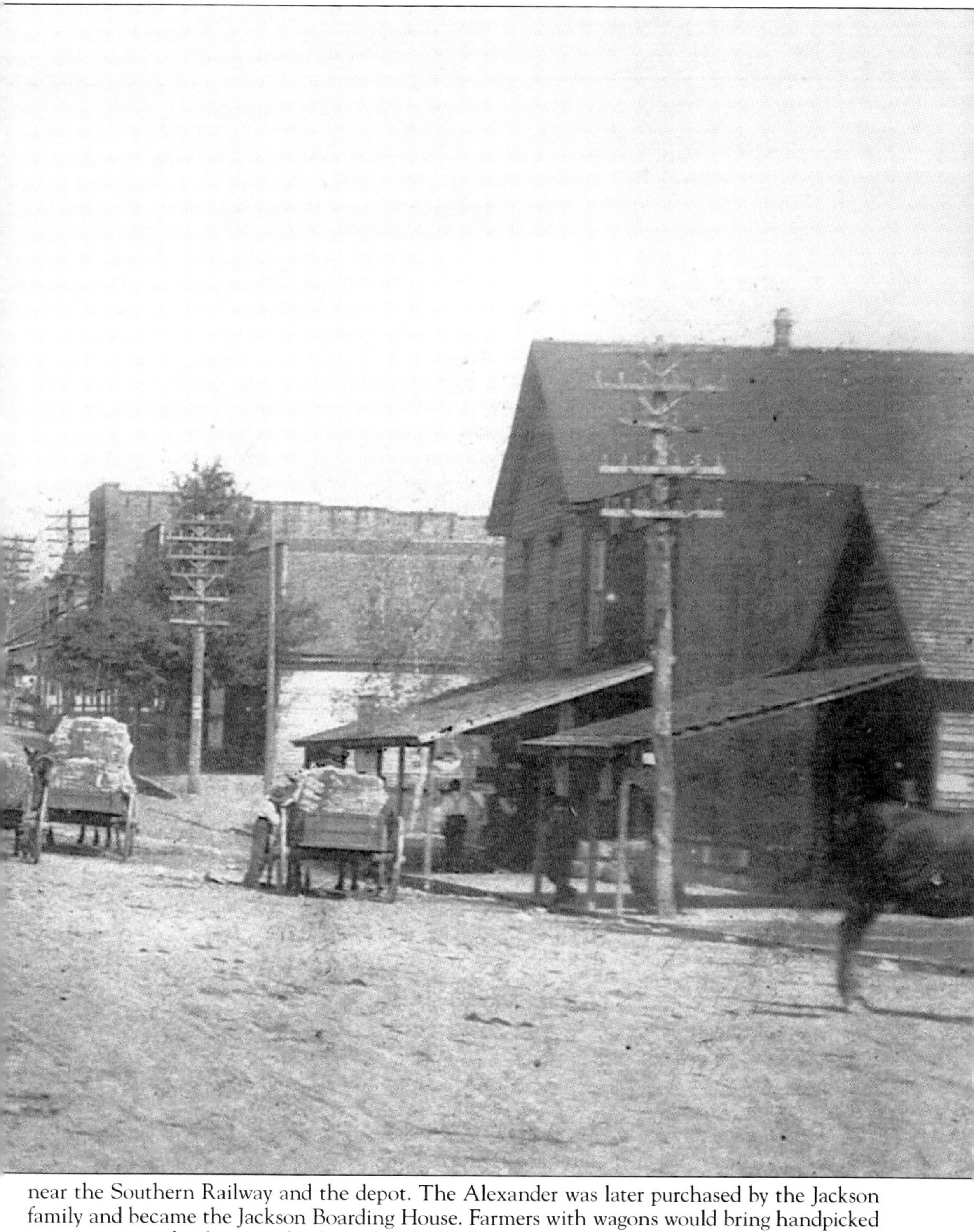

near the Southern Railway and the depot. The Alexander was later purchased by the Jackson family and became the Jackson Boarding House. Farmers with wagons would bring handpicked cotton to town for shipment by the railroad. While in town, they would buy up supplies for the return home. (Courtesy Jimmy Price.)

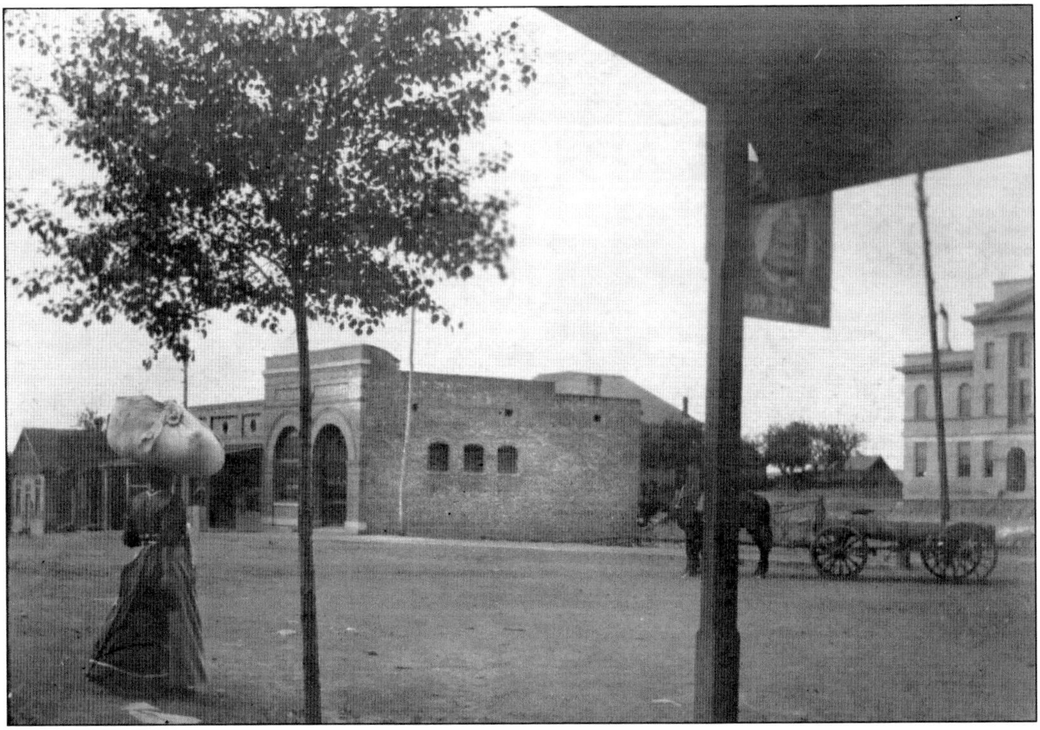

View across Ross Street. This view across Ross Street from near the junction of Ross and Burns Streets looks westward. The Cleburne County Courthouse is in the right of the photograph. The building just to the left and on the corner is the First Bank of Heflin. (Courtesy Pete Wright.)

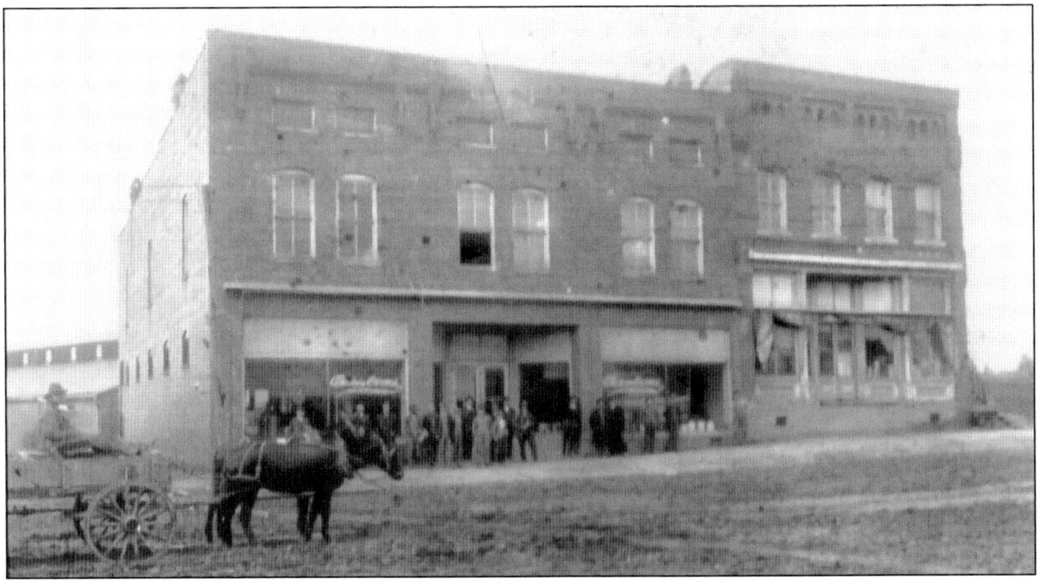

Ross Street, around 1900. This photograph is believed to have been taken around 1900 with the Heflin Railroad Commissary building on the far right. The big building in the center of the photograph is the Atkins and Owens store, which sold farm supplies, seeds, and clothing. An area farmer with his horses and wagon can be seen on the left. The railroad ran to the right and to the rear of the row of buildings. (Courtesy Suzanne Payne.)

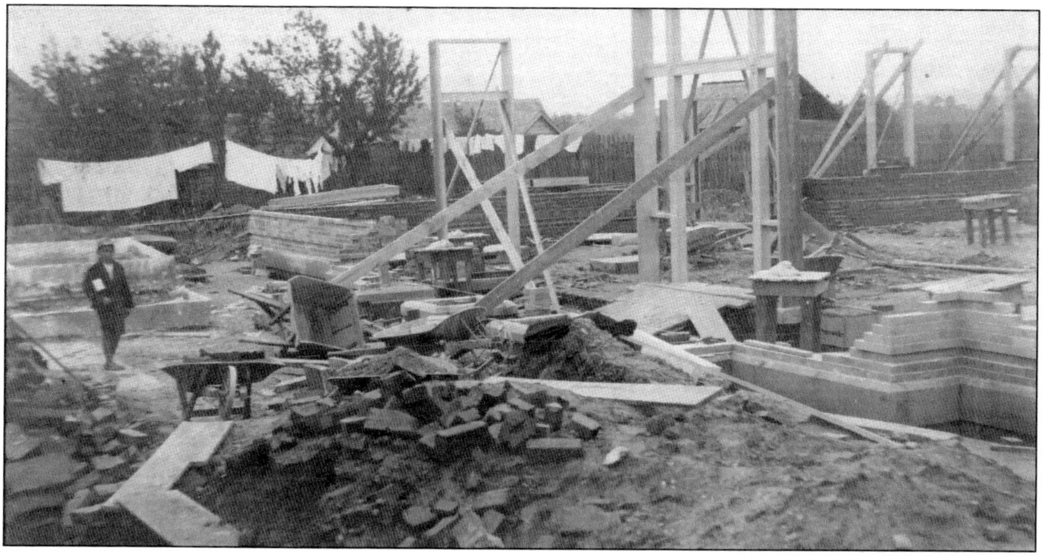

Work Begins on Courthouse. Work began in 1907 on a new Cleburne County Courthouse in Heflin after voters decided to move the county seat from nearby Edwardsville. In this photograph, a worker walks through the construction site. Note clothing items hanging on a line to dry in the background. (Courtesy Lorraine Watson.)

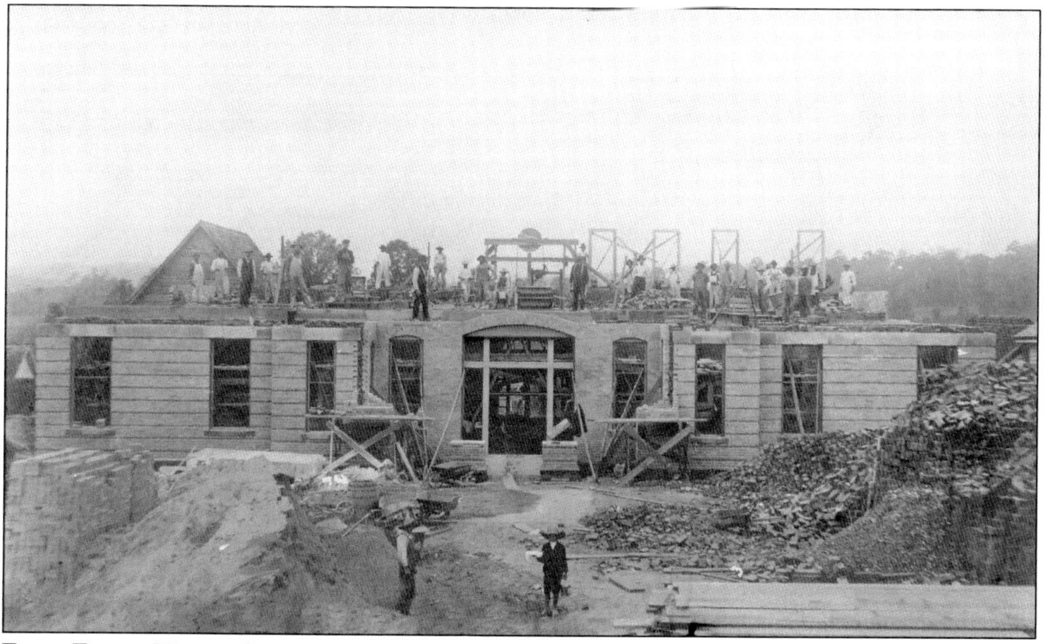

First Floor Nears Completion. Work nears completion on the first floor of the Cleburne County Courthouse. The building was located one block west of Ross Street in what is now downtown Heflin and fronted by Vickery Street. C. W. Carlton was the architect on the project. (Courtesy Lorraine Watson.)

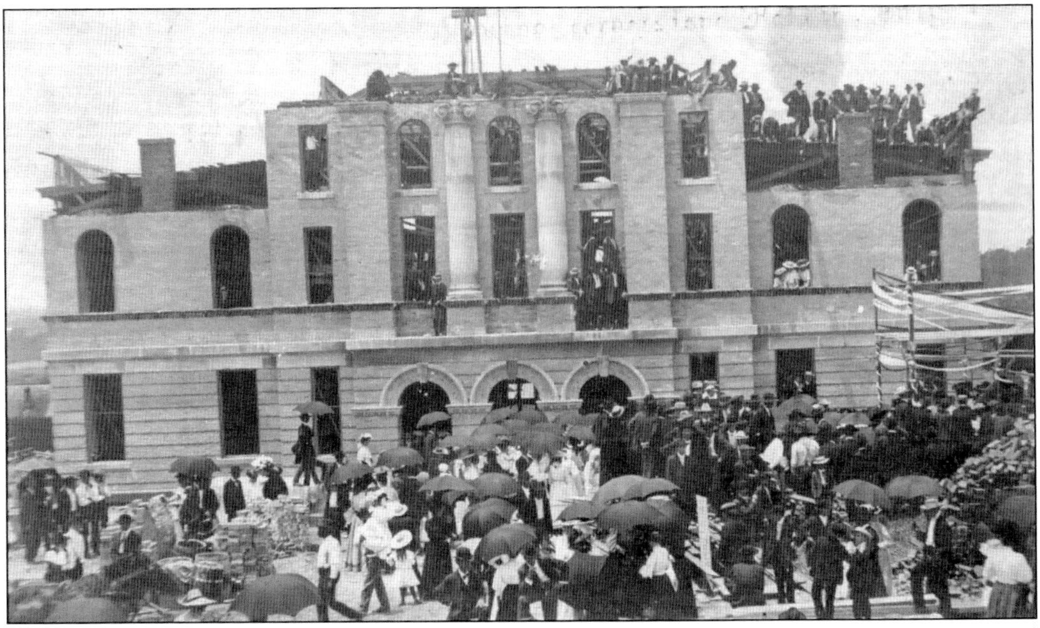

Courthouse Built in 1907. The Cleburne County Courthouse was built in a Classical Revival style and completed in 1907. A dome topped the structure, and two additional wings were added several years later. This photograph was taken during the laying of the cornerstone. An estimated 3,000 people attended the event. The building was placed on the National Register of Historic Places in 1976. (Courtesy Lorraine Watson.)

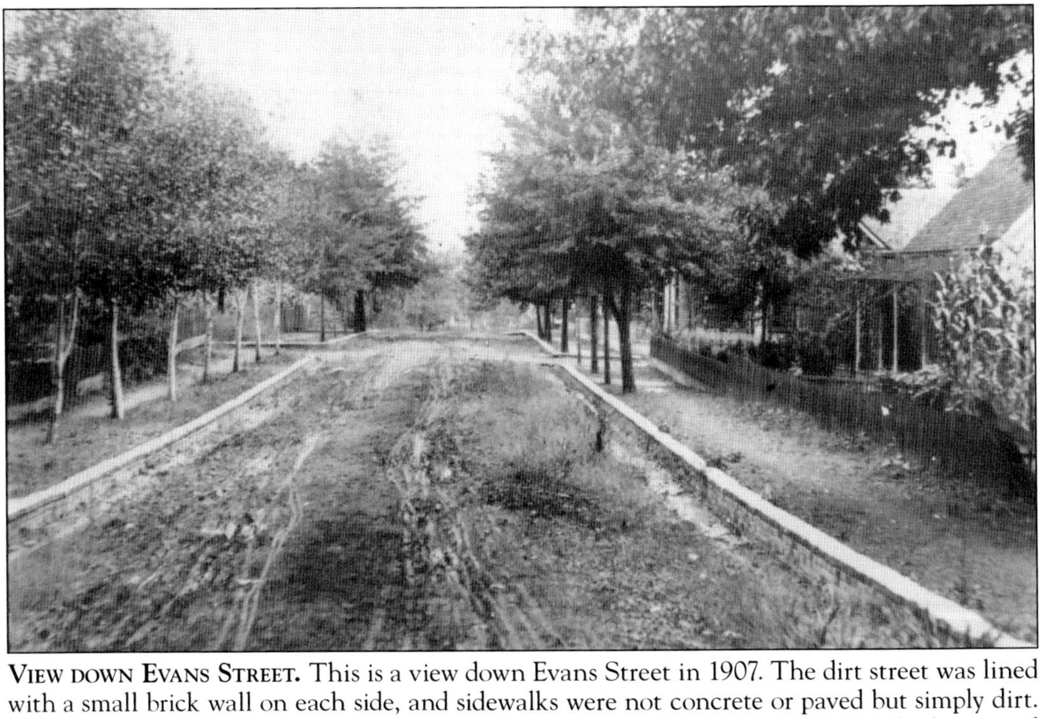

View down Evans Street. This is a view down Evans Street in 1907. The dirt street was lined with a small brick wall on each side, and sidewalks were not concrete or paved but simply dirt. Automobiles would not appear in Heflin until 1914, so the dirt streets were fine for horse and wagons. (Courtesy Pete Wright.)

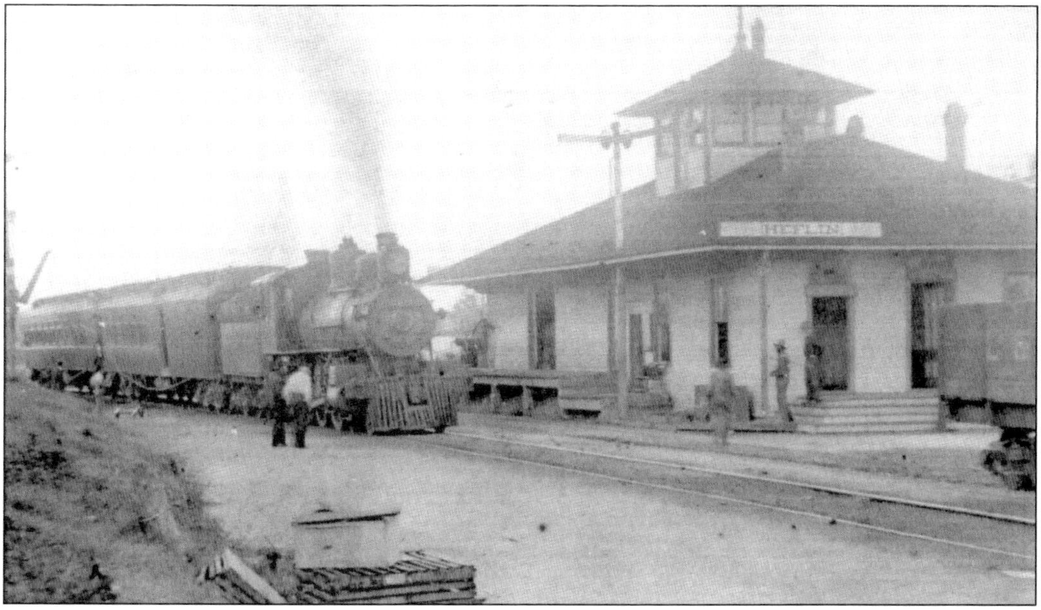

Heflin Depot. The Georgia-Pacific Railroad was completed to Heflin from Atlanta, Georgia, in 1882, and this contributed greatly to Heflin's growth. On May 9, 1917, the Alabama Public Service Commission ordered Southern Railway to file plans "showing improvement for the passenger traffic of the present combination depot at Heflin, Alabama, so as to make said passenger facilities adequate." This photograph is of the Heflin depot as it appeared approximately 1930. (Courtesy Pete Wright.)

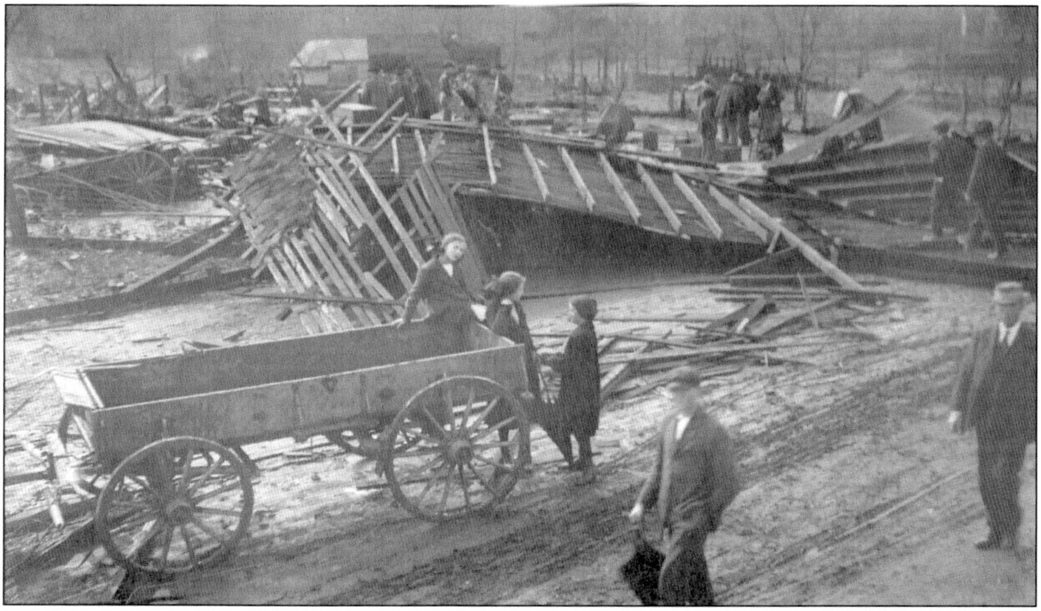

Cyclone. About 6 p.m. on March 21, 1913, "a terrific and death-dealing cyclone" hit Heflin and Edwardsville. The following morning, residents were out looking at the damage. Among those checking the damage was John Lewis Atkins, in the front foreground with umbrella. Behind him, in the bottom right corner, is J. M. Atkins in a suit and hat. (Courtesy Lucile Morgan Public Library.)

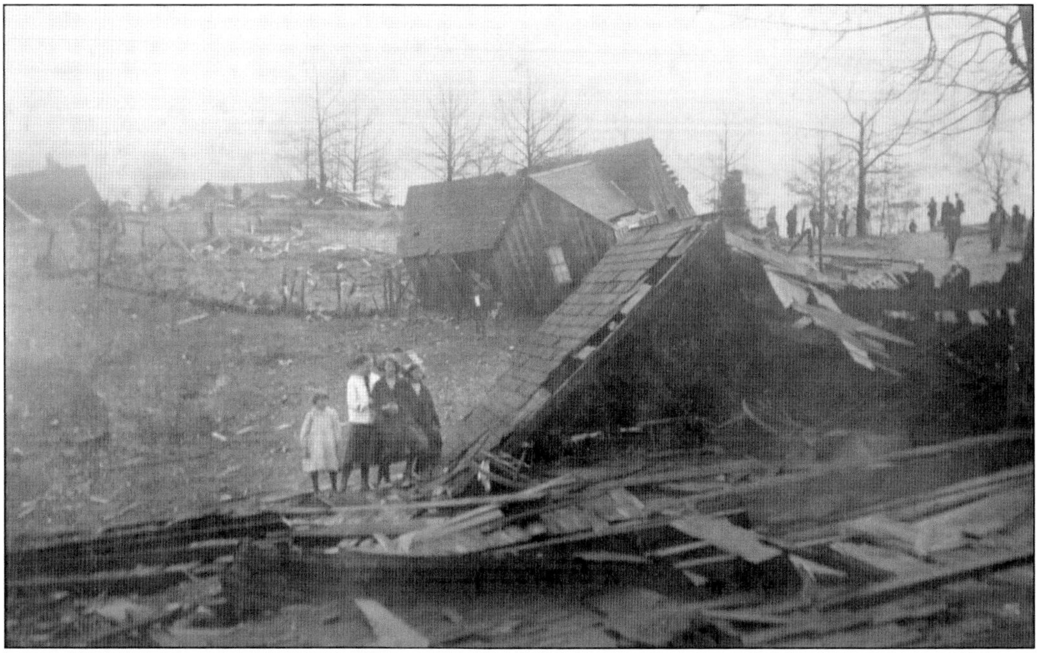

Cyclone Damage. Homes and farm buildings near Heflin and Edwardsville were damaged or destroyed by the cyclone. Newspaper reports told of the storm striking the Lewis Coffey home south of Edwardsville and killing 10 members of the family. Neighbors worked all night and until the following morning to find bodies and prepare them for burial. Some bodies were scattered over acres of land along the path of the cyclone. (Courtesy Lucile Morgan Public Library.)

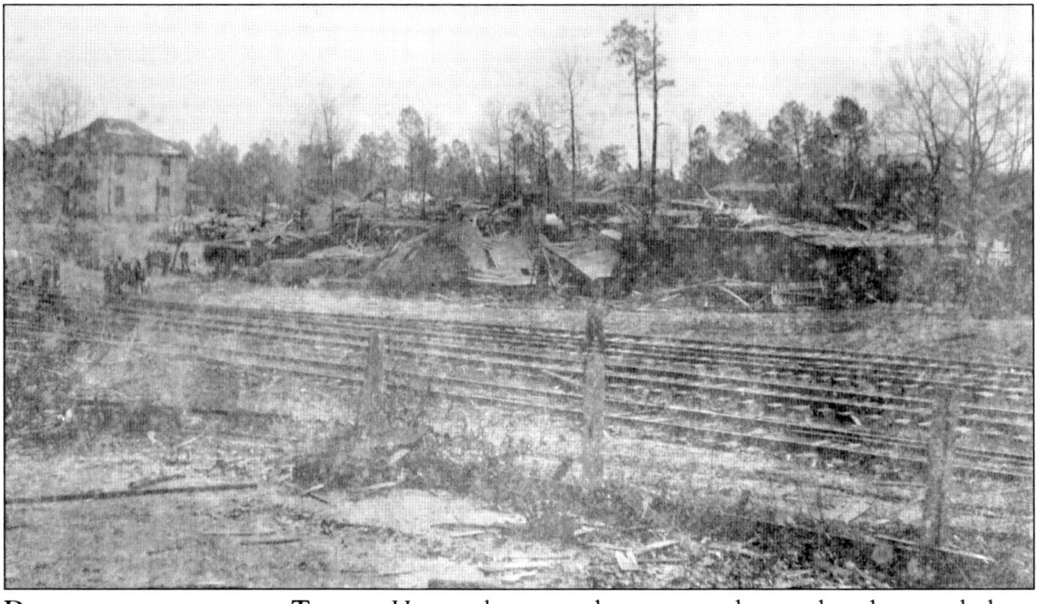

Destruction along the Tracks. Houses, barns, and trees were damaged or destroyed along railway tracks by the cyclone that hit Cleburne County on March 21, 1913. The path was in a northerly direction; it destroyed Heflin's black community and killed 10 people near Edwardsville who were buried in one mass grave at Cane Creek Primitive Baptist Church, 2 miles south of the town. (Courtesy Lucile Morgan Public Library.)

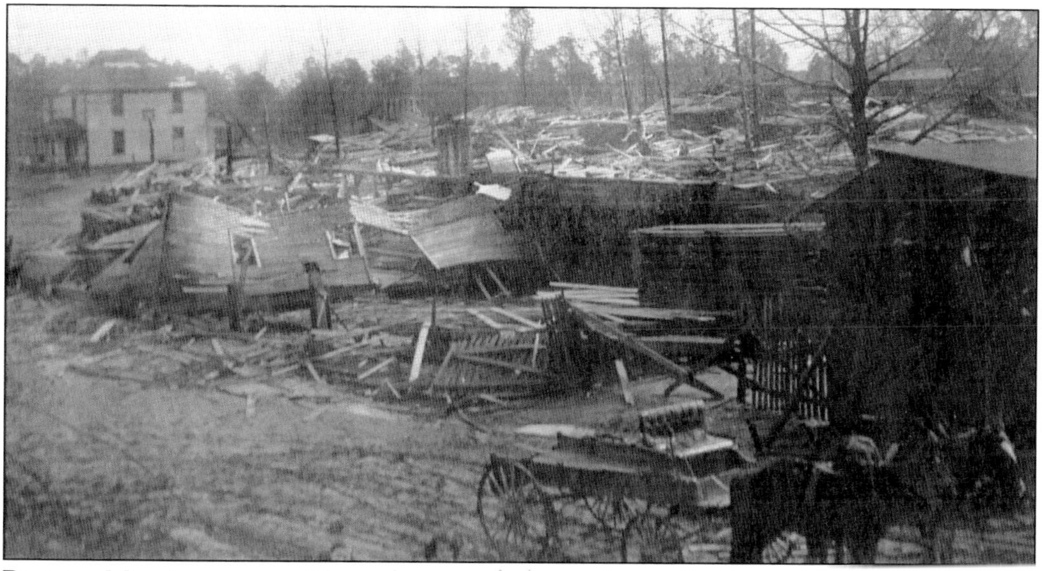

Planing Mill Destroyed. The cyclone struck the outskirts of Heflin and destroyed the Adams Planing Mill, where lumber was planed. The Adams family's two-story home can be seen on the left side of the photograph. The Adamses' daughter Minnie and her husband, Clellon Wager, later owned the home. (Courtesy Lucile Morgan Library.)

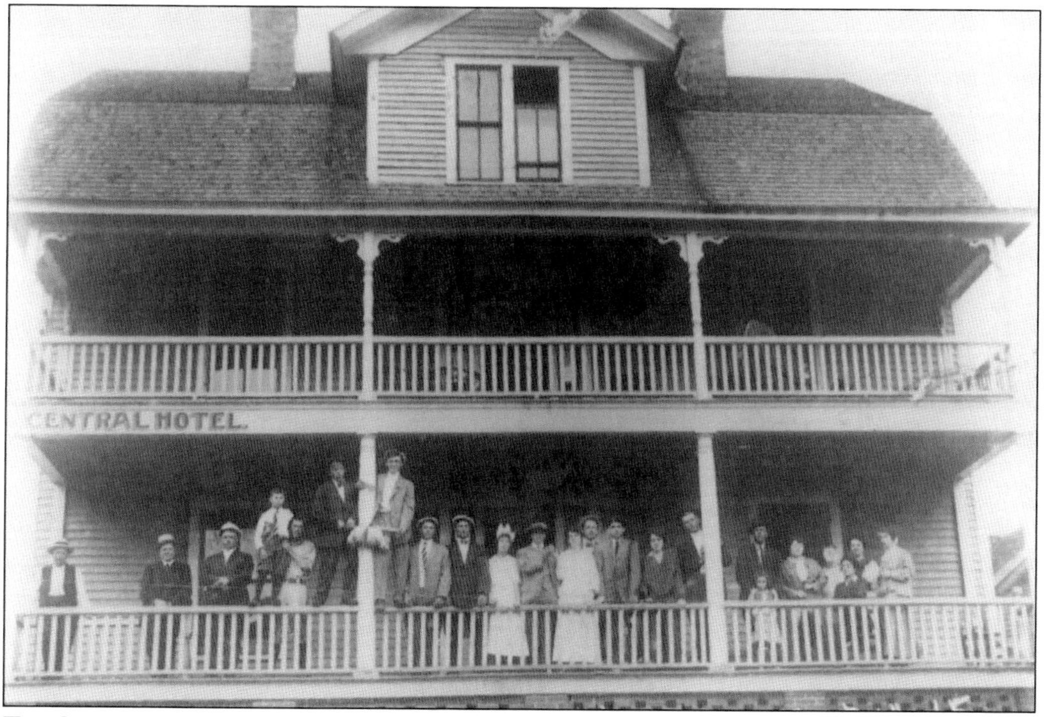

The Central Hotel. Guests and employees of the Central Hotel, located at the corner of Burns and Bell Streets, gathered out front for this photograph on May 31, 1915. The hotel was operated by William Alexander Stephens, seen standing on the far left of the photograph. The three-story hotel had sprawling verandas for guests, and family-style meals were served in the dining room. A dinner bell outside rang three times a day to signal meals. (Courtesy Linda Ayers.)

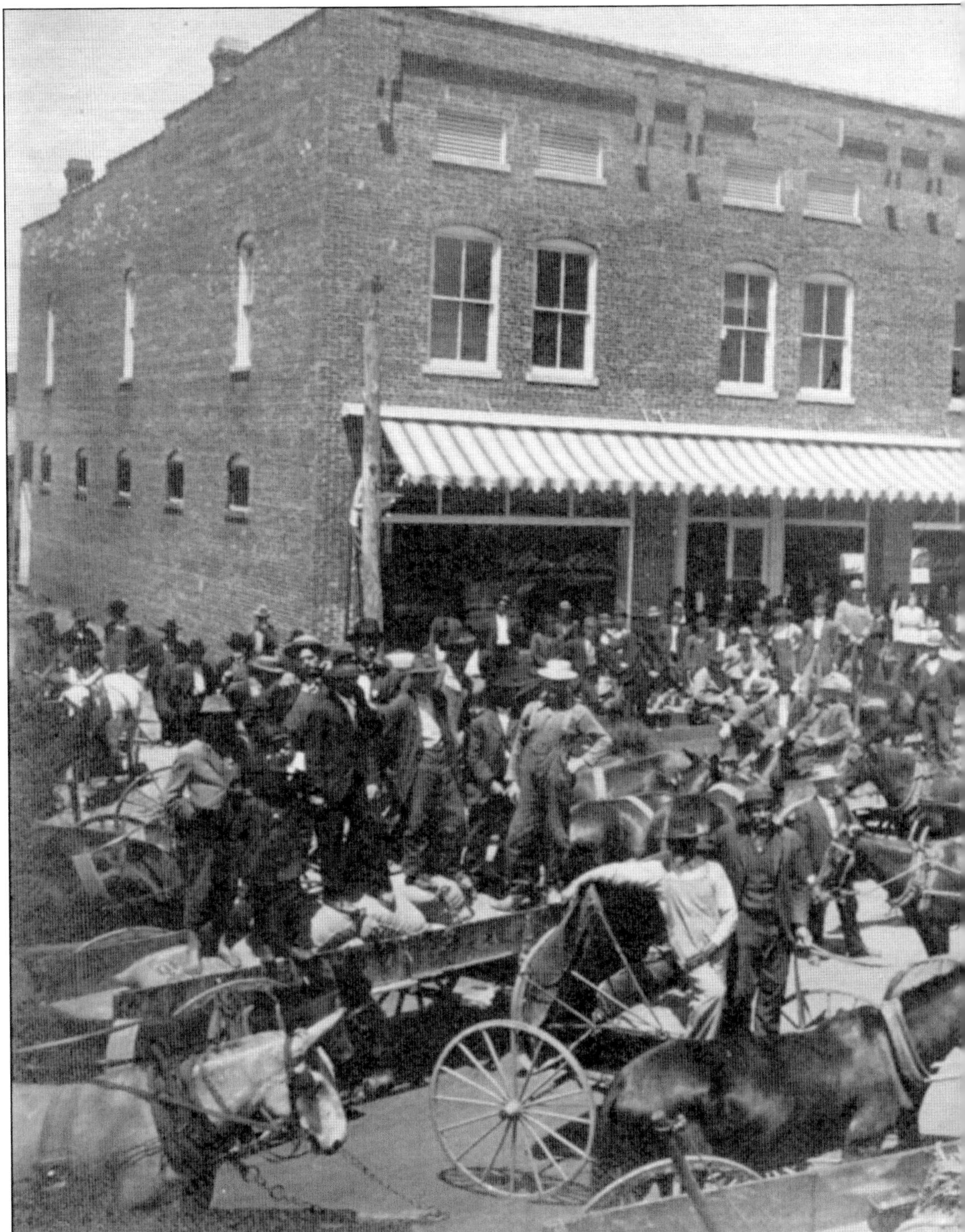

FARMERS IN TOWN. In the late 1800s, downtown Heflin could get a little crowded as farmers from the surrounding rural areas came into town bringing cotton and other goods, which were shipped out on the nearby railroad, in the background. The small building on the right was a dental office, and the large building on the left was the Atkins and Owens mercantile store. They sold farm supplies, lumber and building supplies, and clothing, and they also had cotton scales on which

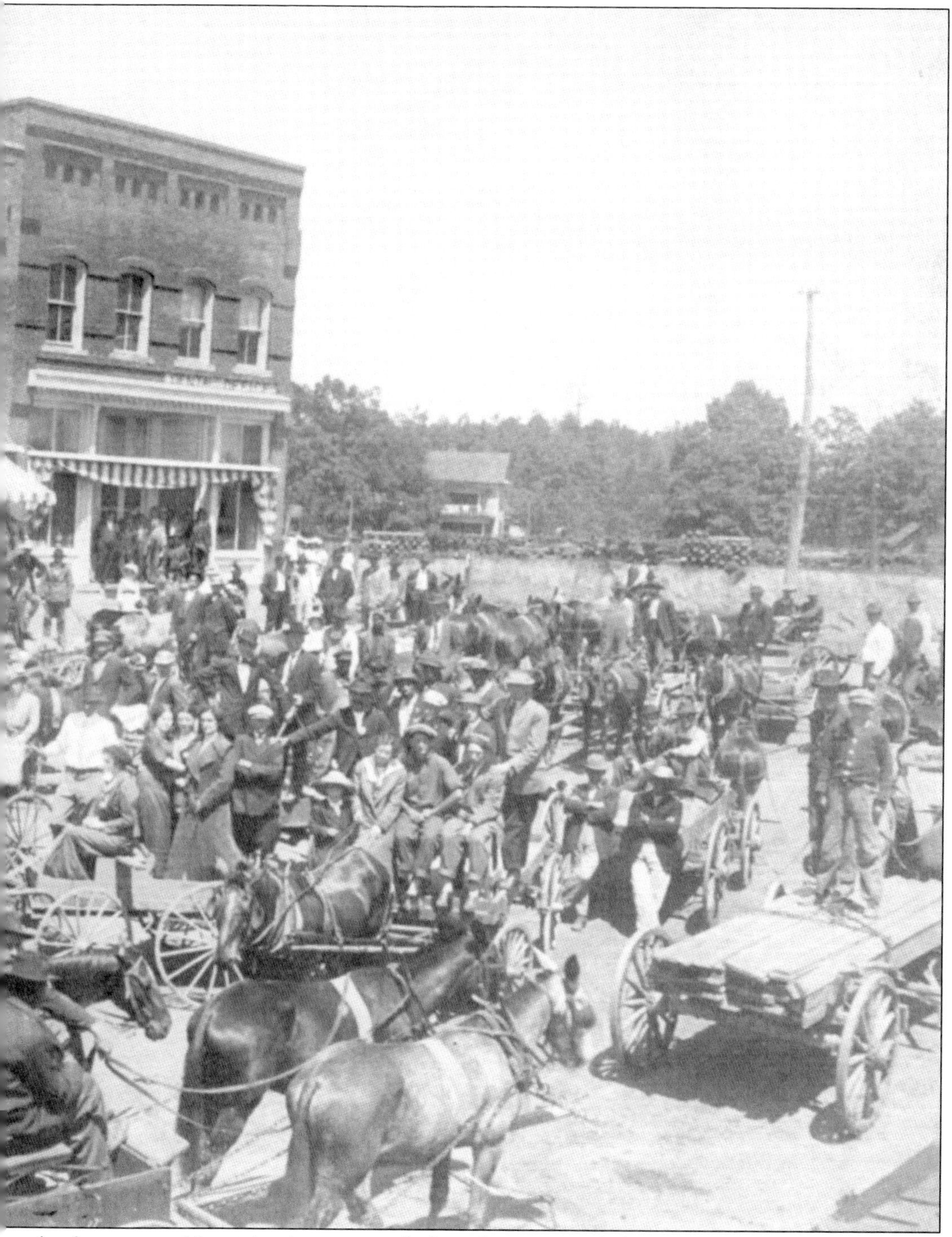

the farmers could weight their cotton before shipment. While in town, the farmers and their families would purchase necessary items to take back home. Over time, Atkins wanted to get out of the business; J. A. Owens bought Atkins's interest in the business, and the store became J. A. Owens Store and continued in business for many years. (Courtesy Jane Beam.)

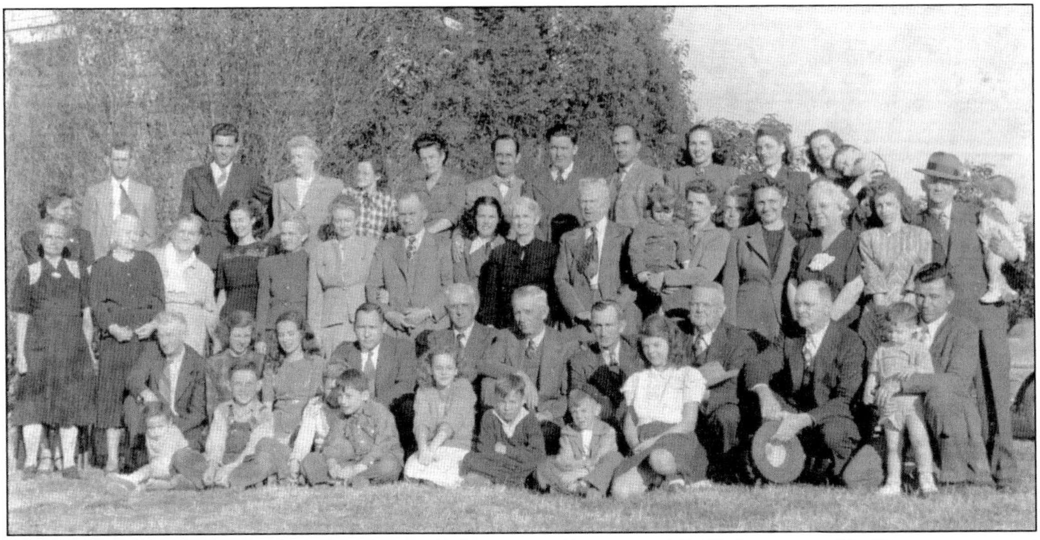

STEPHENS FAMILY REUNION. The Central Hotel, on Burns and Bell Streets in Heflin, was owned by William A. Stephens. In December 1947, the Stephens descendants gathered at the home of A. H. Glasgow in Heflin for a family reunion. The group enjoyed the event and shared many memories of Heflin. (Courtesy Jane Beam.)

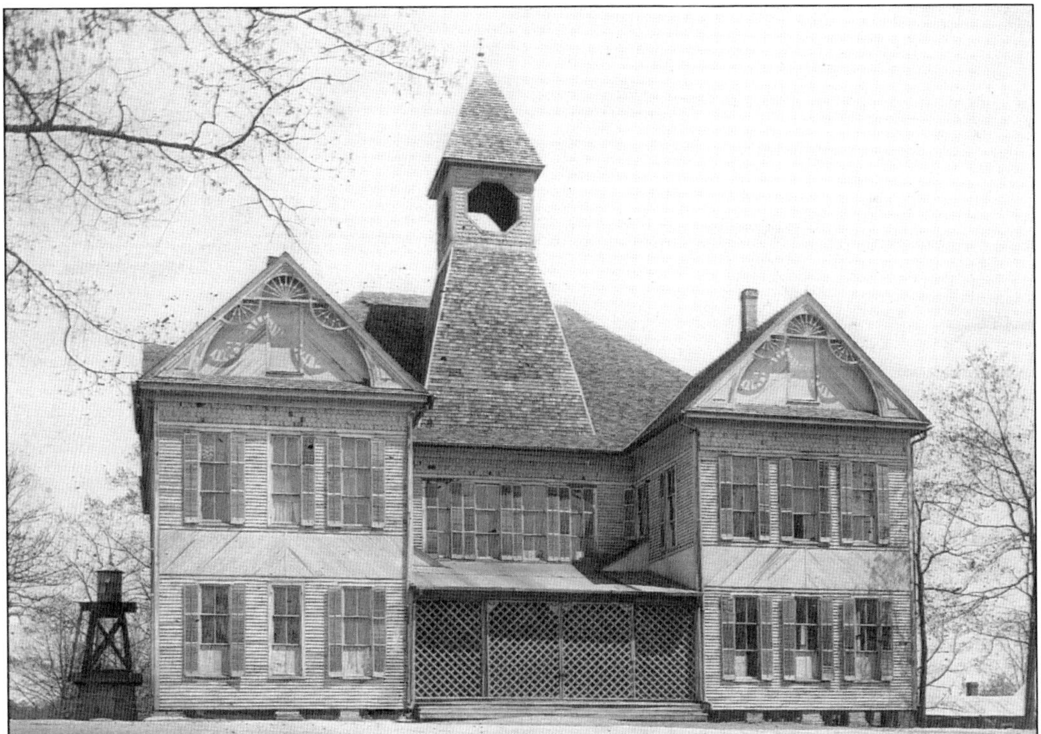

ROSS INSTITUTE. Founded in 1885 with 75 students and originally located in what is now The Pines residential area of Heflin, the Ross Institute later relocated near Heflin City Hall downtown in the building pictured above, built by the city. It was incorporated in 1894 by Act 128 of the Alabama General Assembly. (Courtesy Pete Wright.)

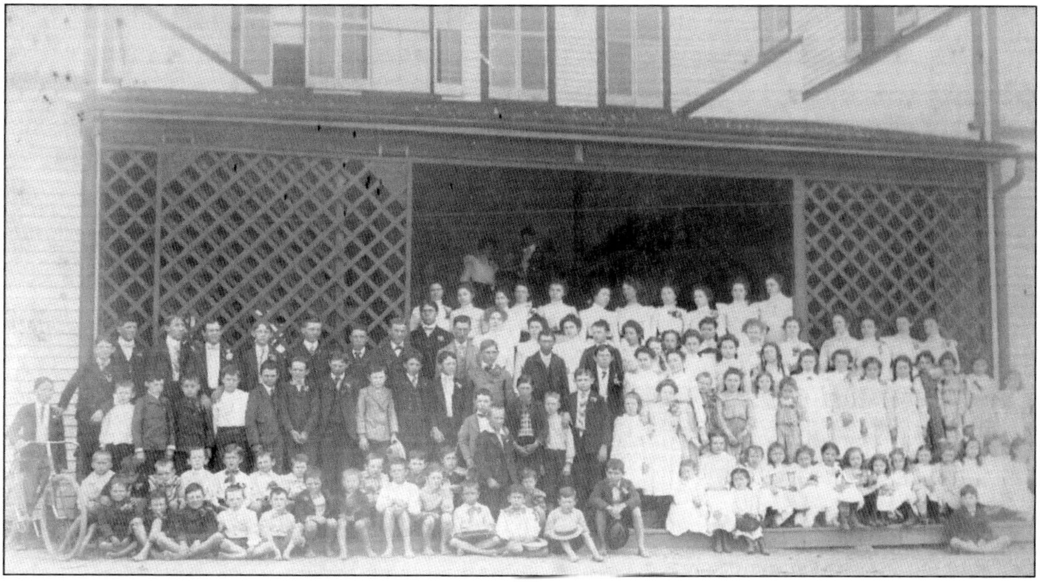

Ross Attendees. Here are some students of the Ross Institute. Following construction of a high school in town, Ross Institute became the elementary school. In 1923, the school was among 78 white and three black schools in the county. The building was later torn down, and Heflin High School vocational building was erected on the site. (Courtesy Lucile Morgan Public Library.)

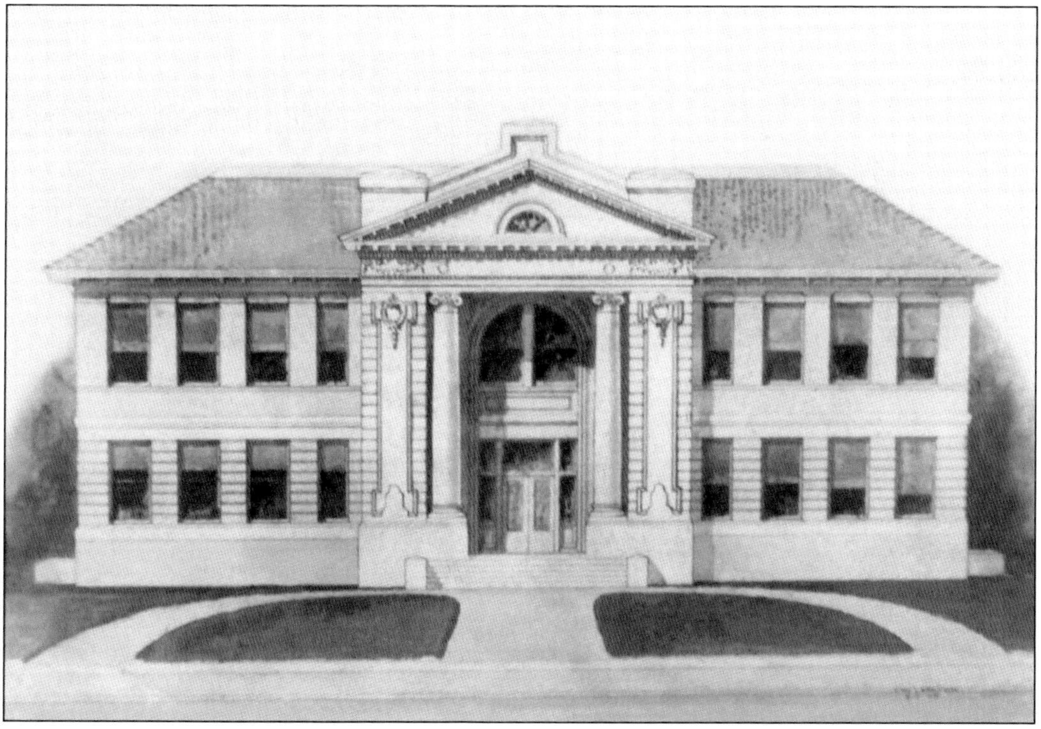

Heflin High School. This postcard drawing, done in 1910, illustrates Heflin High School, located at the corner of Burns and Evans Streets in Heflin. The school was built in 1909. Bonds were sold to finance construction. Today the building houses a privately owned day care facility. (Courtesy Linda Ayers.)

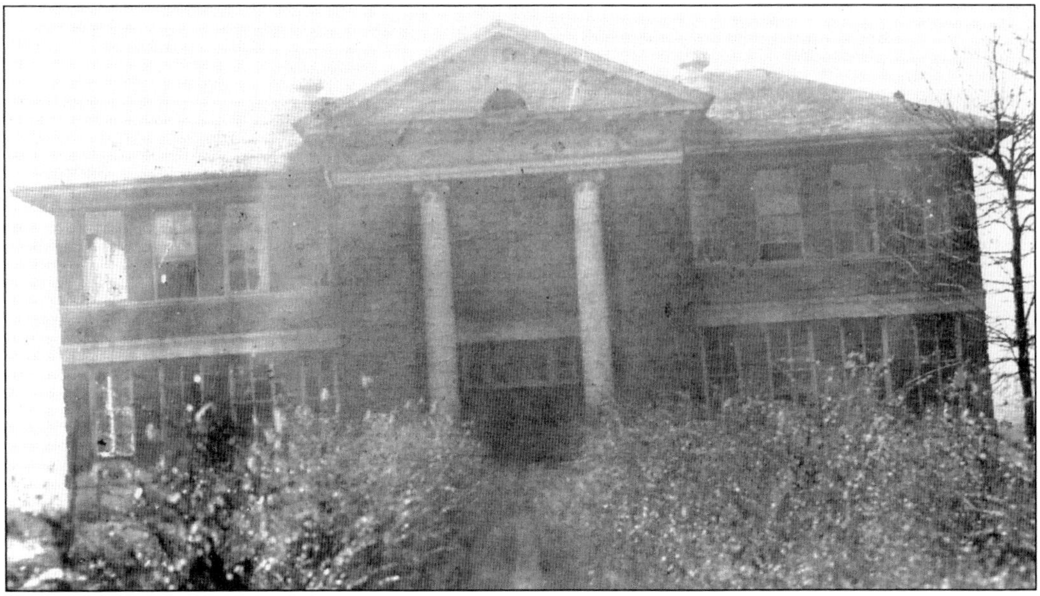

HEFLIN HIGH. Heflin's first high school, Heflin High, was built in 1909 on the corner of Burns and Evans Streets. The school drew students from Heflin and surrounding areas because classes ran for nine months instead of the four to six months out in the county, where children were expected to help plant and harvest crops. Ross Institute became the town's elementary school. (Courtesy Carolyn Parker.)

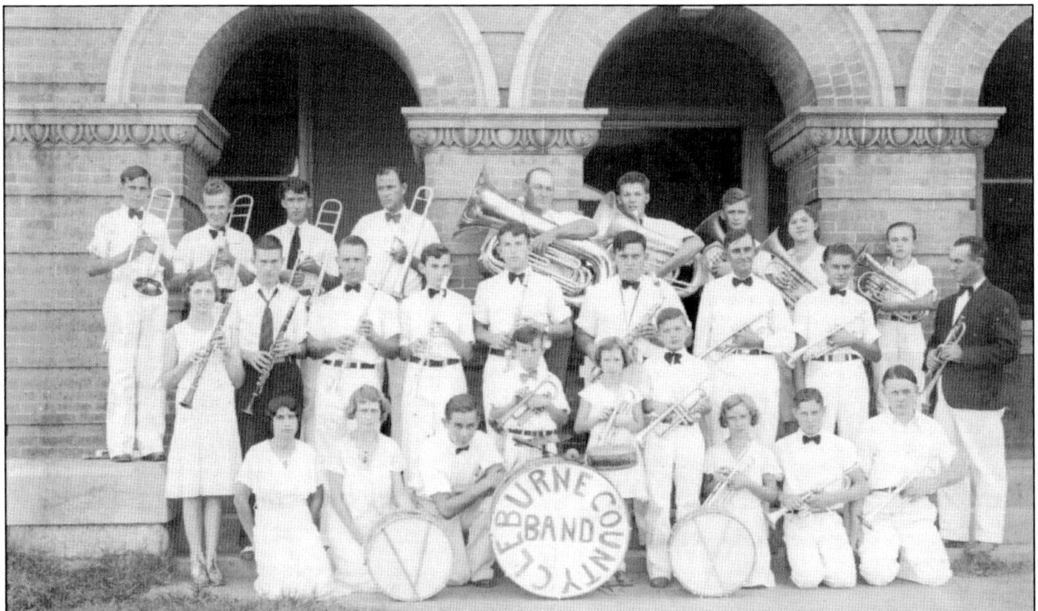

CLEBURNE COUNTY BAND. This is a 1933 photograph of the Cleburne County Band in front of the Cleburne County Courthouse. Members included, from left to right, (first row) all unidentified; (second row) Bobby Jean Burgess, Ralph Jones, unidentified, Louis Langford, Bill Wright, unidentified, ? Langford, and two unidentified; (third row) Maurice Clay, Alwyn Akins, Ray Cole, ? Cole, three unidentified, Merle Wager, and unidentified. (Courtesy Lucile Morgan Library.)

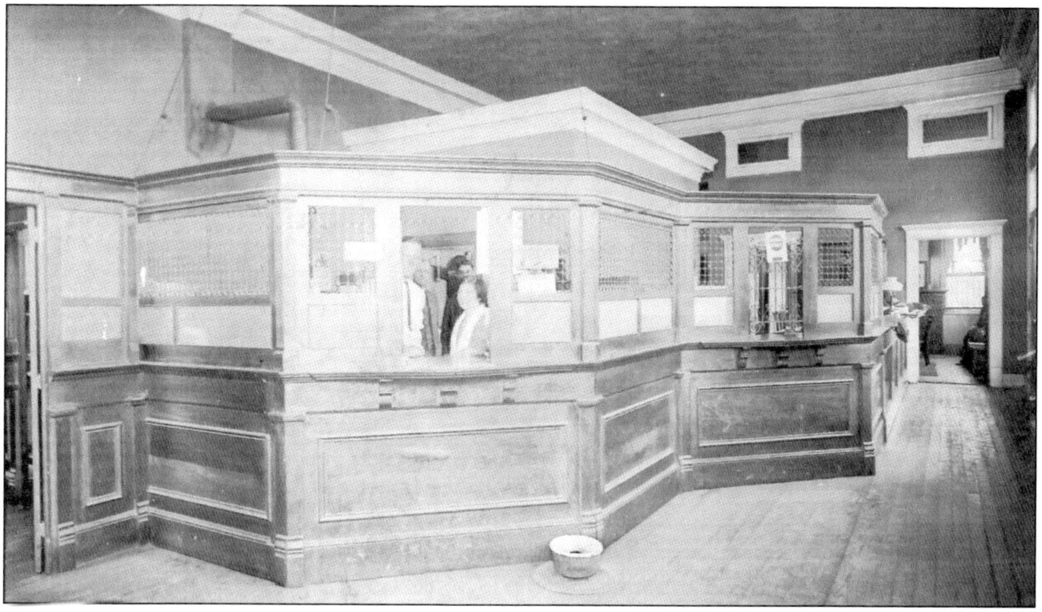

Bank Lobby. Customers to the First Bank of Heflin entered this lobby of the bank that was located at the corner of Ross and Hunnicutt Streets. The building is now a dentist office. The bank incorporated on February 2, 1905. J. M. Atkins was the first president. Later presidents included B. W. Pruett, John Lewis Atkins, R. O. Atkins, J. Ralph Hamilton, and Robert R. Pope. (Courtesy Lucile Morgan Public Library.)

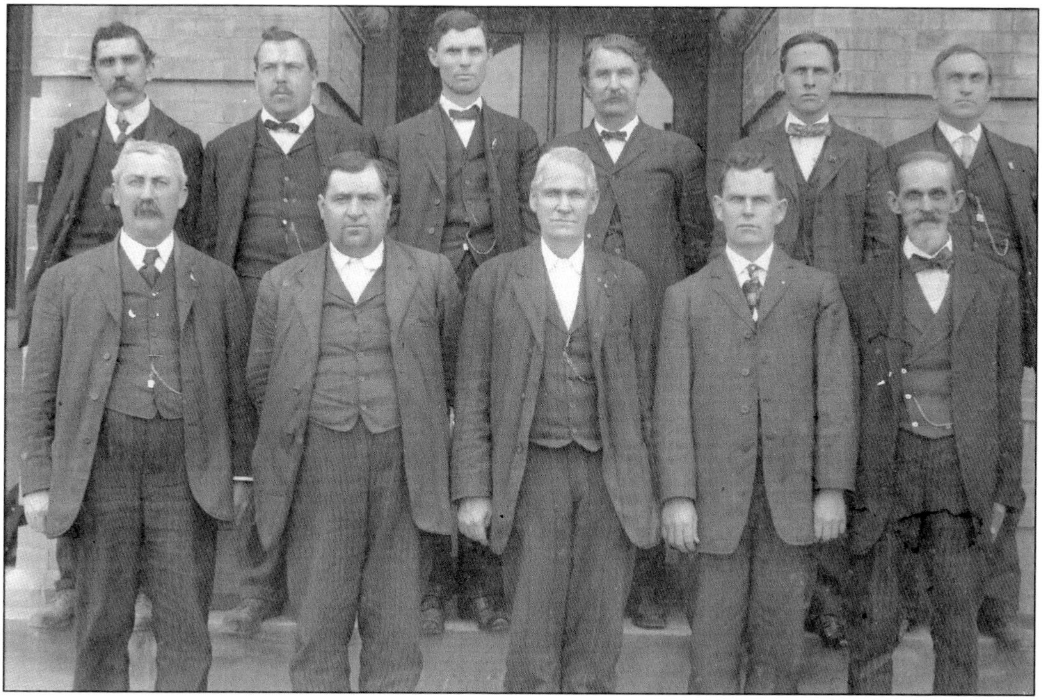

County Officials. These men are standing on the steps of the Cleburne County Courthouse in Heflin some time between 1904 and 1910. A. H. Glasgow (first row, fourth from left) was the Cleburne County superintendent of education from 1904 to 1910. (Courtesy Jane Beam.)

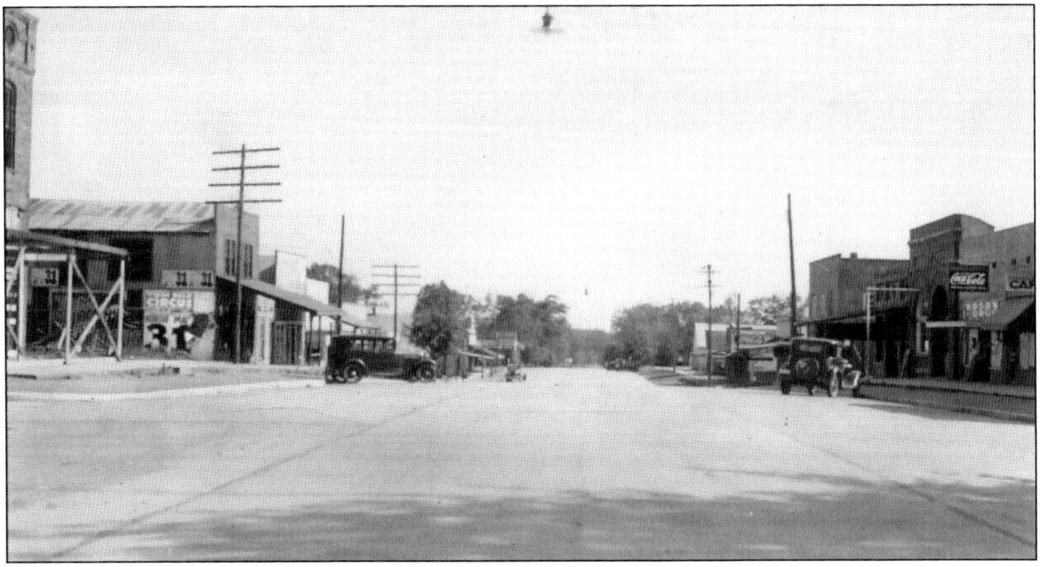

ROSS STREET, EARLY 1930S. This photograph was taken in the middle of Ross Street in front of Wright's Drugs, looking west some time in the early 1930s. On the right side of the street can be seen a café and Woods Drugstore. Farther down was the old post office building and gas company along with White's Grocery, and on the left side, just the edge of the two-story Hunnicutt Building is visible, along with the theater and the power company. (Courtesy Pete Wright.)

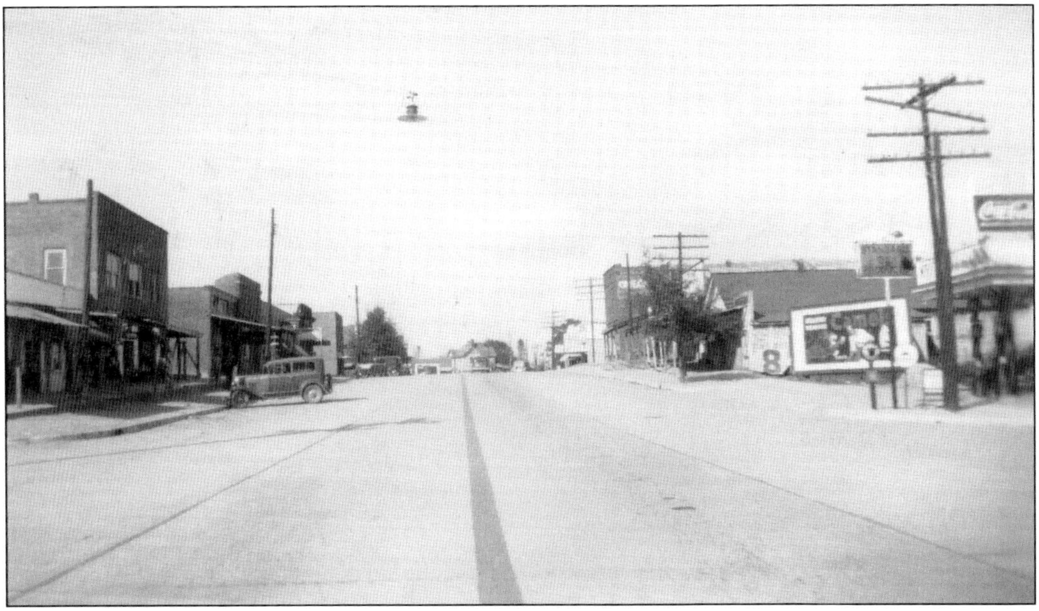

EASTWARD VIEW DOWN ROSS STREET. On the right side of this early-1930s look down Ross Street is Chandler and Edwards, a Standard Oil service station, and in the distance the Hunnicutt Building, which housed, at one time or another, a furniture store, Masonic hall, and law offices. By this time, Heflin had a bowling alley, tennis court, theater, and croquet courts. The Bankhead Highway, also known as U.S. Highway 78, was paved in 1933, greatly improving transportation through town. (Courtesy Pete Wright.)

1918 PAYROLL. The Town of Heflin received $345 for its March and April 1918 payroll from the "special fund for school purposes," according to this payroll record. J. R. Barker, chairman of the Cleburne County Board of Education, approved the payment to the town treasurer of Heflin on May 4, 1918. (Courtesy Lucile Morgan Public Library.)

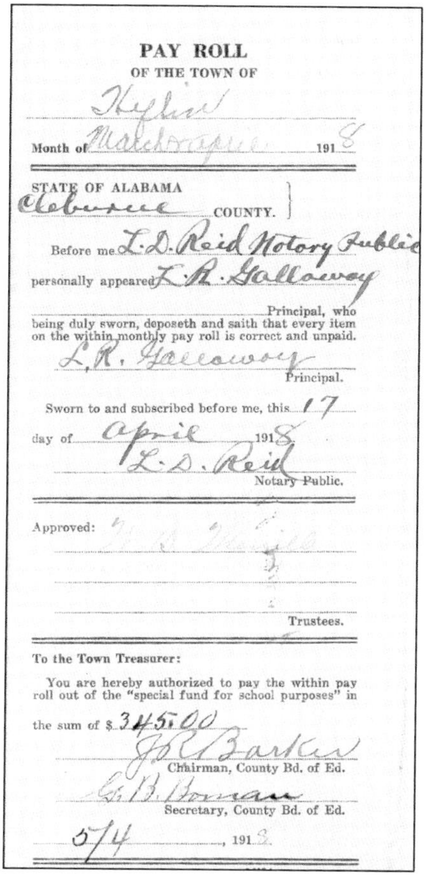

PAY ROLL
OF THE TOWN OF
Heflin

Month of March-April 1918

STATE OF ALABAMA
Cleburne COUNTY.

Before me L. D. Reid Notory Public
personally appeared L. R. Galloway
Principal, who being duly sworn, deposeth and saith that every item on the within monthly pay roll is correct and unpaid.

L. R. Galloway
Principal.

Sworn to and subscribed before me, this 17
day of April 1918
L. D. Reid
Notary Public.

Approved: [illegible]

Trustees.

To the Town Treasurer:

You are hereby authorized to pay the within pay roll out of the "special fund for school purposes" in the sum of $345.00

J. R. Barker
Chairman, County Bd. of Ed.

G. B. Bowman
Secretary, County Bd. of Ed.

5/4, 1918

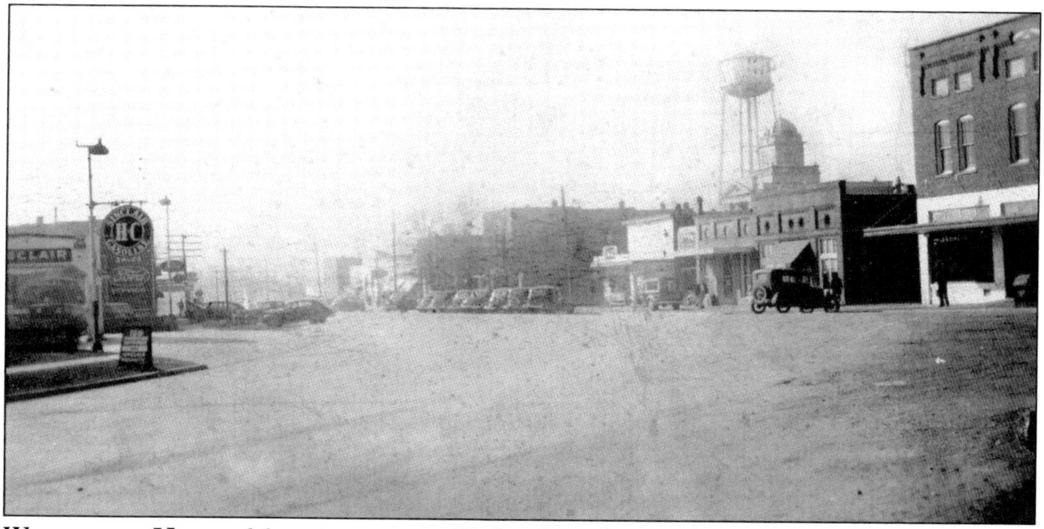

WELCOME TO HEFLIN. Motorists entering Heflin from the east during the 1930s and 1940s were welcomed with this scene in the large curve coming into town. On the right-hand side of the street can be seen Owens's store, a funeral home, S. A. Edwards, Burt Harris's popcorn and peanut stand, a croquet field, the Harper Building, and the Bank of Heflin. On the left was Paul Harper's Sinclair gas station. (Courtesy Carolyn Parker.)

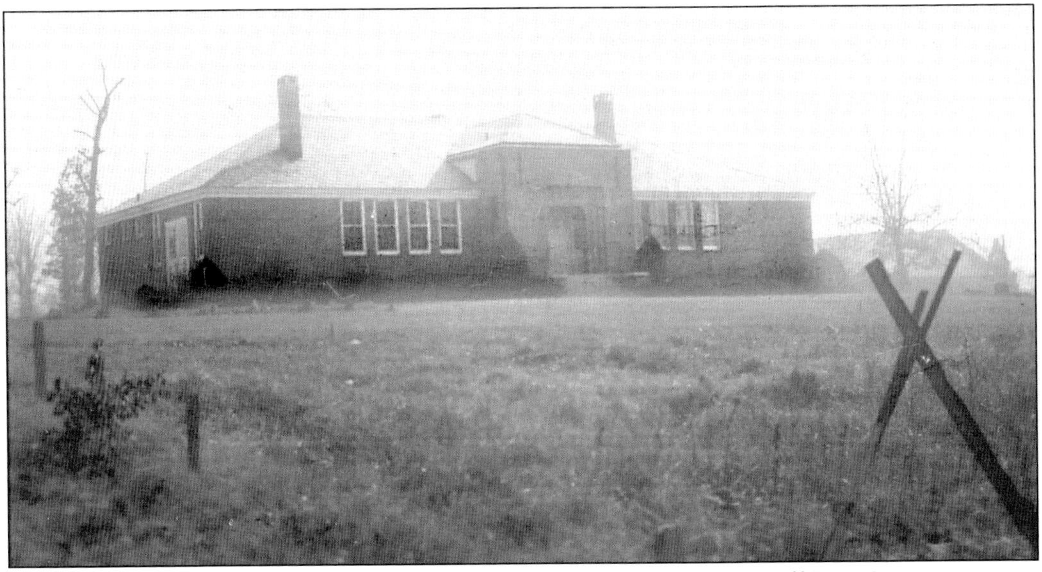

HEFLIN VOCATIONAL DEPARTMENT. The old Ross Collegiate Institute, off Ross Street, was torn down to make way for construction of the Cleburne County High Vocational Department. Girls met on the right side of the building for classes in home economics, while boys met in the left side to learn agricultural trades. (Courtesy Carolyn Parker.)

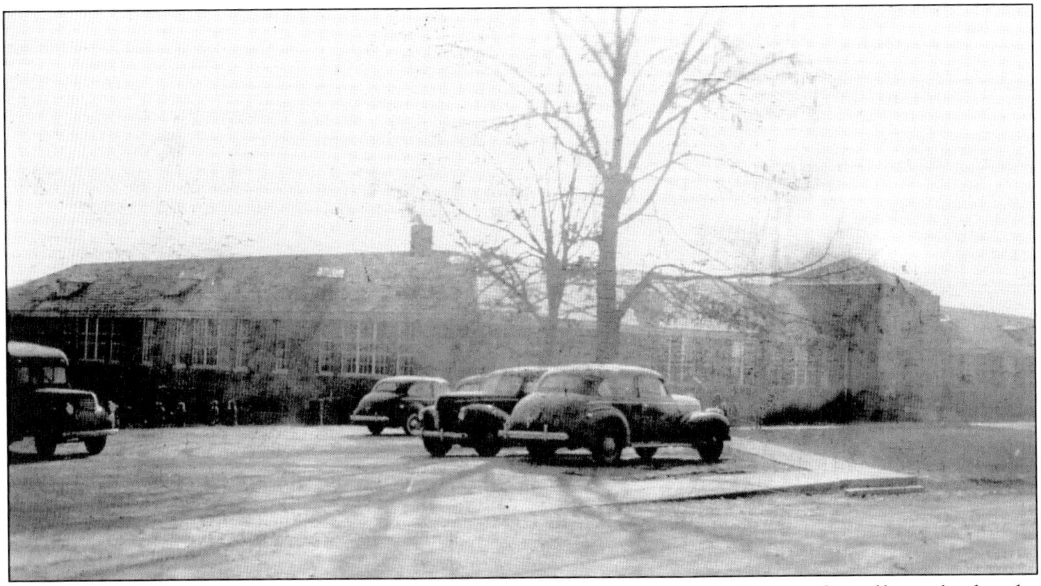

CLEBURNE COUNTY HIGH. Due to growing enrollments and consolidation of small rural schools, a new high school was built in Heflin in 1936 on Willoughby Way, and it became Cleburne County High. Junior high students met in the left half of the building, and seniors met in the right side. The old Heflin High on Burns Street became Cleburne County Elementary. (Courtesy Carolyn Parker.)

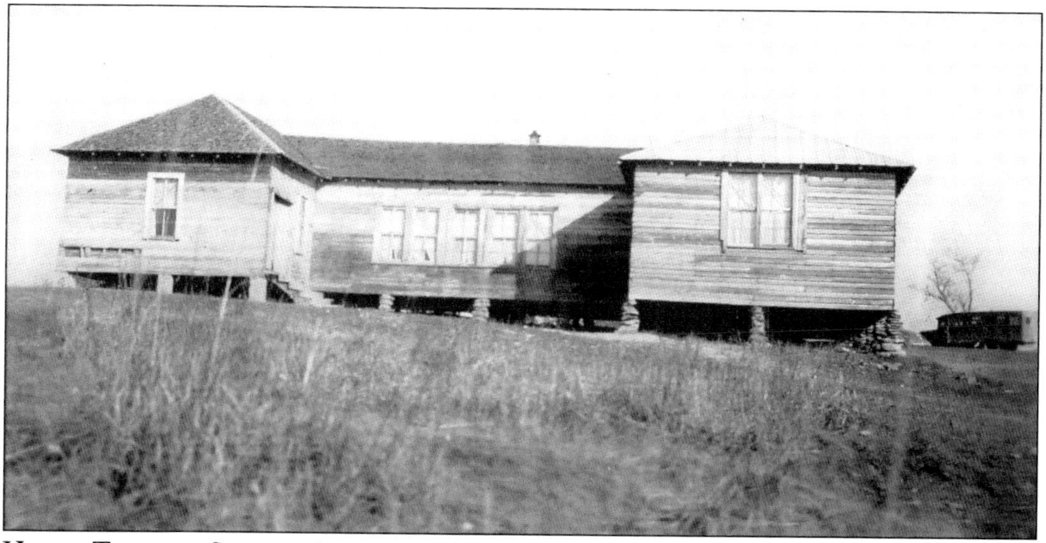

Heflin Training School. A separate school for African Americans was built in Heflin. The Heflin Training School served the black community and was consolidated with Cleburne County High in the mid-1960s. Early teachers and principals included John Harris, R. M. Allen, T. J. Freeman, Ora Wilson, William Brown, Abraham Perkins, and Katherine Driver. (Courtesy Carolyn Parker.)

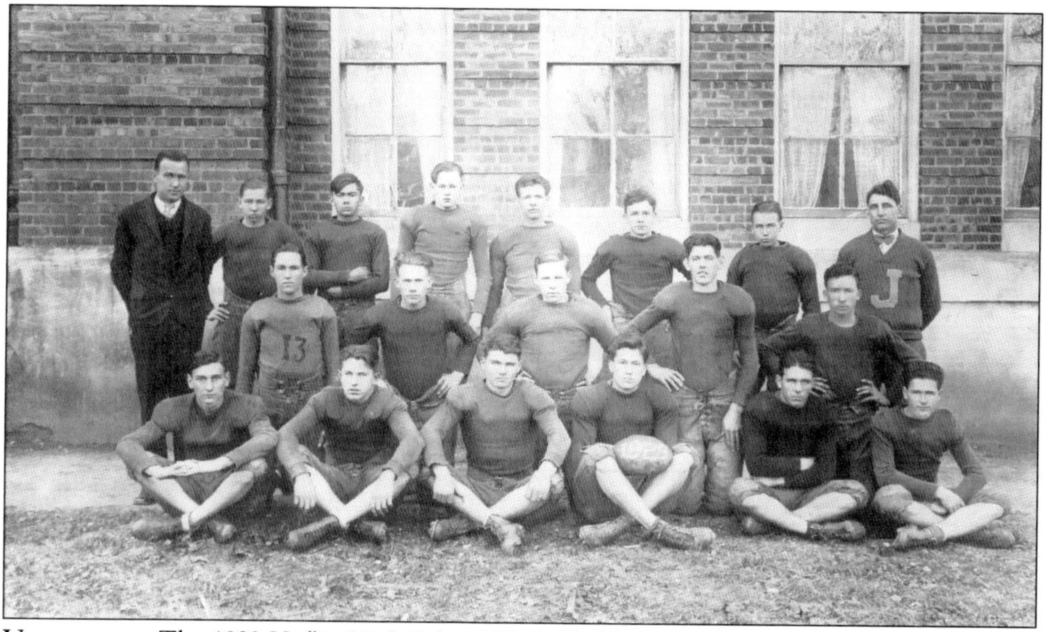

Undefeated. The 1929 Heflin High School Tigers, led by coach Foster Lockridge, won all but one game, and that one ended in a tie. Seen here from left to right are (first row) Louie Wessinger, Bill Wright, Sam Young, Robert Tolleson, Bill Pounds, and Hoyt Wright; (second row) Harold Adams, "Smiley" Bennett, Casey Jones, Knox Campbell, and "Zeke" Owen; (third row) Heflin High School principal Joe Petterson, Frank Cunningham, Lindley Ayers, Owen Crumpton, Ralph King, Ed Owen, Tom Owens, and coach Foster Lockridge. The picture was taken on the north side of the high school on Burns Street on January 30, 1930. (Courtesy Lucile Morgan Public Library.)

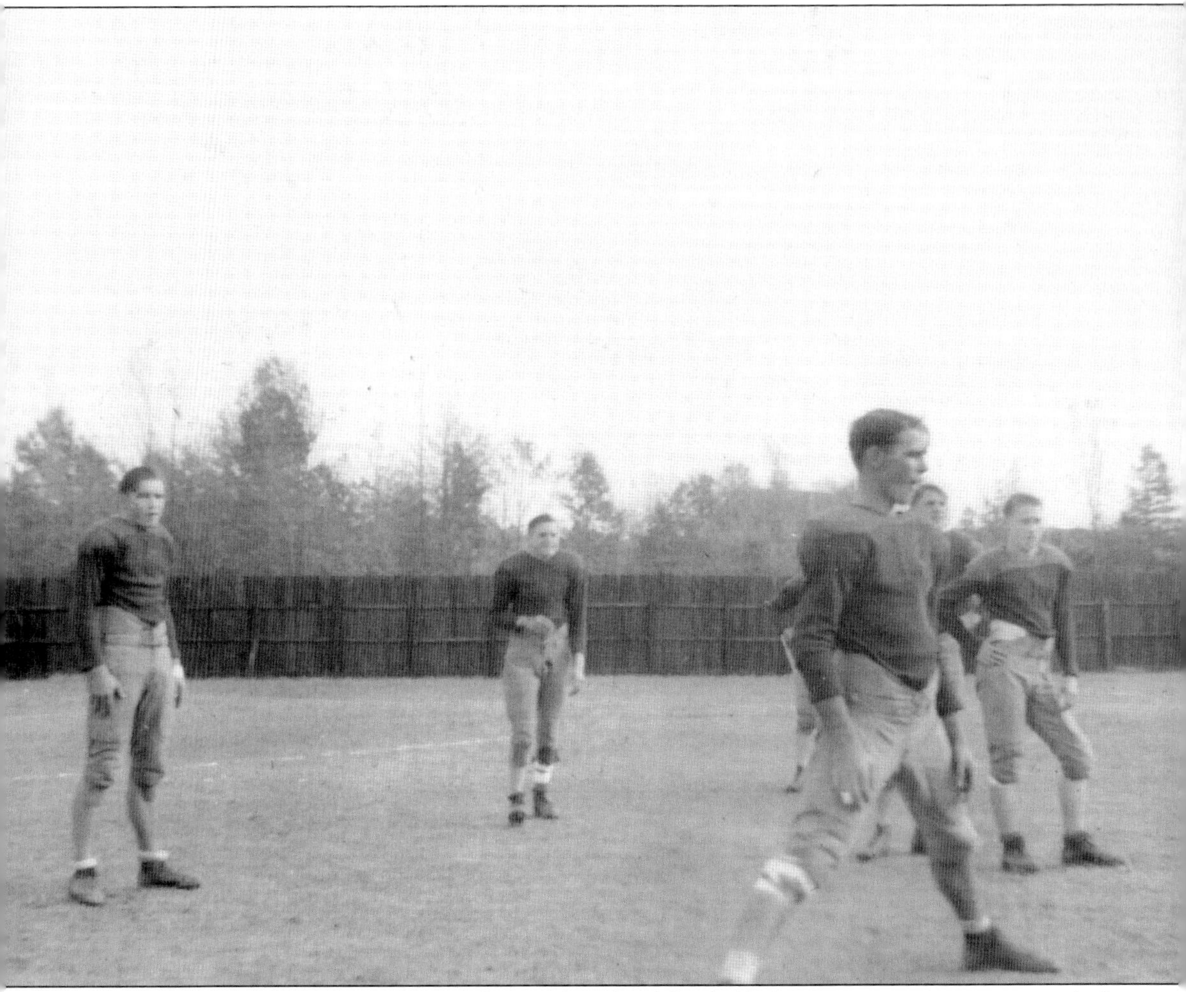

PRACTICE TIME. This group of Heflin High School football players gets in some practice before their next game. The team did well in the late 1920s and early 1930s. Coach Foster Lockridge led the team for a number of years. (Courtesy Leesa Cheatwood.)

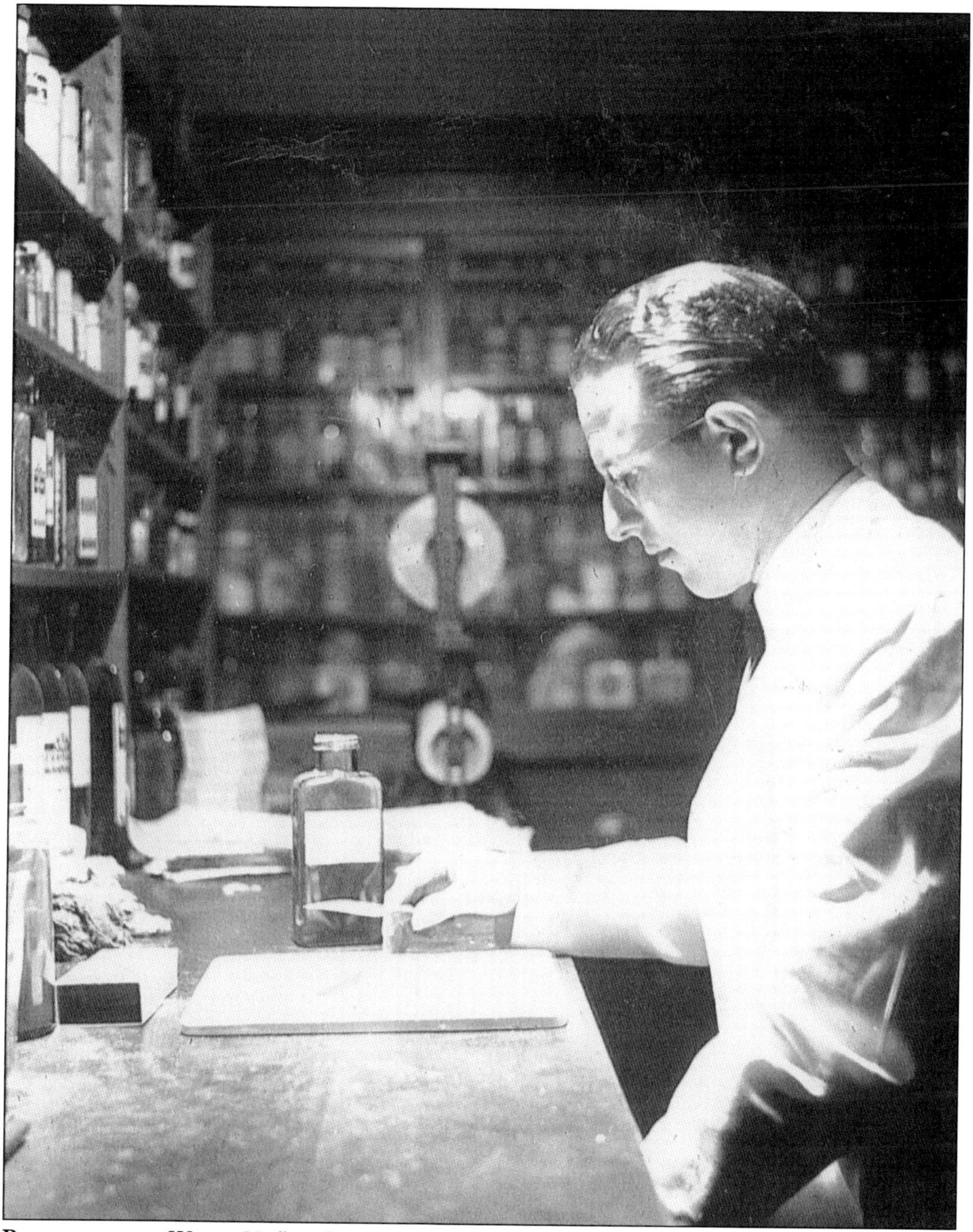

PHARMACIST AT WORK. Heflin pharmacist W. W. Wright is shown here in his drugstore. Wright Drugs has been in business in Heflin since 1902. Dr. Lee Roy Wright opened the drugstore, and his son followed. In the early 1920s, gasoline for automobiles could be purchased from drums located at the rear of the drugstore. A telephone office was also in the rear of Wright Drugs. (Courtesy Pete Wright.)

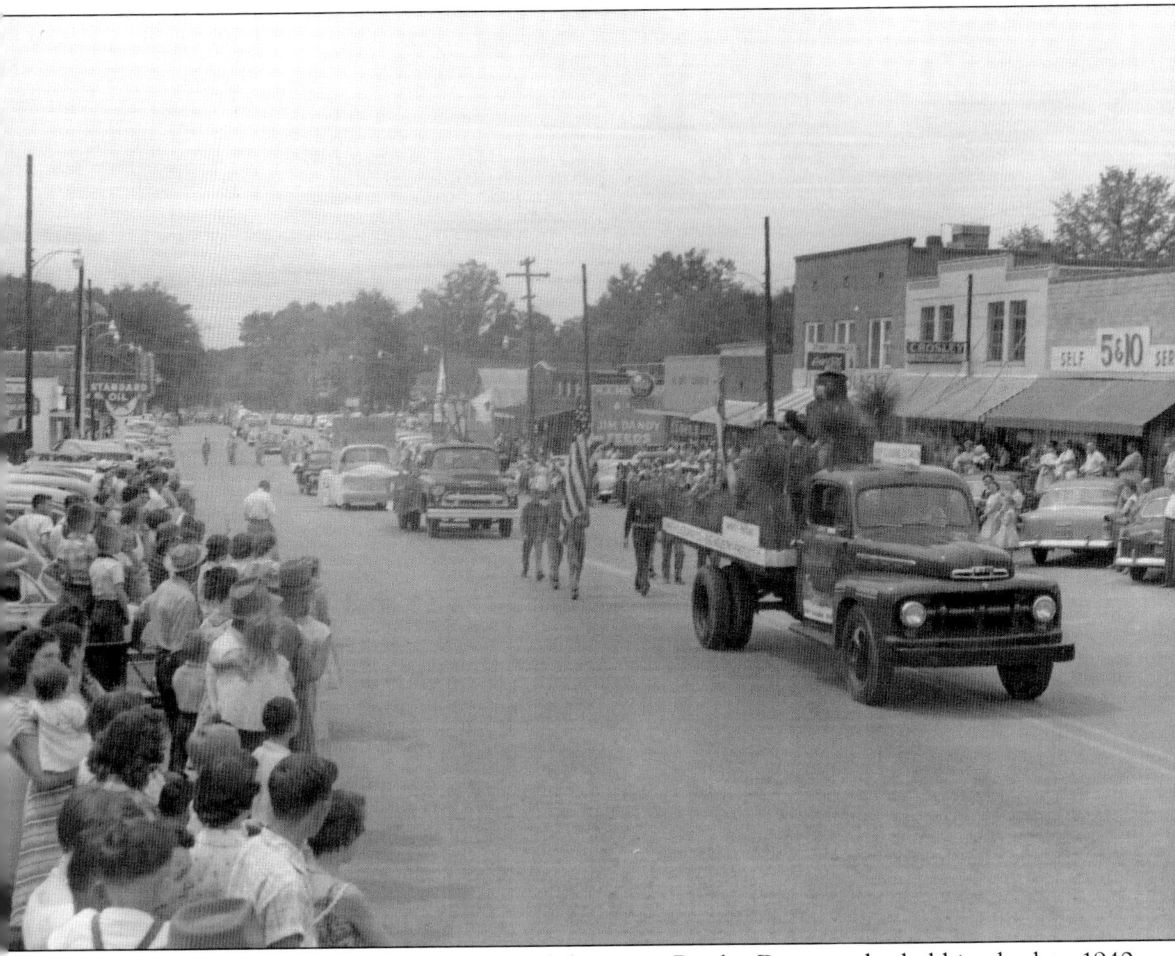

Downtown Parade. Pictured is one of the many Broiler Day parades held in the late 1940s and early 1950s to promote the poultry industry in Cleburne County. There were many events, including the selection of a Broiler Day Queen. Tyson Poultry operated a processing plant just south of town until it burned in early 2007. (Courtesy Pete Wright.)

Three

COMMUNITIES
FOCUSED ON RURAL ACTIVITIES

Cleburne County has always been considered rural, and the largest city, Heflin, with a population of around 3,000, is termed a bedroom community, as most employed residents commute outside the county to work in nearby Anniston or into parts of Georgia. Life in much of Cleburne County focuses on farming and outdoor activity. Farm-related businesses such as blacksmiths, farm supply stores, and Extension Service programs have served the needs of rural dwellers. Almost half the western side of the county is included in the Talladega National Forest, which has attracted locals and visitors to many outdoor activities, such as hiking, fishing, camping, and picnicking. The Tallapoosa River, which flows through the county, offers fishing, swimming, and canoeing opportunities.

Since settlers first arrived in the county, churches and schools were vital parts of the community, and school programs such as Future Farmers of America and Future Homemakers of America attracted many student participants. School graduations, Friday night football games, and family reunions became the staples of life. Some of the communities that sprang up in Cleburne County included Sugar Hill, a very old settlement, and Belltown, located in rich bottomland along the Tallapoosa River. Communities located in the eastern part of the county were Abernathy, Macedonia, and Hopewell.

Abernathy was settled in 1855. Macedonia was settled by families from Georgia. Macedonia Baptist Church was built in the 1880s and quickly became the center of the Macedonia community. A corn mill was located near the church, and oxen were used for farming. Lumber was also important to the local economy.

Hopewell was settled in the 1890s and was incorporated with a mayor and council. The community thrived as the Vanderbilt Timber and Mining Company built a railroad from Tallapoosa, Georgia, to take advantage of local timber. Six coke ovens were in use to burn charcoal. Between 1904 and 1906, Hopewell had a hotel, four stores, a cotton gin, a gristmill, a millinery store, doctor and dentist offices, and a calaboose. A large cotton and fertilizer market was served by 20 to 30 wagons that brought in cotton from west Georgia and the Alabama counties of Clay and Randolph. Other communities included Hightower, Lecta, and Trickem Valley.

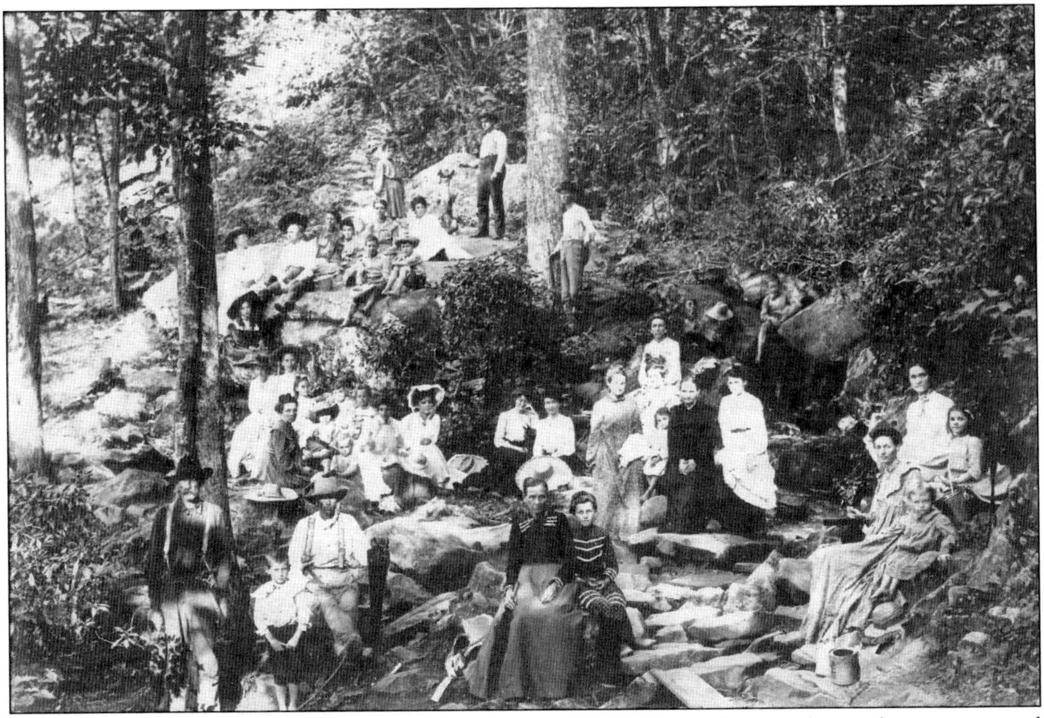

Forest Picnic. The mountains and forests of western Cleburne County have always attracted visitors, such as this group out on a picnic. Cheaha Mountain is the highest point in the state at 2,413 feet. A portion of the 392,567 acres of the Talladega National Forest are in Cleburne County. (Courtesy Lucile Morgan Public Library.)

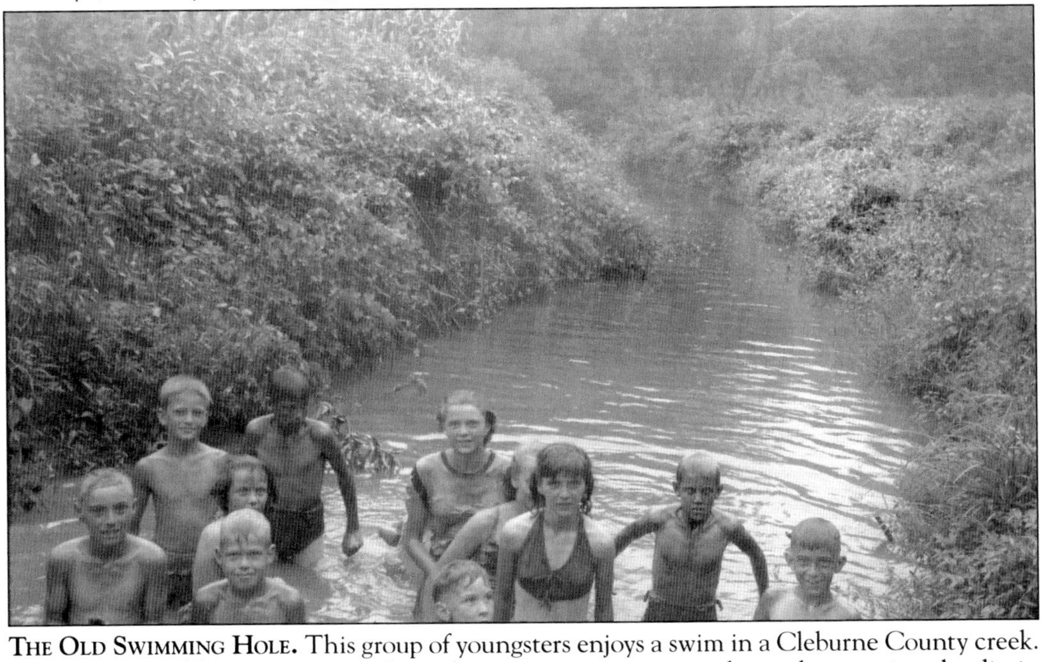

The Old Swimming Hole. This group of youngsters enjoys a swim in a Cleburne County creek. There are no public swimming pools in the county, so youngsters have always enjoyed a dip in local creeks, ponds, or the Tallapoosa River. (Courtesy Cleburne County Extension Office.)

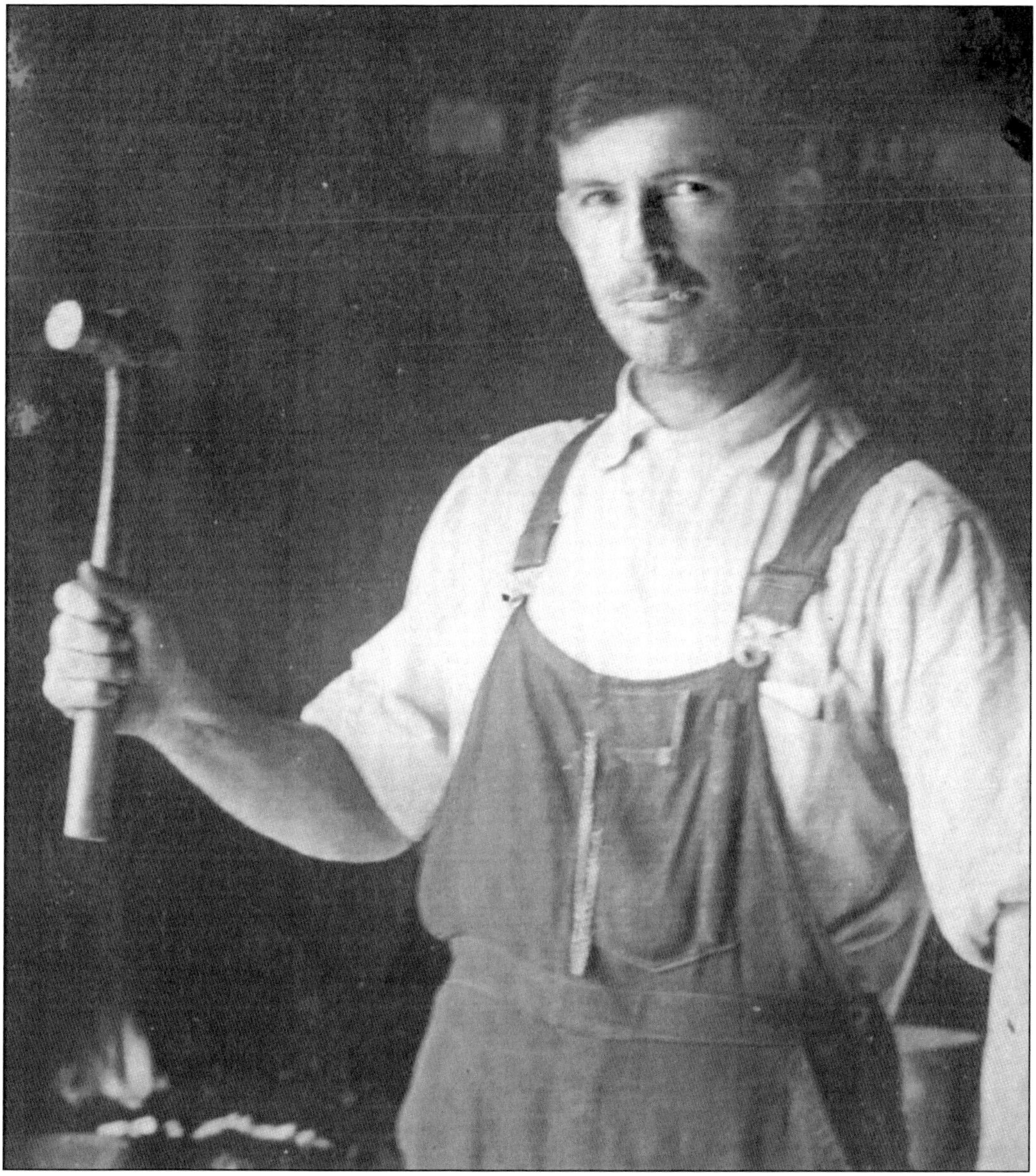

Blacksmith at Work. Before the advent of motorized vehicles, the talents of a local blacksmith were important in keeping horses shod and farm equipment working. Blacksmiths were very important to rural communities. John Zachary Grubbs was a blacksmith in the Oak Level community around 1903. Grubbs was born in the community in 1878. He married Daffie Lane Parker of Oak Level in 1900, and the Reverend Wilson Parks Howell performed the ceremony. The Grubbs had eight children, and Daffie died in 1928. "Zackie," as some called Grubbs, lived until 1957. In the mid-1800s, the community of Oak Level was home to Oak Level Academy. A large group of children attended while their parents worked as mechanics, hatters, tobacconists, carpenters, millwrights, and farmers. Over time, the school grew with increased attendance, but in 1930, only grades one through six were taught, and junior high students transported to Fruithurst. (Courtesy East Alabama History Museum.)

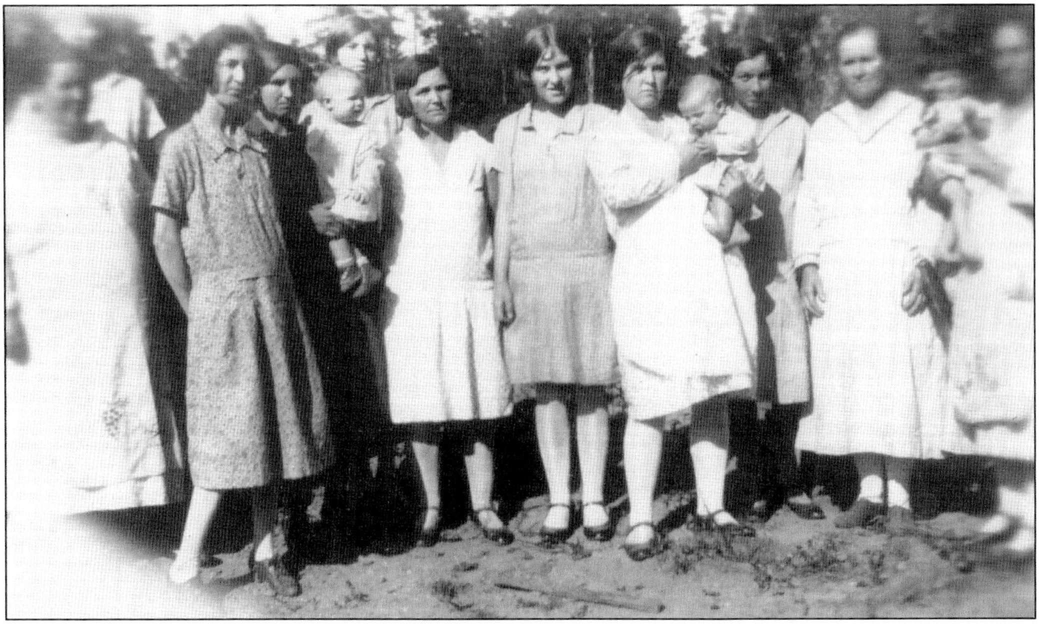

Grantley Club Organizes. Ladies Extension Homemakers Clubs were active in rural areas of Alabama. This photograph was taken of the Grantley club the day they organized. Alabama Extension will mark its centennial in 2014. One of the major focuses of Extension work has been using cutting-edge research from the state's land-grant university system to improve the working conditions of farmers and homemakers. (Courtesy Cleburne County Extension Office.)

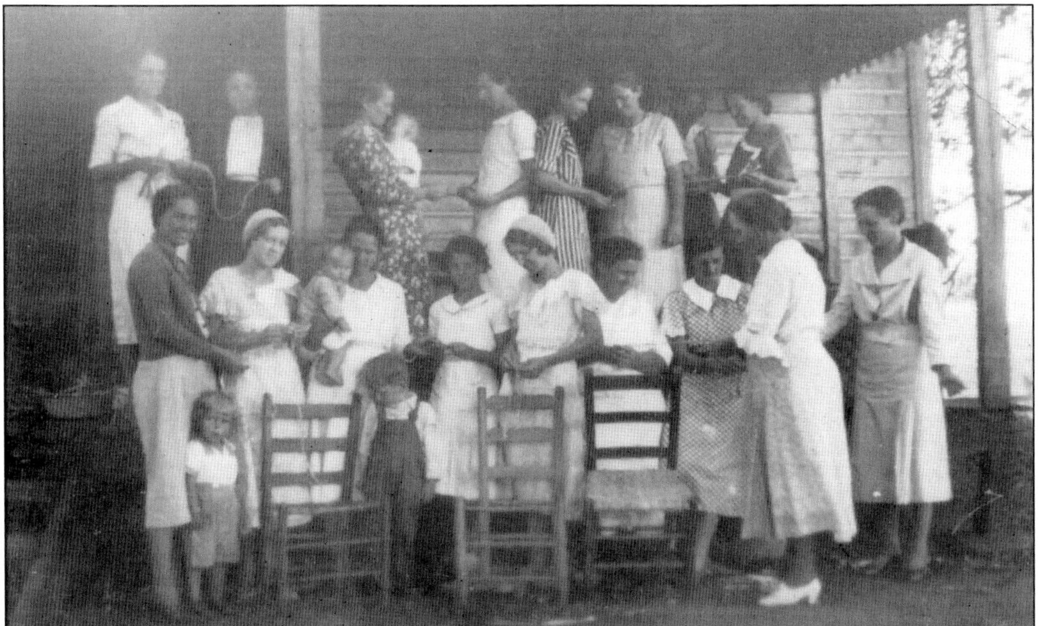

Re-Seating with Corn Shucks. The photograph above shows Howle's Grove Club re-seating chairs with corn shucks. Extension agents would go into communities and work with farmers and homemakers, introducing them to programs, activities, and techniques that would improve their lives. (Courtesy Cleburne County Extension Office.)

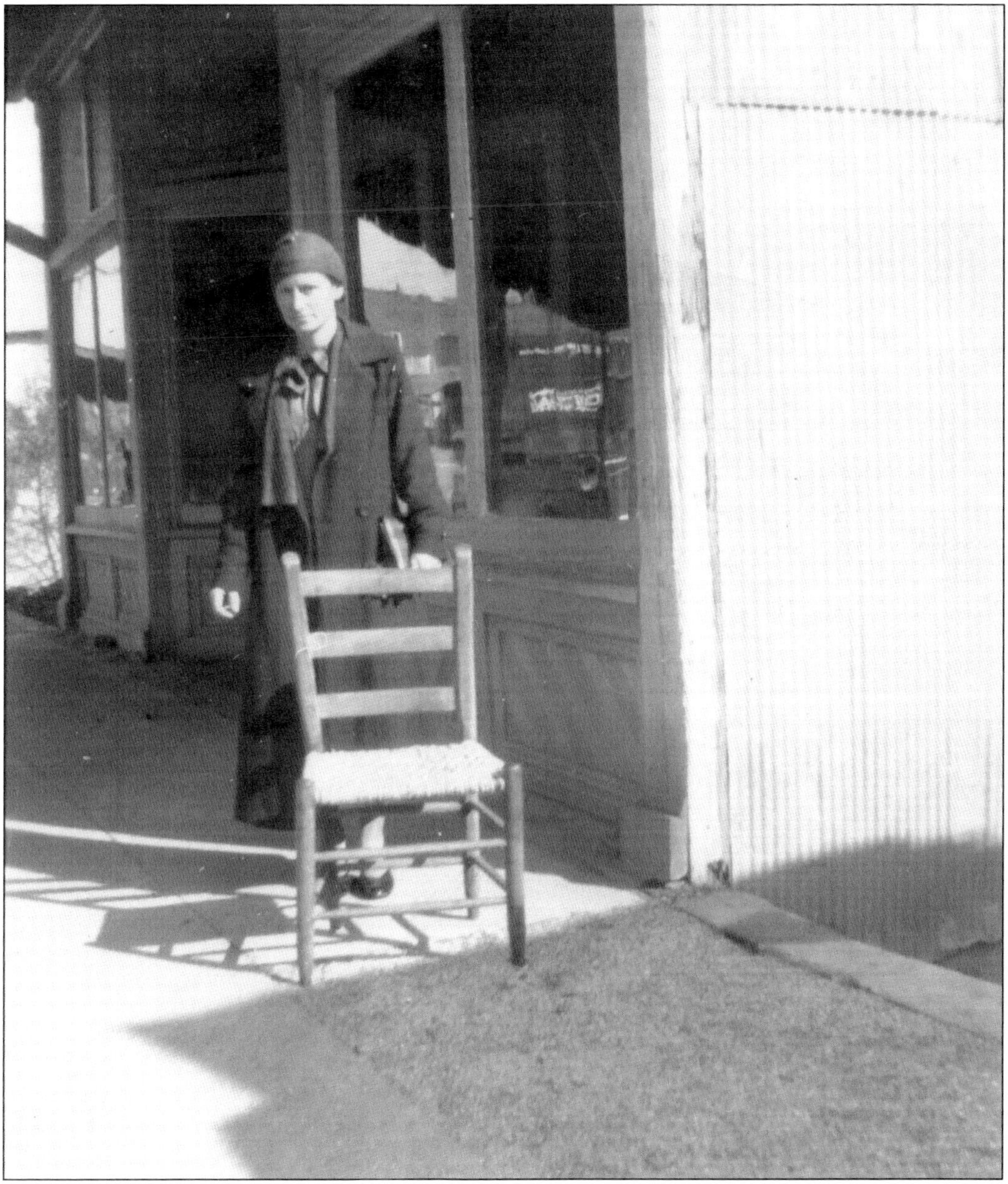

Velma and the Chair. Velma Perry of Route 3 in Heflin proudly displays one of the chairs she re-seated with corn shucks as part of an Extension System program in Cleburne County during the early 1900s. The Alabama Cooperative Extension System was formed in 1914. Extension initially focused on improving the bleak economic prospects of Alabama farmers, most of whom raised cotton under the persistent threat of the boll weevil. As funds permitted, home demonstration agents were employed to provide farm wives with practical assistance with food preservation and other home-related improvements. Eventually, program areas were expanded to include assistance with dairy, livestock production, agronomy, horticulture, farm marketing, and plant and animal diseases. Youth outreach, typically in the form of Boys and Girls Clubs, also comprised an integral part of extension work. In 1914, forty-three of Alabama's 67 counties were served by agents. (Courtesy Cleburne County Extension Office.)

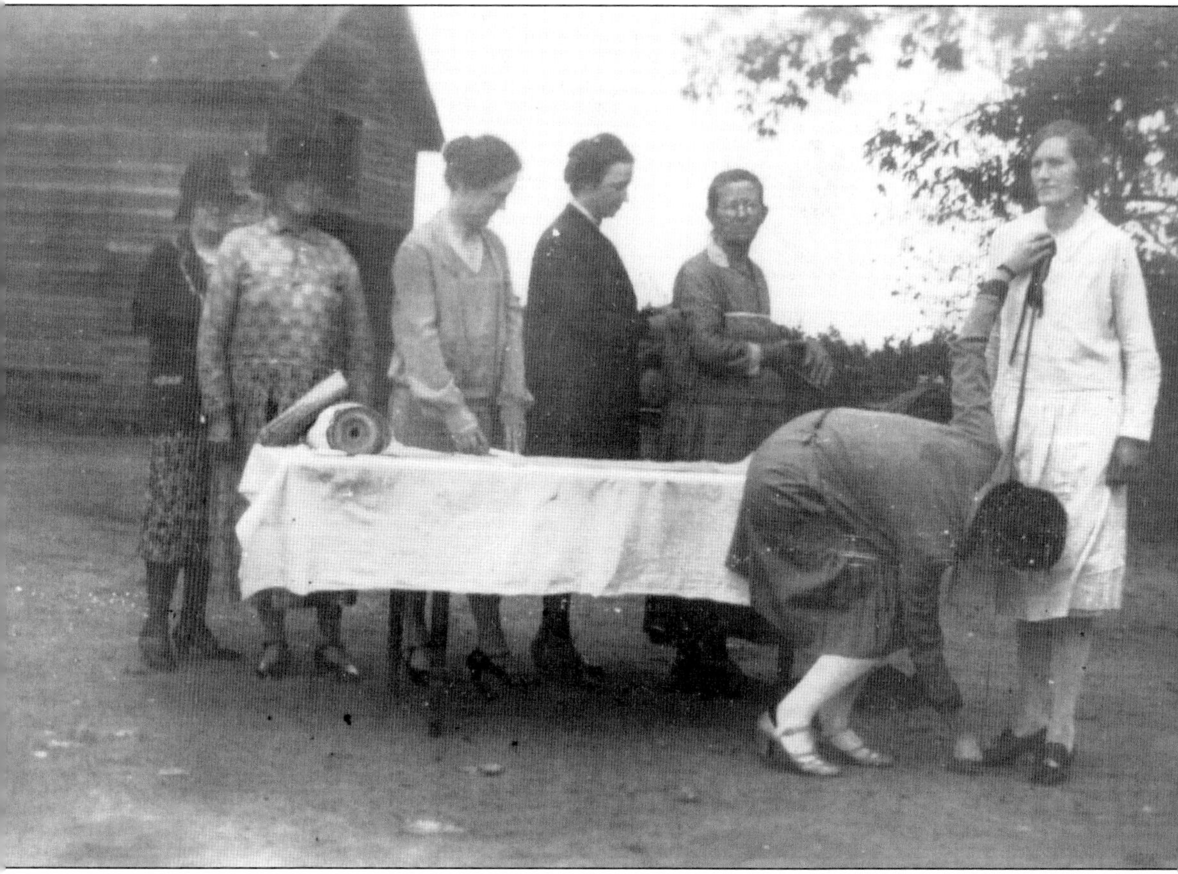

Cutting Patterns. These Hightower Extension Homemaker Club women try, for the first time, to cut clothing patterns, measure, and sew clothing. Seen here from left to right are participants Mrs. J. E. Walker, Mrs. J. R. Thomason, Mrs. Jeff Howle, Mrs. J. W. Fowler, Mrs. Walker, unidentified, and Mrs. W. J. White. The programs offered by the extension service were designed to help women become better homemakers. These programs involved cooking, sewing, and general life skills. Extension agents would go into the rural communities of Cleburne County and meet with a group of women who would participate in a learning experience. Club competitions in dressmaking, cooking, food preparation, and other activities helped women get to know their neighbors and gave them pride in their accomplishments. By the 1920s, Extension agents were operating out of fully staffed and equipped offices in many counties. (Courtesy Cleburne County Extension Office.)

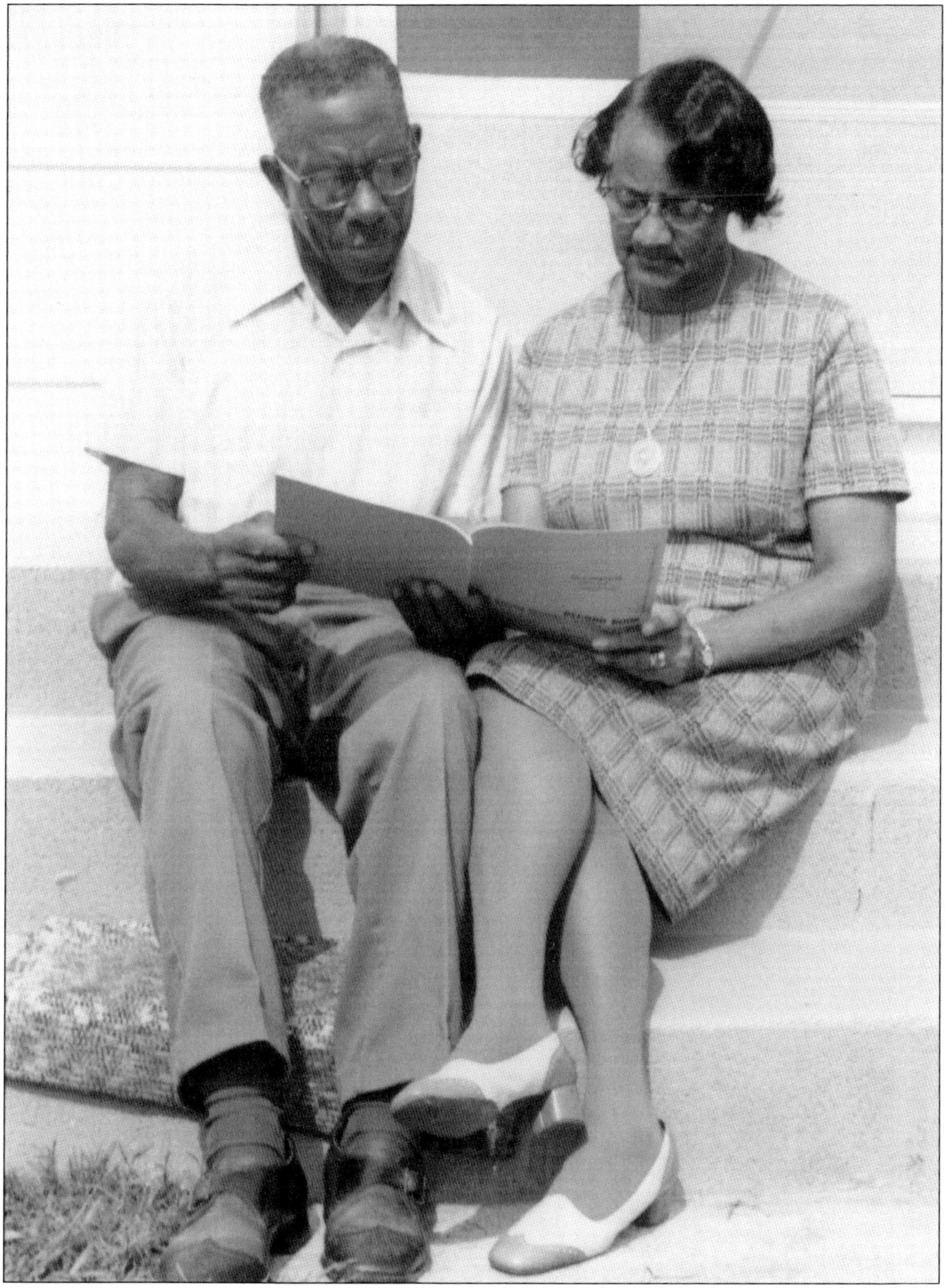

HOME MANAGEMENT. James and Vera Stephens of the Chulafinnee community share information on home management provided by the Cleburne County Extension Office. During the late 1940s and early 1950s, the office provided Cleburne County residents with a wealth of information on farming practices, flowers, yard care, budgeting, home management/planning, and other information helpful to rural communities. The Stephens family was one of many in the county that benefited from the educational programs and material offered. (Courtesy Cleburne County Extension Office.)

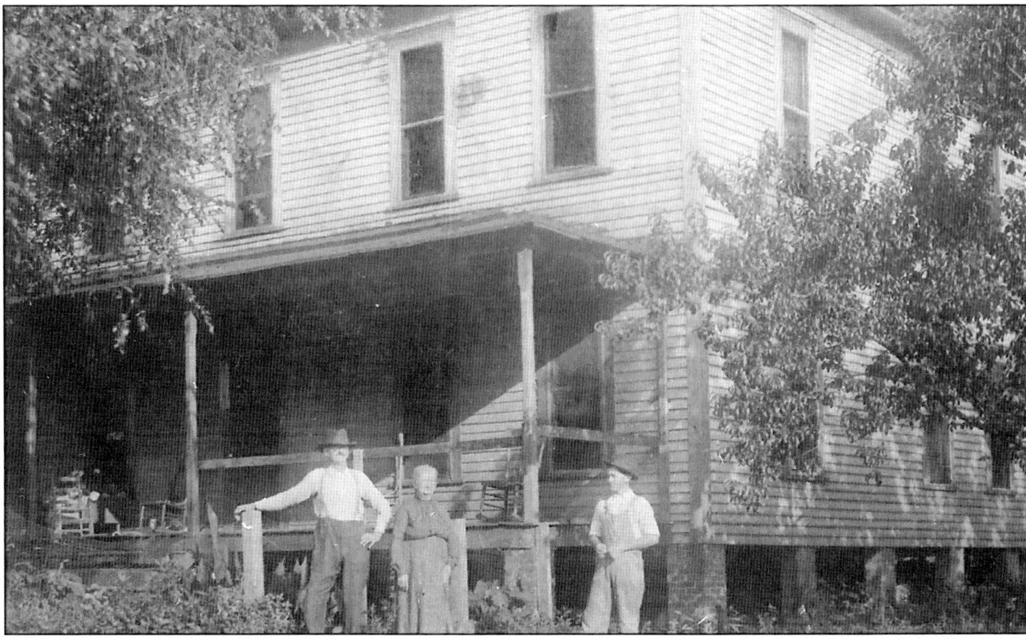

Hotel Proprietor. Melvin Franklin Smith stands in front of the hotel he operated in the Hopewell community in eastern Cleburne County. With Smith are his wife, Almedie, and son Walter. Smith also ran the first saloon in Cleburne County. The saloon was located inside the hotel. Smith was a tailor as well, and there is a story about a fight breaking out in the bar and a patron getting his ear cut off. Smith, using his sewing talents, sewed the man's ear back on. (Courtesy Patsy Smith.)

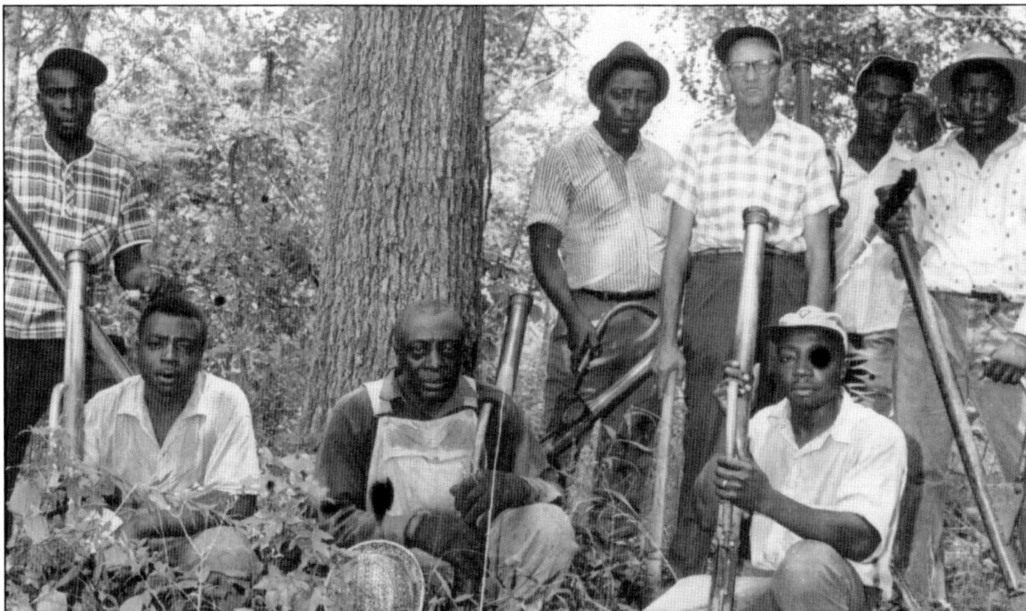

Tree Planting Crew. This eight-man crew helped plant trees in areas of the Talladega National Forest. Seen from left to right are three unidentified crew members, ? Trammell, T. D. Jerdan, and three unidentified crewmen. (Courtesy Cleburne County Extension Office.)

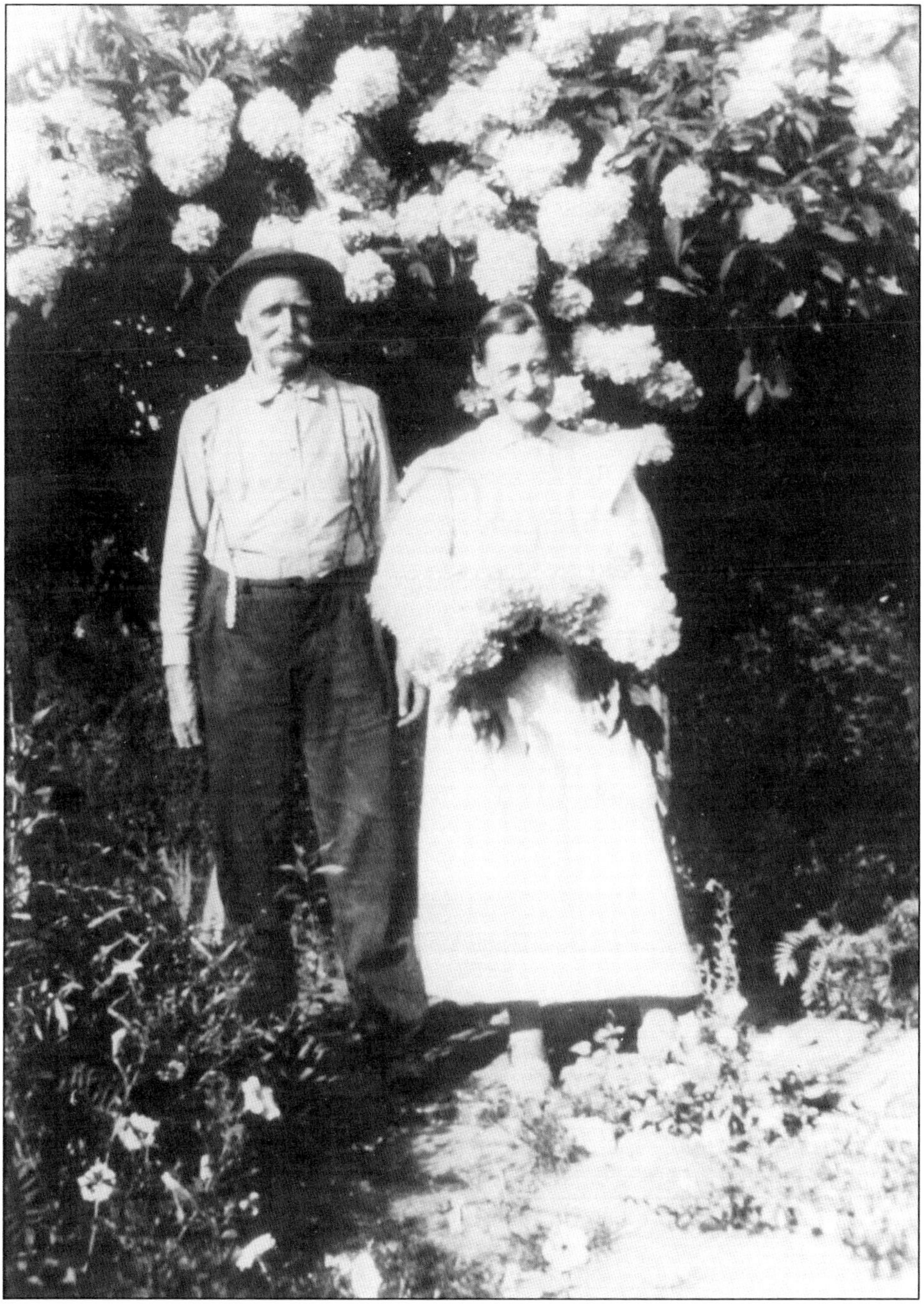

AMONG THE FLOWERS. Heflin Route 6 residents P. F. Currie and his wife, Leona, were very proud of these "snowball" bushes on their property. The August 1, 1908, edition of the *Cleburne New Era* reported that Currie, along with W. W. Little, "carried three bales of cotton to Heflin on Friday." On January 12, 1922, Currie was reported in an Anniston hospital due to an illness. The Curries were well-known in the area. Snowball bushes were extremely popular landscape plants. They were easy to grow in drought and the hot Southern climate, and they bloomed from spring until fall. Growing flowers was and continues to be a popular hobby for county residents. (Courtesy Cleburne County Extension Office.)

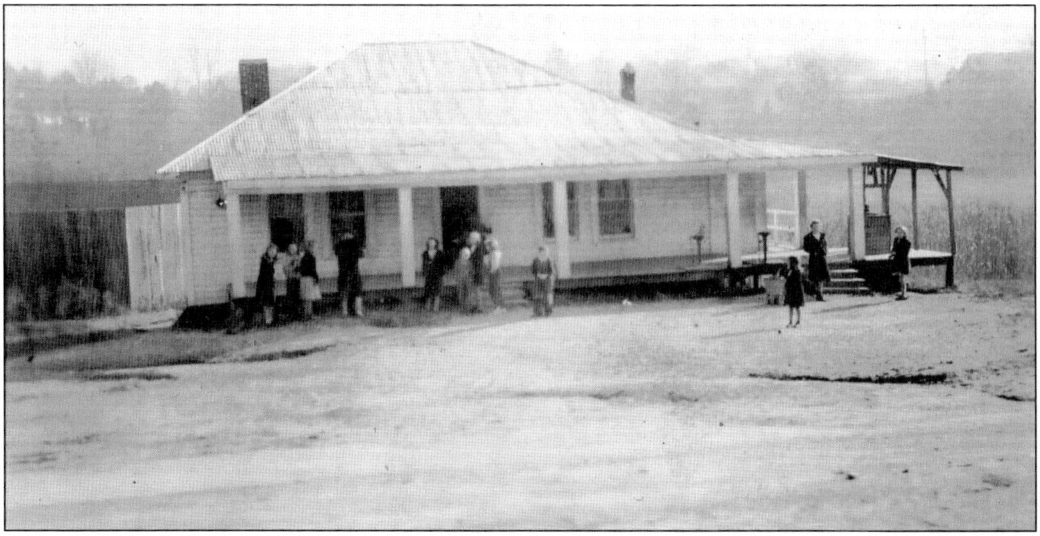

Rural Home. This house is typical of many of the rural homes found in Cleburne County before 1950. Tin roofs were popular, and most houses in rural areas and communities did not have running water. Note the well to the right of the home. Water was drawn from the well using a bucket and a rope. Large porches afforded a place of comfort during the South's typically hot days, as there was no air-conditioning. (Courtesy Carolyn Parker.)

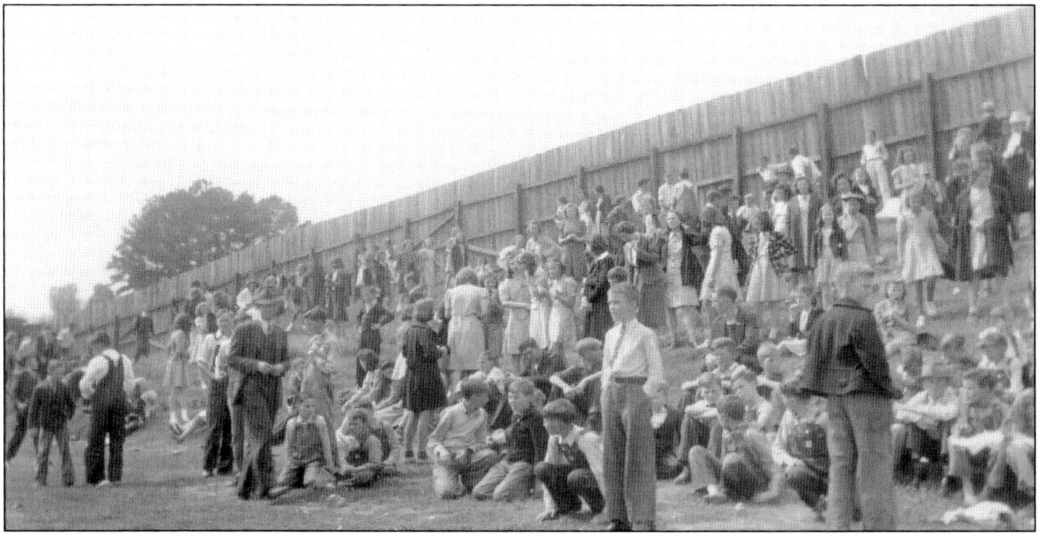

4-H Rally. Extension System 4-H clubs were very popular in the late 1940s and 1950s with Cleburne County school students. This is a 4-H club rally pictured in 1950 at Cleburne County High School. Students came from surrounding county schools to participate in the rally that would feature contests, entertainment, and food. (Courtesy Cleburne County Extension Office.)

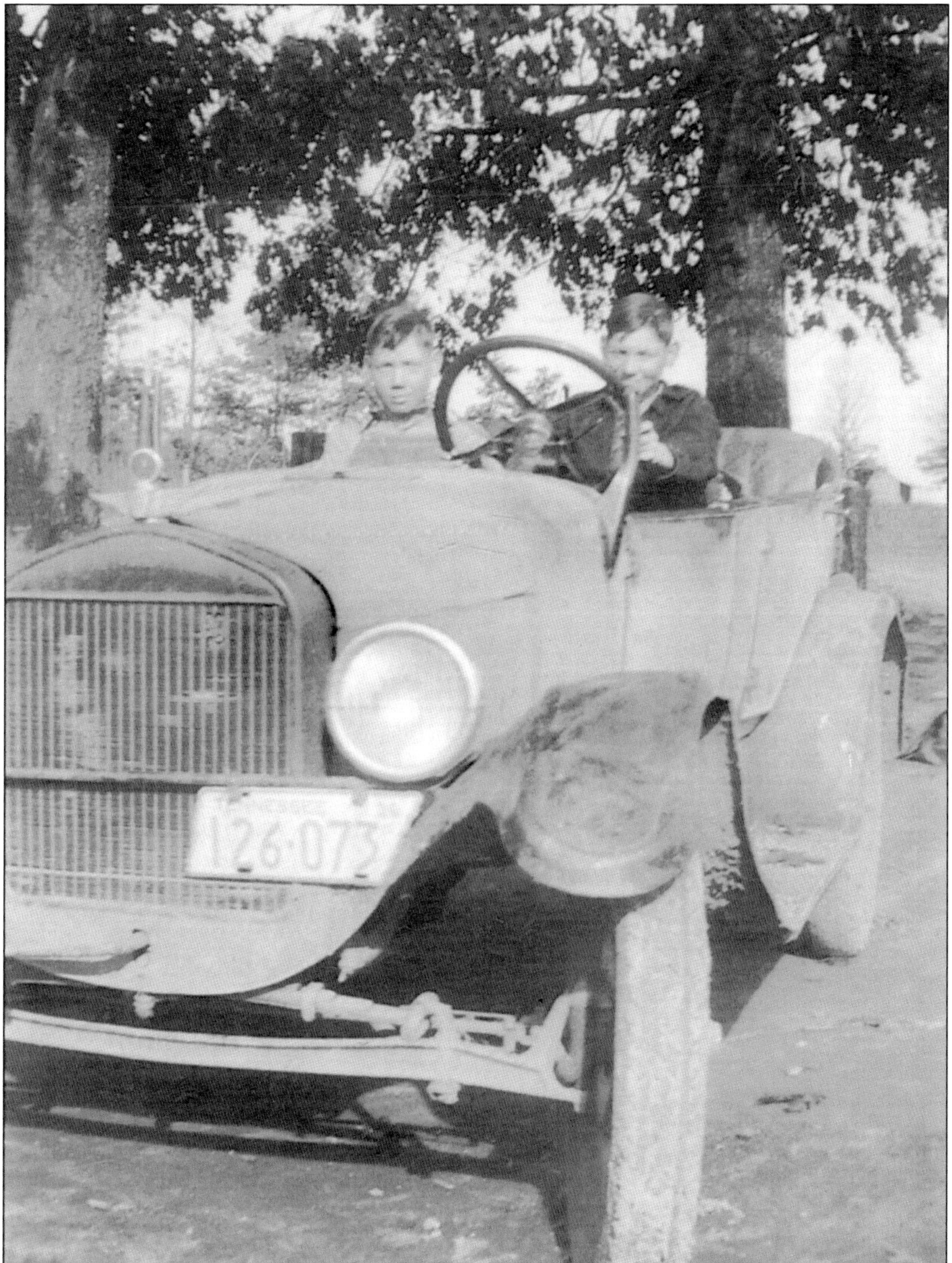

Ready for a Ride. Young Rufus (left) and Fornie Walker pretend they are old enough to drive and on a trip as they sit in a Model T for this 1936 photograph. The automobile belonged to Fornie's father, P. J. Walker. Fornie was born in Edwardsville and celebrated his 88th birthday in May 2010. (Courtesy Vertie Walker.)

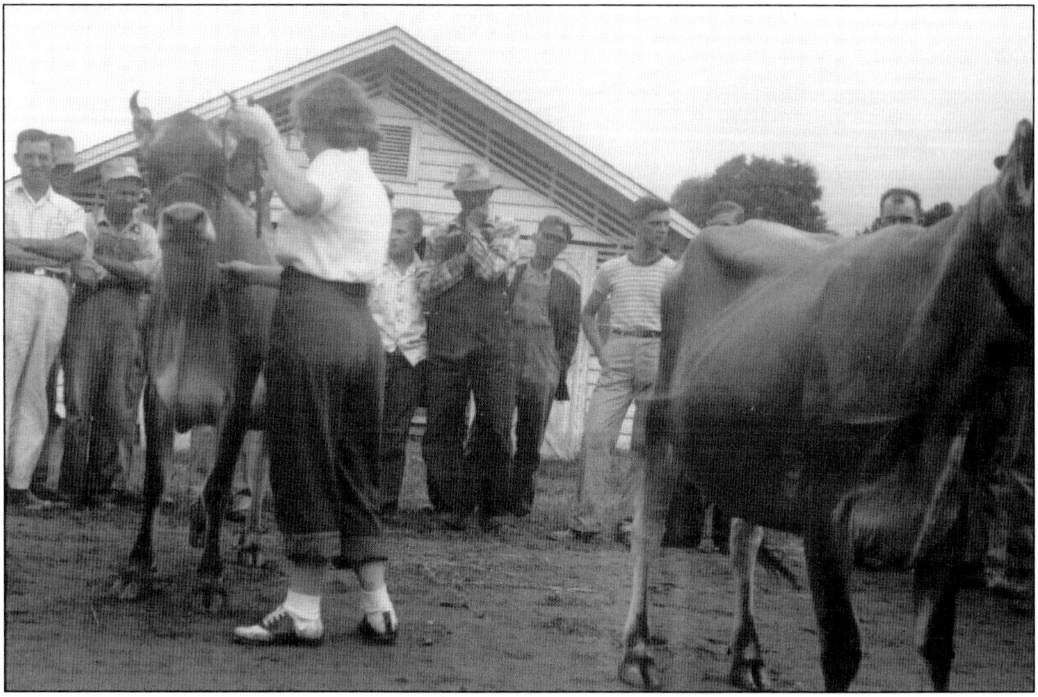

JUDGING COWS. Cleburne County was mostly agricultural during the 19th century, and its farmers produced mostly corn, oats, wheat, cotton, and cattle. Timber was, and remains, a major industry as well. Many students in Cleburne County schools participated in 4-H club programs that taught the raising of cattle, sheep, and hogs. Contests were held to judge cows the youth had raised, with prizes and ribbons being awarded. (Courtesy Cleburne County Extension Office.)

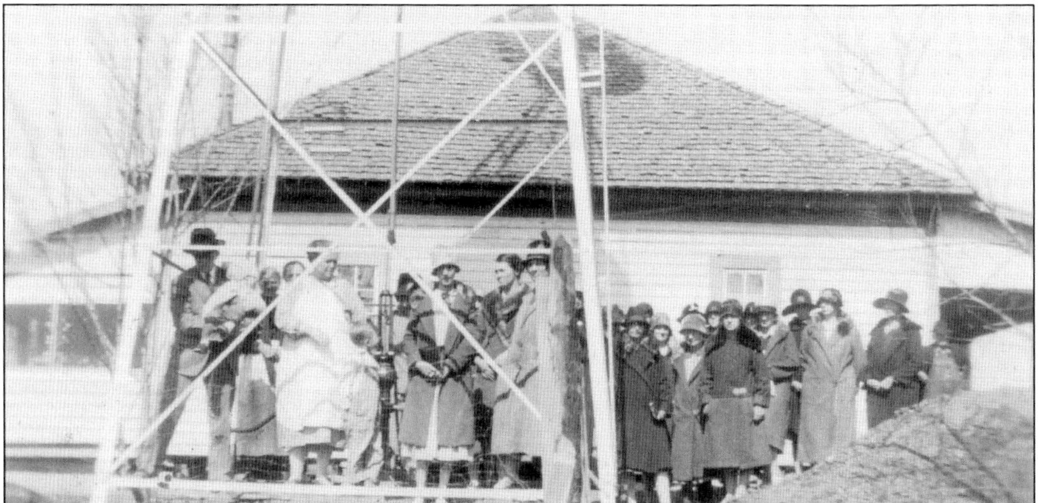

WINDMILL. Some farmers installed windmills to pump water and provide electricity. The *Cleburne News*, on January 24, 1935, called attention to attorney Wiley Clark McMahan's "modern and convenient home, the least expensive and most conveniently arranged in the county, as it is equipped with a complete lighting plant, radio, and a home water system operated by a big windmill, an abundance of fruit, vineyards, and good pastures, situated on an 80-acre farm." (Courtesy Cleburne County Extension Office.)

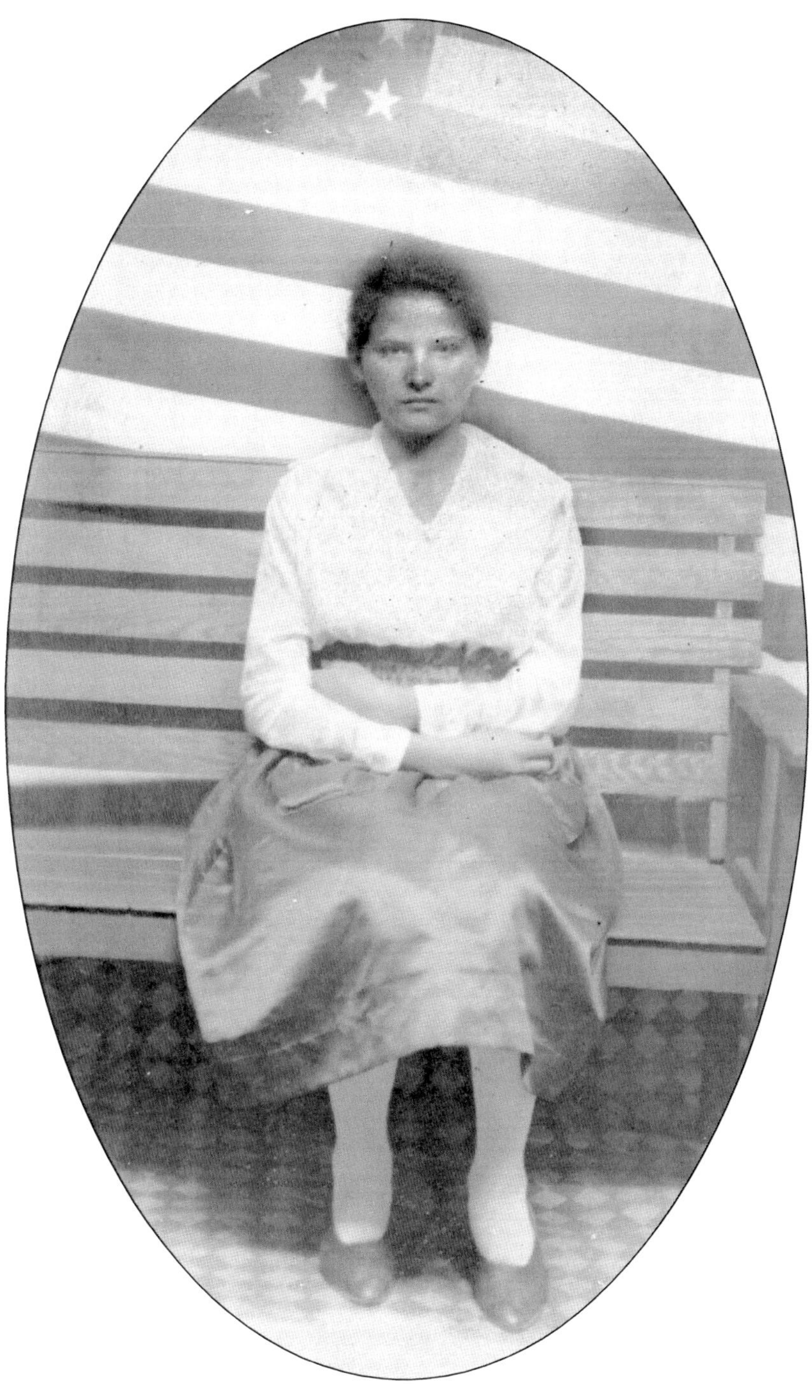

YOUNG EDWARDSVILLE WOMAN. Vera Walker was a young woman in Edwardsville when this photograph was taken in 1902. She was the daughter of Joe Walker. The Walkers were a well-known family in northern Cleburne County, and there is a Walker Cemetery in the Abernathy community. Many family photographs taken during this time period were done by traveling photographers who, using a few props, would photograph families outside their homes. (Courtesy Vertie Walker.)

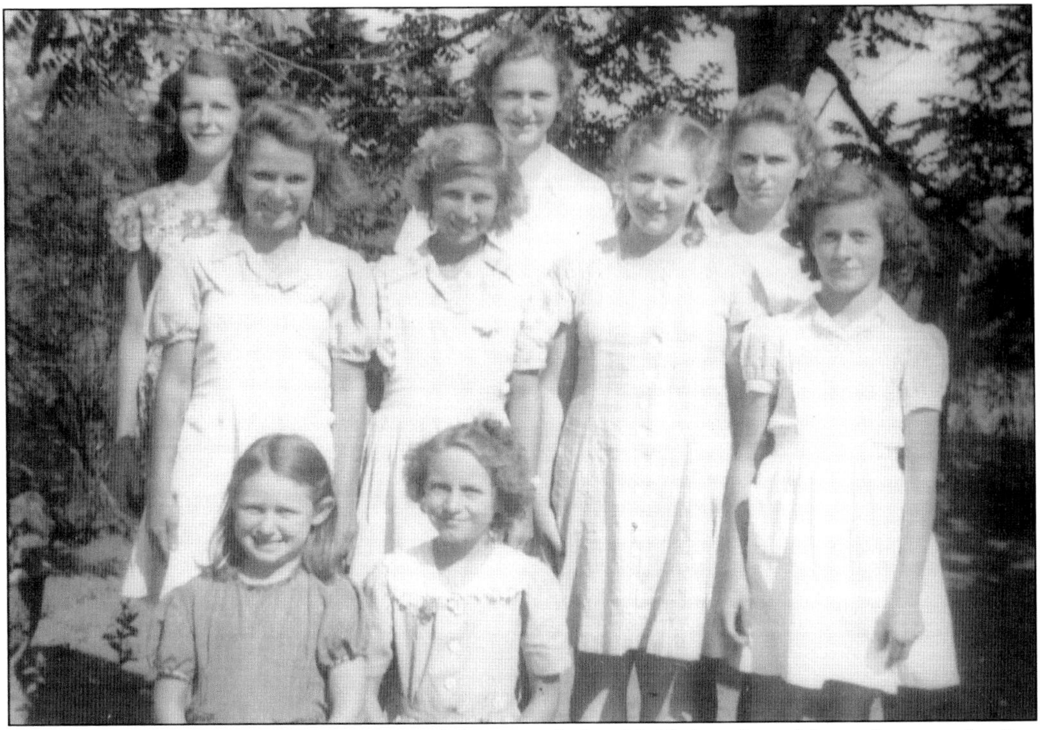

YOUNG HEPSABAH MEMBERS. Members of the Hepsabah 4-H Club gathered for a photograph after a demonstration by Launa Wright and Miriam Thrash. This group had four summer meetings. The 4-H clubs were very popular among school students in Cleburne County as they involved various demonstrations and programs. (Courtesy Miriam Turner.)

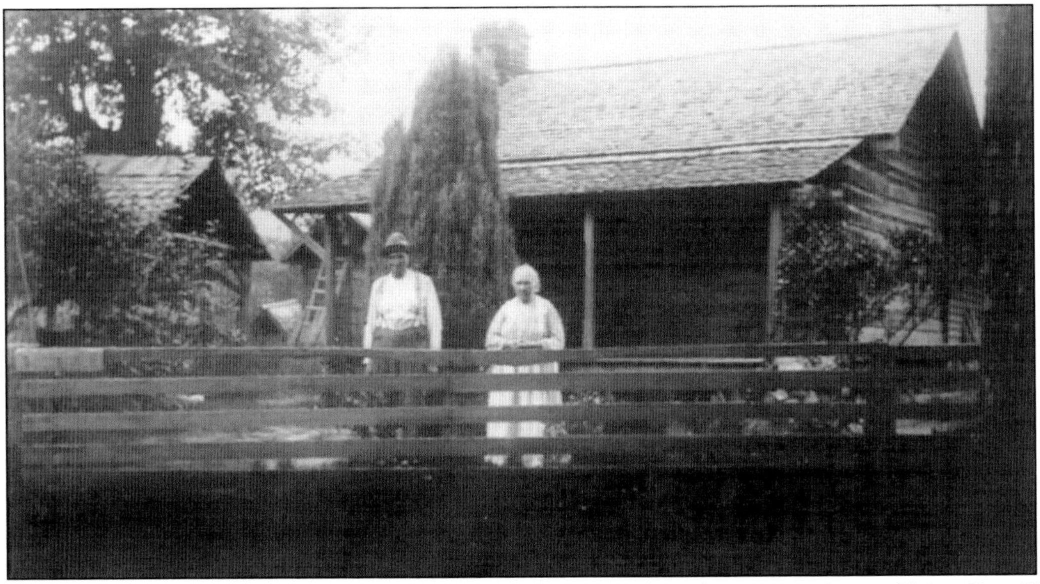

CIVIL WAR VETERAN. Heflin resident Lucile Jacobs's great-uncle and great-aunt Jim and Mary Ferrell stand outside their log cabin in Ranburne. Ferrell was a Civil War veteran who owned 40 acres about 3 miles outside of Ranburne. Ferrell was a private in Company I, 48th Alabama Regiment, Newmar Pounds Guard, mustered into service on April 26, 1862. (Courtesy Lucile Jacobs.)

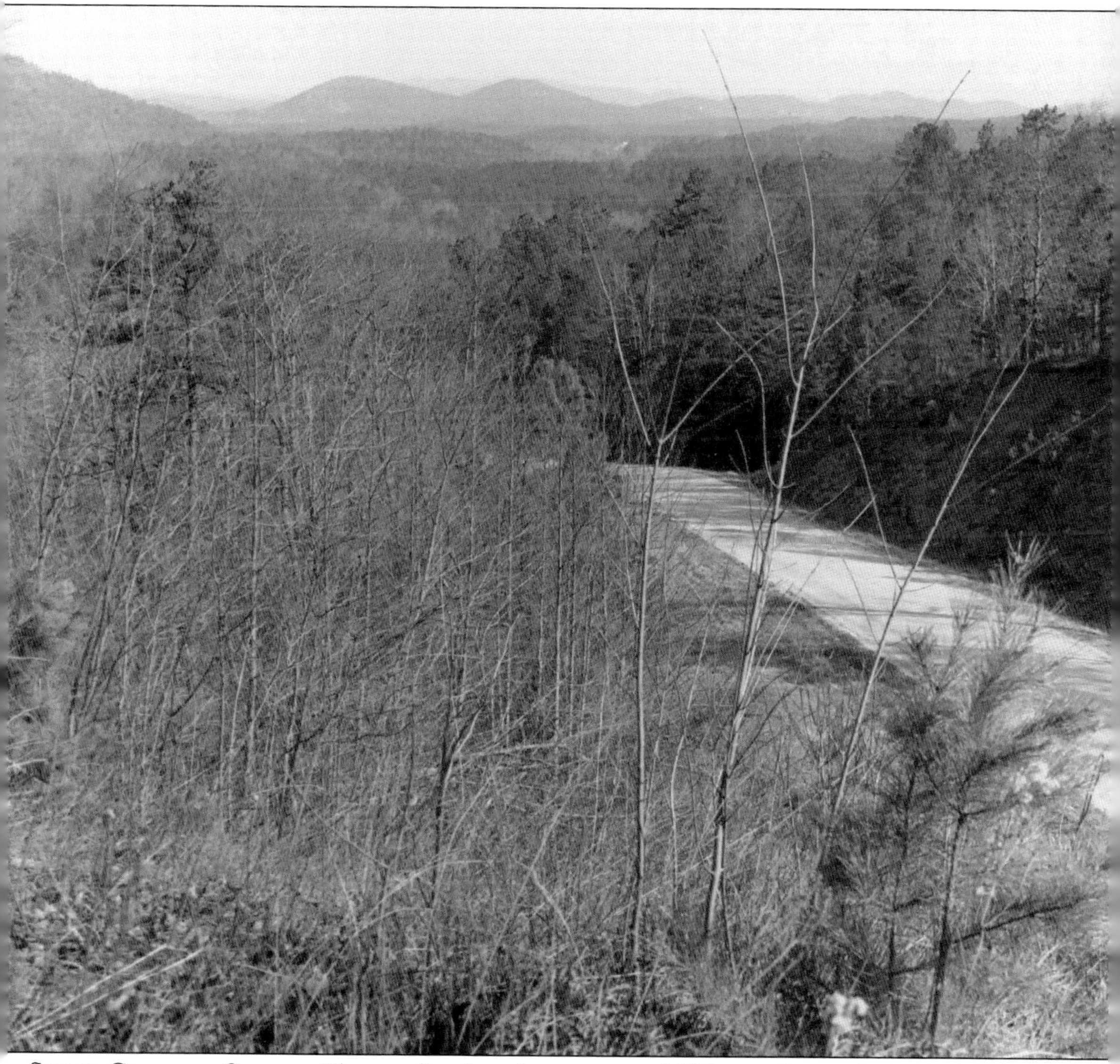

Scenic Cleburne County. The woodlands and mountains of Cleburne County have attracted settlers and visitors alike. This typical rural road was like many in the county in the late 1940s and early 1950s. This particular view from a hillside along the Talladega Scenic Drive leading from Heflin to Cheaha State Park gives a glimpse of Cheaha Mountain, the highest point in the state. The road runs 26 miles along the backbone of Cheaha Mountain. Motorists can stop at scenic overlooks for views of rural settlements and rock outcroppings. The entire highway is within the Talladega National Forest, and Cheaha State Park is accessed by the road. The roadway is now a part of the Appalachian Highlands Scenic Byway. (Courtesy Cleburne County Extension Office.)

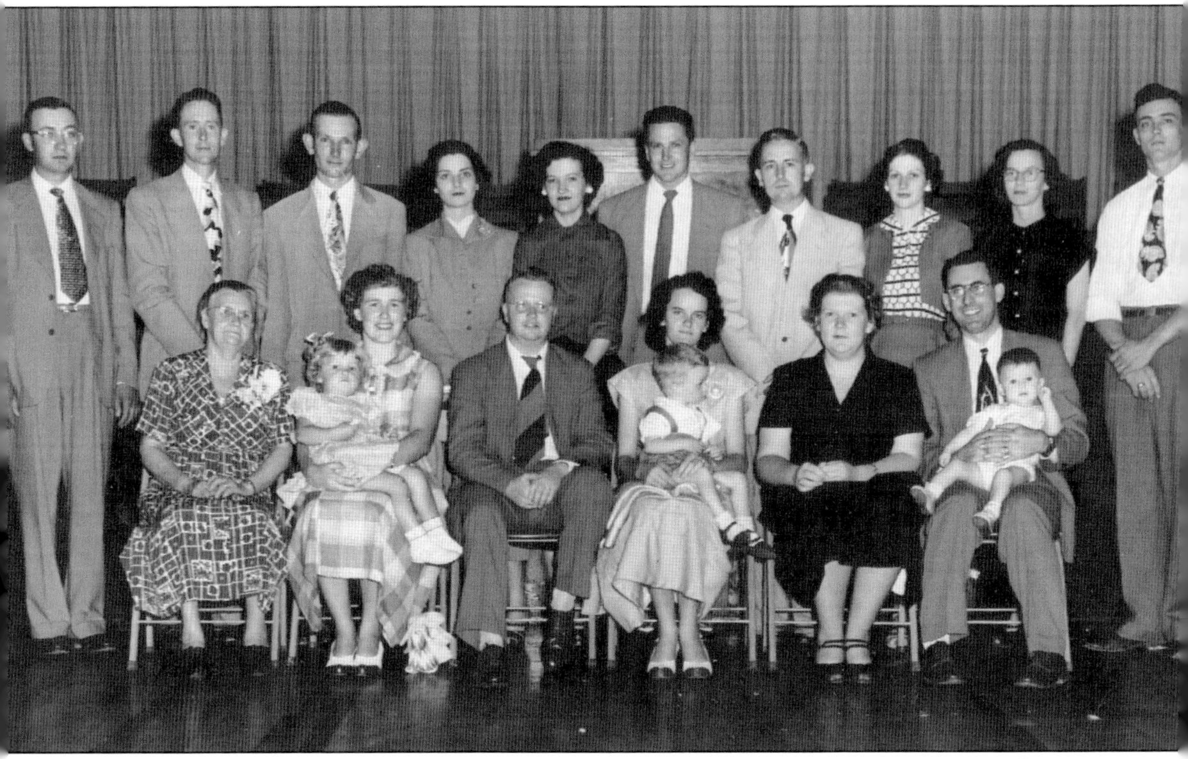

Class of 1946. Class reunions are very popular among Cleburne County residents. Seen here attending a Cleburne County High School reunion in 1947 are (first row) teacher Lucy Turner, unidentified, Willie Freeman, Jean Durham, and two unidentified; (second row) Forrest Turner, Arnold Freeman, three unidentified, Norman Thrash, and four unidentified. (Courtesy Miriam Turner.)

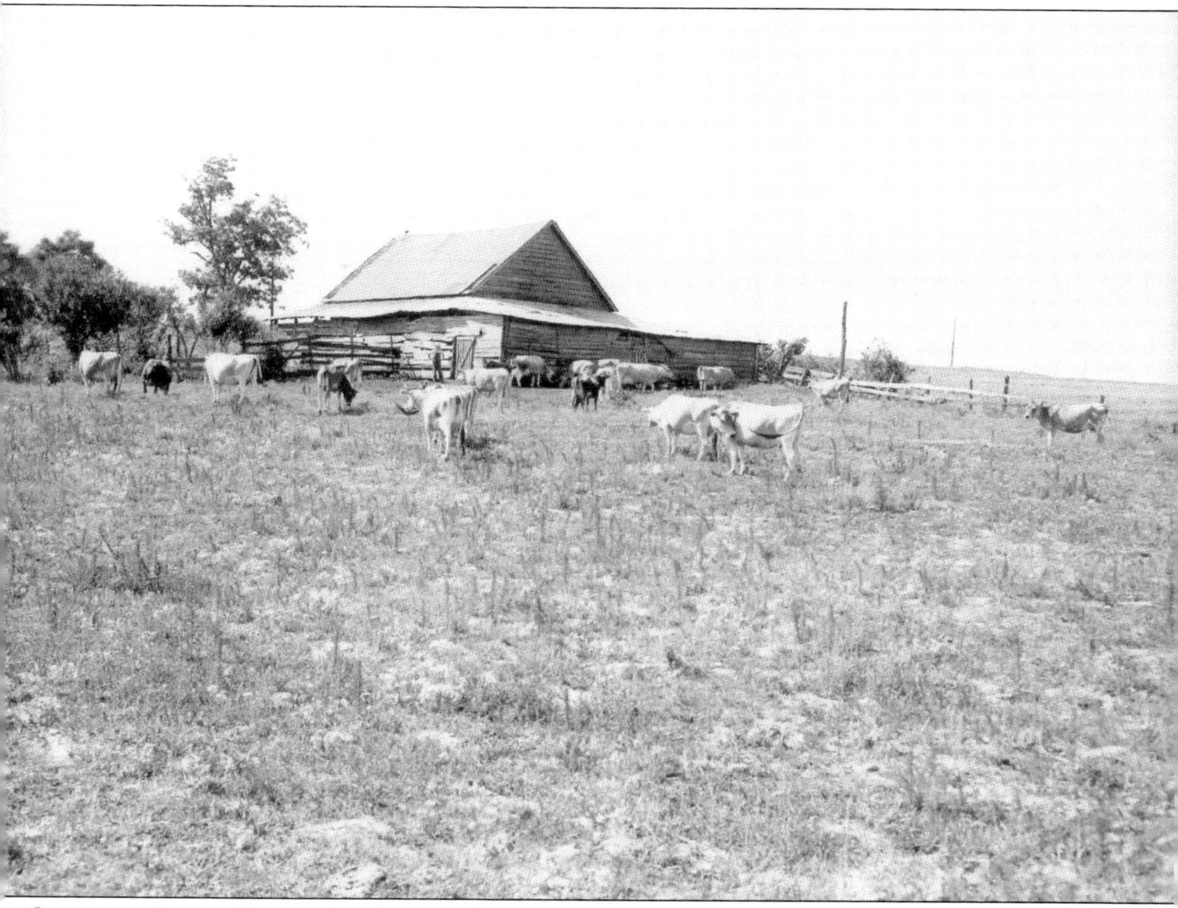

Cleburne Cattle Farm. This photograph taken in the late 1940s illustrates a family cattle farm in Cleburne County. Like many areas of the nation, family farming has been on the decline. The most recent figures indicate that the average farm in the county has 136 acres, with only 28 cattle or calves per every 100 acres. Of these of cattle, only 1.14 percent are milk cows; most are raised for slaughter. (Courtesy Cleburne County Extension Service.)

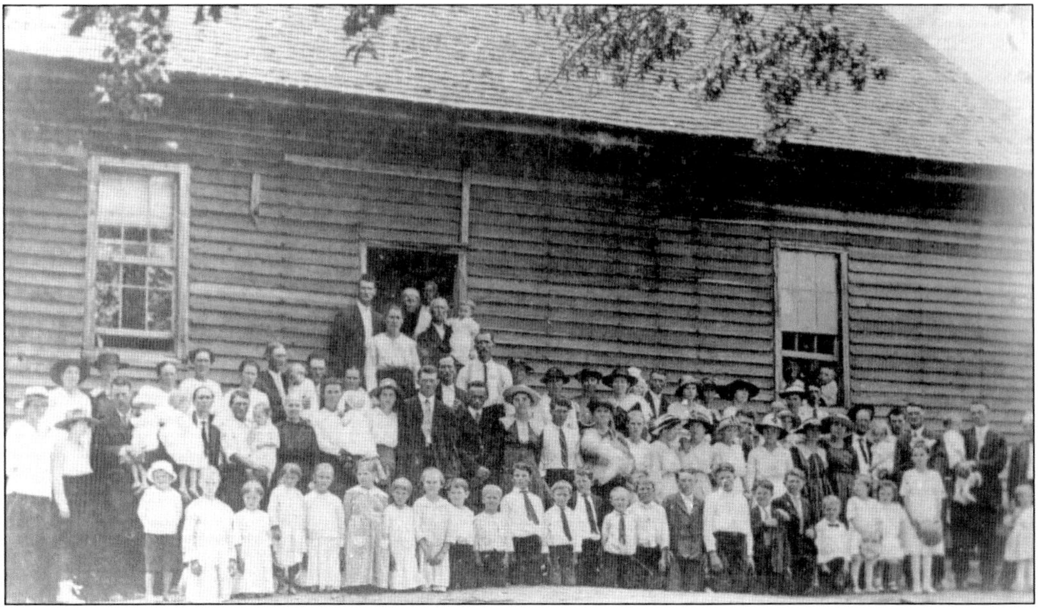

Homecoming Day. Homecoming day at Crossroads Church, sometimes called Bethsadia, is pictured around 1900. The church was built by the Walker family, who moved into the area from Georgia. Land for the church was donated by the Coleman family. The church received its name from being located at the intersection of two roads. (Courtesy Vertie Walker.)

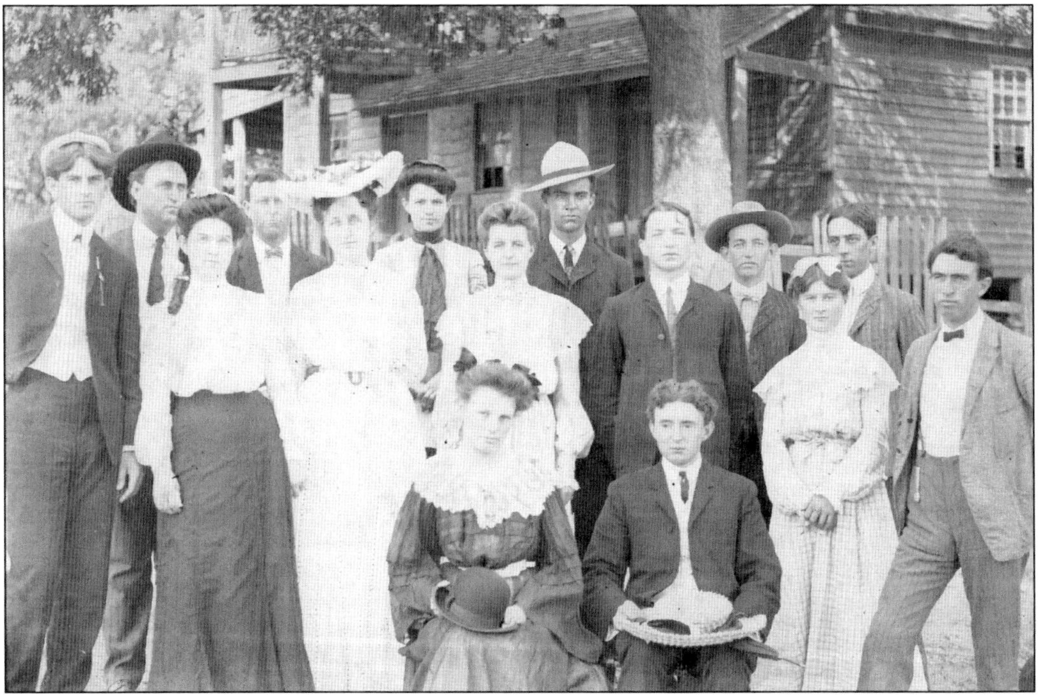

Institute Graduates. These students attended and graduated from the Cleburne Institute in Edwardsville, which was a private school for boys and girls. The school was incorporated on February 18, 1891, by founder professor D. Adams Sox. H. G. Barnes and C. M. Garrett served as principals of the school in 1894. The school closed some time prior to 1921. (Courtesy Lorriane Watson.)

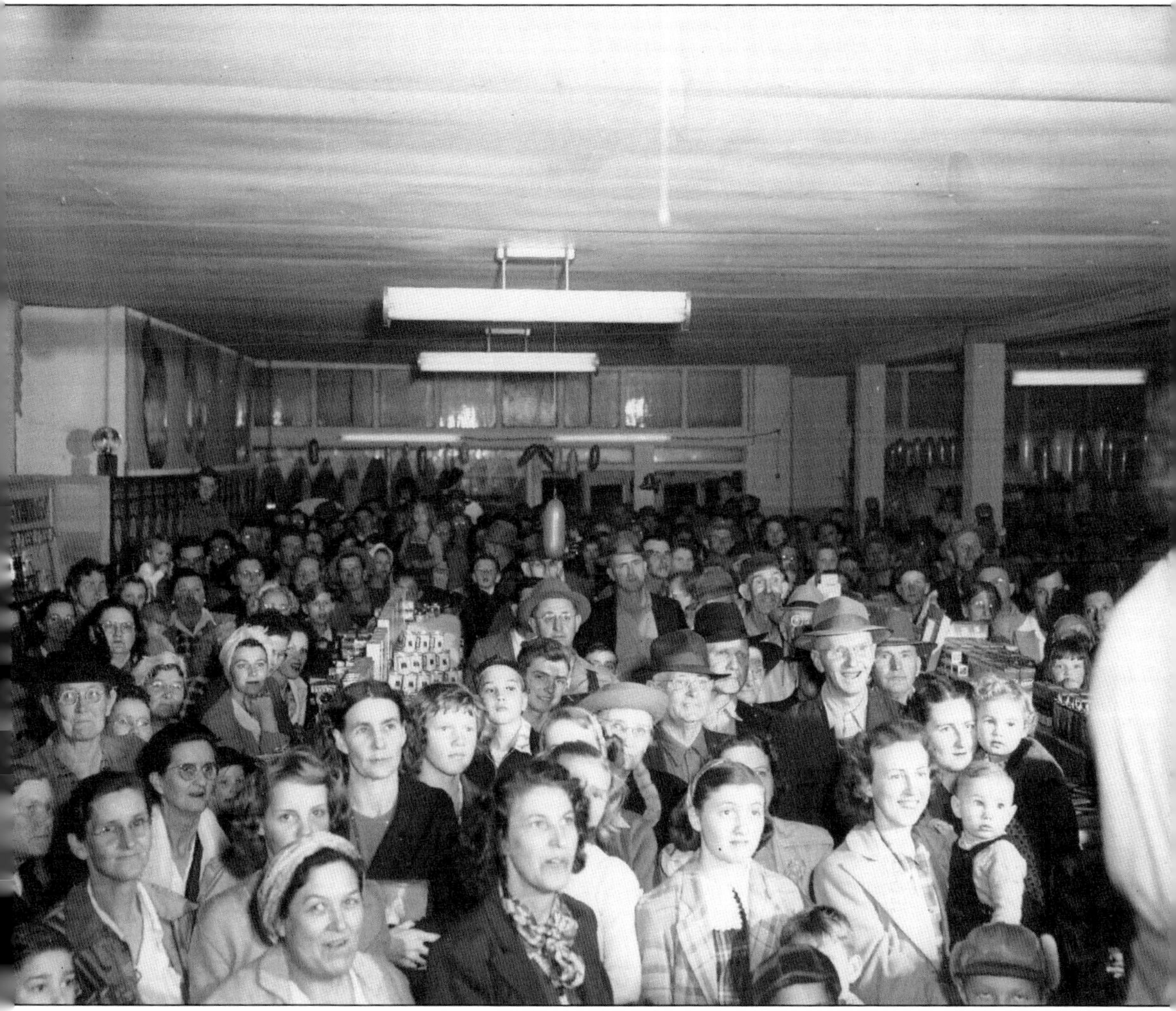

Store Promotion. During the 1940s and 1950s, stores in Heflin would have promotions to attract crowds and business. Shoppers would register for prizes and gather to learn who the lucky winners were. In this Cleburne County store, shoppers eagerly wait to hear their name called. (Courtesy Pete Wright.)

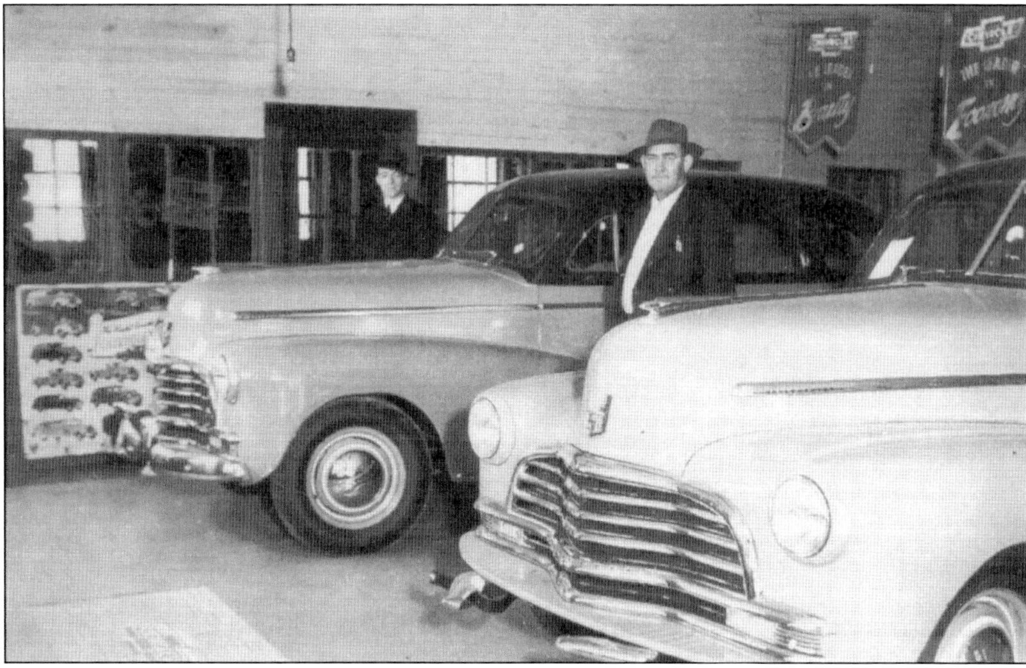

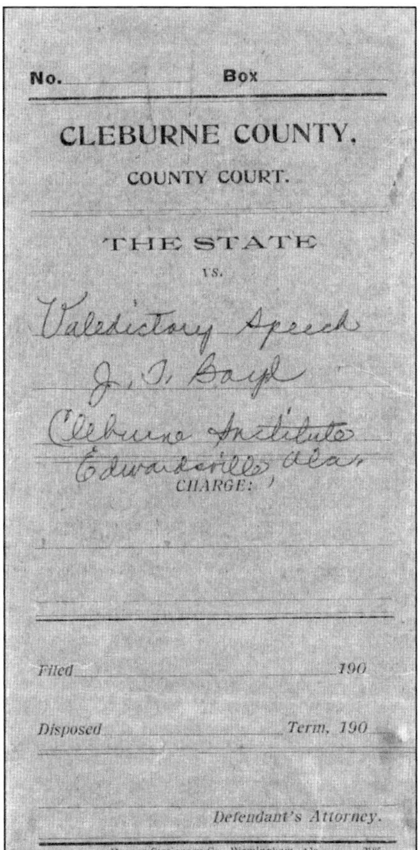

No. Box

CLEBURNE COUNTY,

COUNTY COURT.

THE STATE

vs.

Valedictory Speech

J. D. Boyd

Cleburne Institute

Edwardsville, Ala.

CHARGE:

Filed 190

Disposed Term, 190

Defendant's Attorney.

Rogers Stationery Co., Birmingham, Ala. 2185

FIRST AUTOMOBILE DEALERSHIP. James D. McGriff (1897–1964) was the owner of Heflin's first automobile dealership and founder of McGriff Motor Company. He is shown here with one of his famous 1940s-era Chevrolets. McGriff became a local hero when he accompanied Cleburne County sheriff W. I. Owen and attorney Pelham Merrill on a cross-country trip to California to catch a man who had murdered one of Heflin's prominent citizens in the 1930s. McGriff furnished a car for the trip off his showroom floor and took turns driving the Chevrolet back to Alabama. At times during the trip, he sat in the backseat handcuffed to the assailant until the trio arrived back in Heflin. (Courtesy East Alabama History Museum.)

VALEDICTORY SPEECH. J. D. Boyd placed his valedictory speech from the Cleburne Institute on June 14, 1893, in this county charge envelope. The institute was a private school for boys and girls in Edwardsville. In his speech, Boyd thanked the instructors "for your paternal care, for your faithful counsel, and your affectional instruction." (Courtesy Lorraine Watson.)

Four

Edwardsville
Home of the First Courthouse

Around 1828, the fertile land along Cane Creek had attracted many settlers from South Carolina and Georgia, and by 1860, the Cleburne County community of Fair Play was a bustling center of commerce with several mechanics, blacksmiths, mercantile stores, a post office, and a "vendor of spirits." As more settlers entered the area, a great number of them located between Cane Creek and Town Creek. One of the families was that of William Edwards. As the area developed, the town of Edwardsville came into existence. The town consisted of 10 dry good stores, grocery stores, three saloons, two drugstores, two livery stables, a branch bank, two blacksmith shops, a hotel, a telegraph office, a post office, a gristmill, a cotton gin, several doctors and dentists, a photographer, a school, and several churches.

A year after Cleburne County was created, the Alabama General Assembly appointed J. R. Northcutt, Sidney Carruth, J. W. Wiggonton, A. W. Denman, and Joel Cosper as commissioners to organize the county and locate the county seat. Three sites were considered for the county seat: Edwardsville, Story, and Salem. An election was held in February 1867, and Edwardsville was selected. That same year, William Edwards, James Baber, and James Thompson each donated 10 acres for the establishment of the town. The name Edwardsville was selected in honor of Edwards. County officers were selected, and a county surveyor, with assistants, was directed to locate a public square and lay out town lots within the donated land, three-quarters of a mile from the courthouse in all directions. A small wooden courthouse was built along with a three-room jail built of logs.

Edwardsville Methodist Seminary was established in 1896, and three years later, enrollment had grown to 80. By 1912 and 1913, students were coming from other parts of the state and boarding in dormitories and local homes to attend the school. Subjects covered included reading, writing, arithmetic, Latin, logic, history, geography, nature study, drawing, and music. Tuition ranged from $1 to $2 per month; board in private homes cost from $9 to $12 per month. In December 1905, an election was held to move the courthouse from Edwardsville to Heflin.

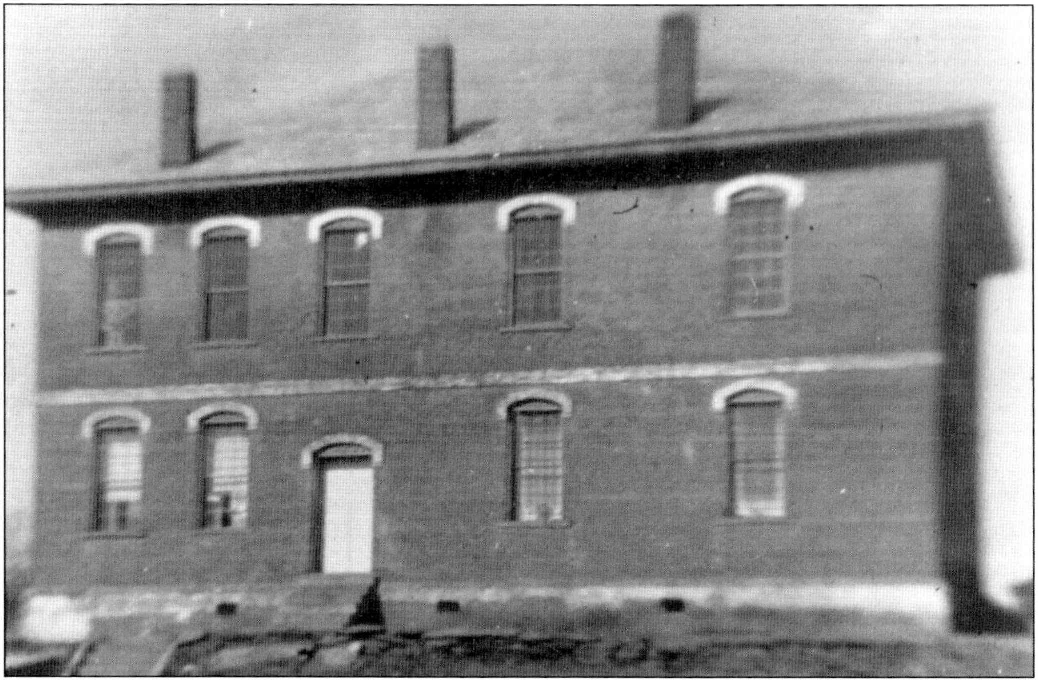

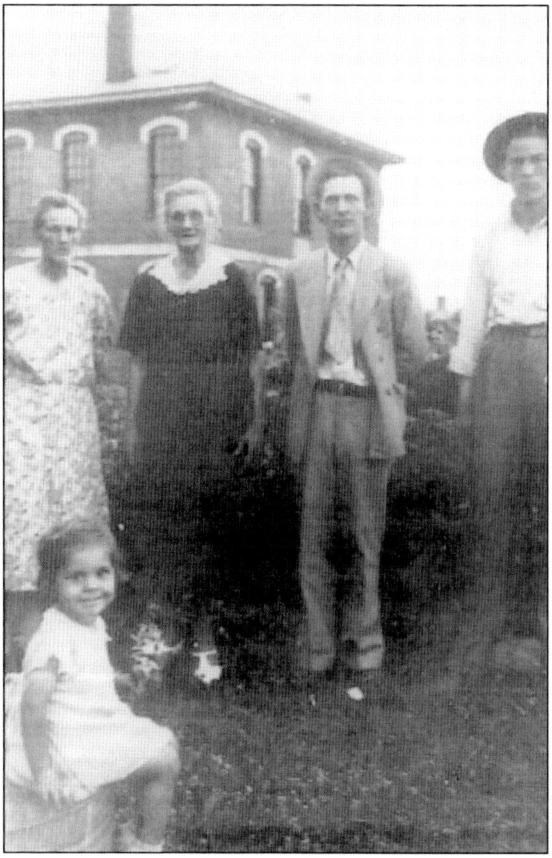

First Courthouse. The first courthouse was built in Edwardsville, as the town was the first county seat. After voters voted to change the county seat to Heflin and a new courthouse was built there, this structure became Edwardsville School, offering grades one through six. The building burned in the early 1960s. (Courtesy Charlotte Funderburk.)

Visit Courthouse. Visitors to the Cleburne County Courthouse in Edwardsville included, from left to right, Ida Woodward, ? Woodward, Lenard Star, and unidentified. The little girl is Lavern Star. Up until 1905, the county seat was at Edwardsville. During the fall of 1905, an election was held to move to Heflin. The election was appealed to the Alabama Supreme Court. The court, on July 1, 1906, decided to approve the change. (Courtesy East Alabama History Museum.)

PROBATE JUDGE. Cleburne County probate judge Thomas Burton was from Edwardsville, but he served after the county seat was moved to Heflin and a new courthouse built. Judge Burton donated land for the Baptist church in Edwardsville, and he was involved with the Baptist Association during its early days. (Courtesy Charlotte Funderburk.)

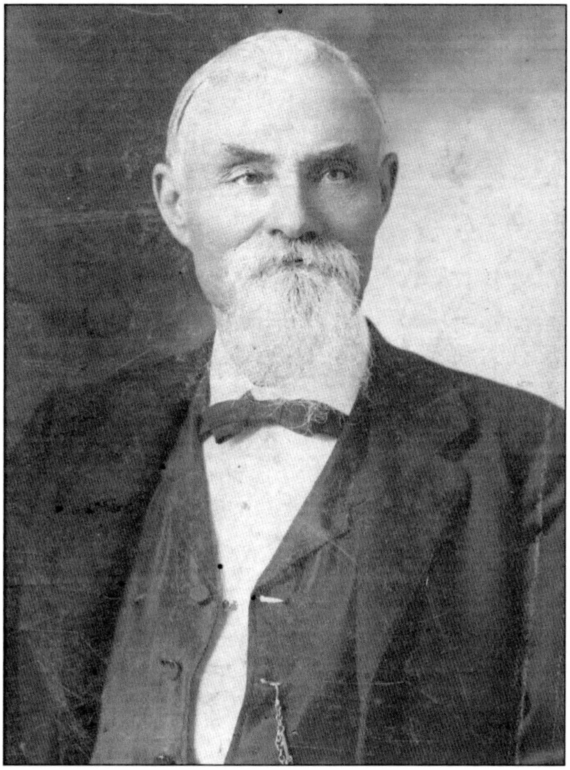

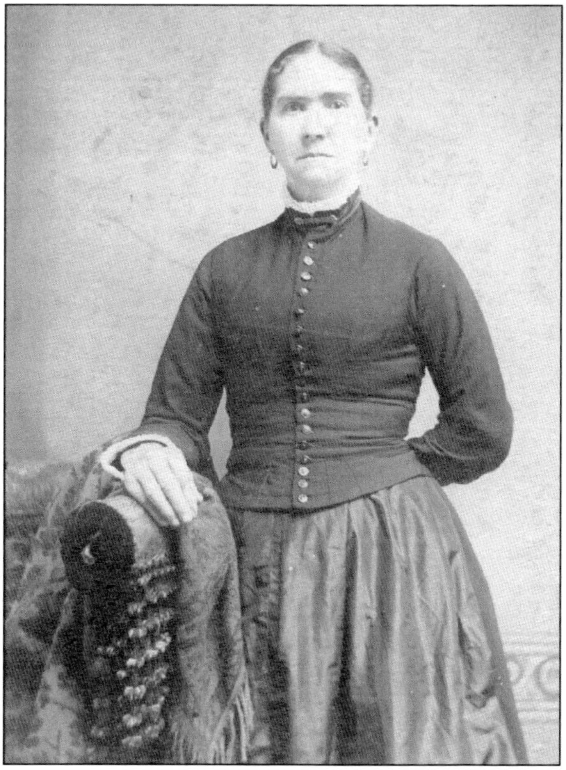

LEADING LADY. Charlotta Jane Owen Burgess was from one of the leading families of Edwardsville. Her descendants continue to live and be active in the community. After the county seat was changed to Heflin, Edwardsville begin to suffer a decline, as much business and commerce followed the building of a new courthouse there. (Courtesy Charlotte Funderburk.)

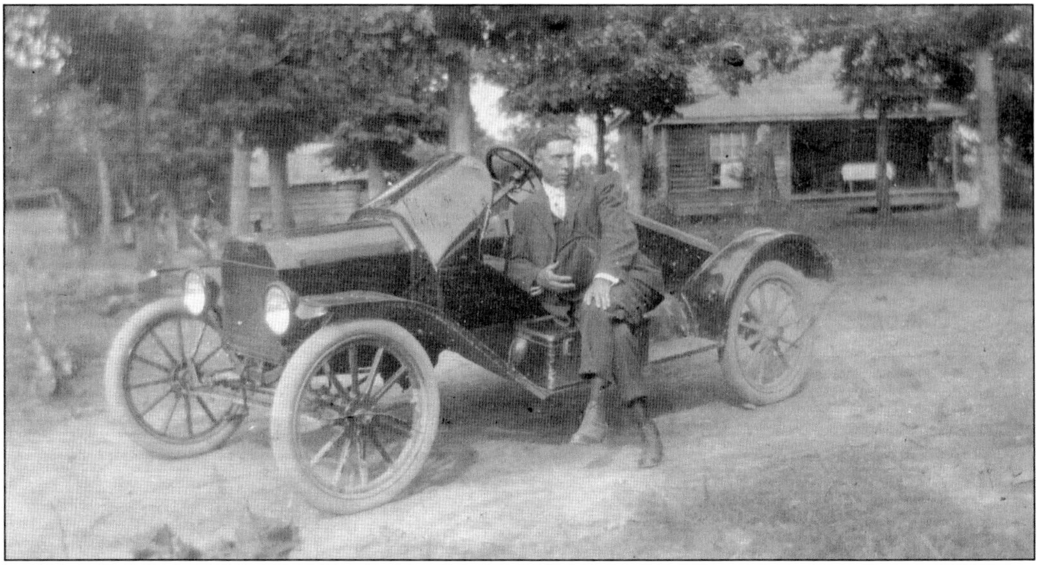

Sporty Driver. This photograph of a man relaxing on what was probably considered the sports car of its time was taken somewhere in Edwardsville, but the date is unknown. Cars began to appear more frequently as Cleburne County's roadways were improved. There are many stories of early automobiles and school buses being pulled out of the mud by farmers and their mules. (Courtesy Charlotte Funderburk.)

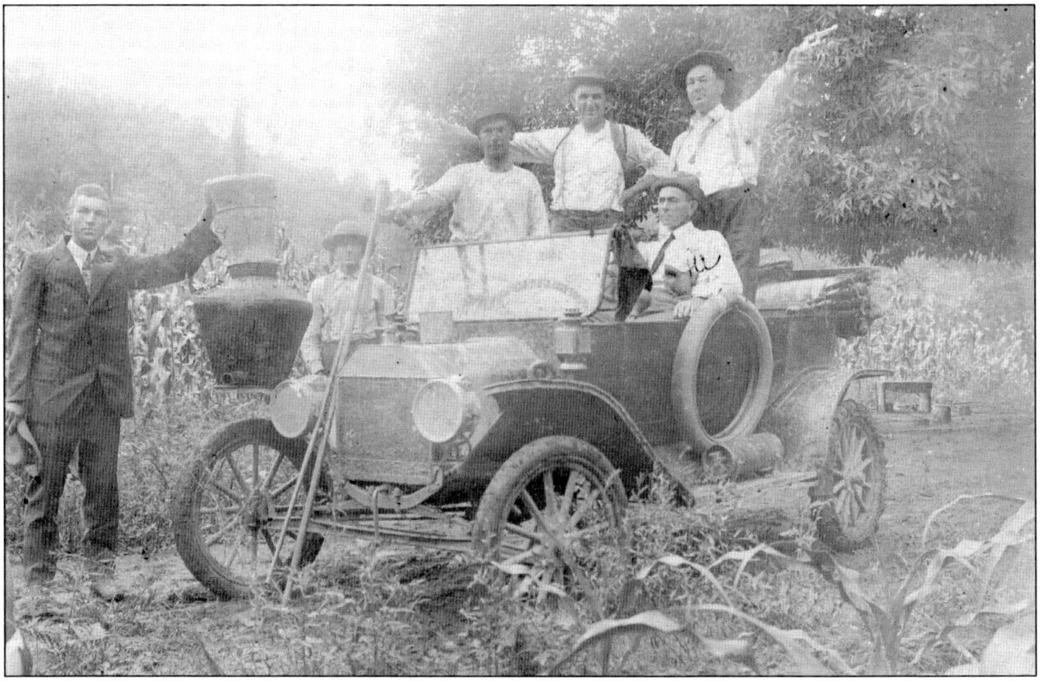

First Car in Town. The first car in Cleburne County was this Model T owned by Will Burgess of Edwardsville. Here Burgess gives federal revenue officers a ride to raid an illegal whiskey still. Burgess made international headlines when this vehicle stalled on the railroad track in Edwardsville and became the first-known fatal accident between an automobile and train. A man named Hilton, Burgess's passenger, died in the accident. (Courtesy Charlotte Funderburk.)

EDWARDSVILLE WOMAN. Nellie Burgess Elliott was an Edwardsville resident. She moved to Birmingham, Alabama, in the early 1920s. The *Cleburne News*, on February 12, 1925, reported her returning to Edwardsville for the funeral of her father, W. A. Burgess. Her husband worked in the mica mines in the southern half of Cleburne County. (Courtesy Charlotte Funderburk.)

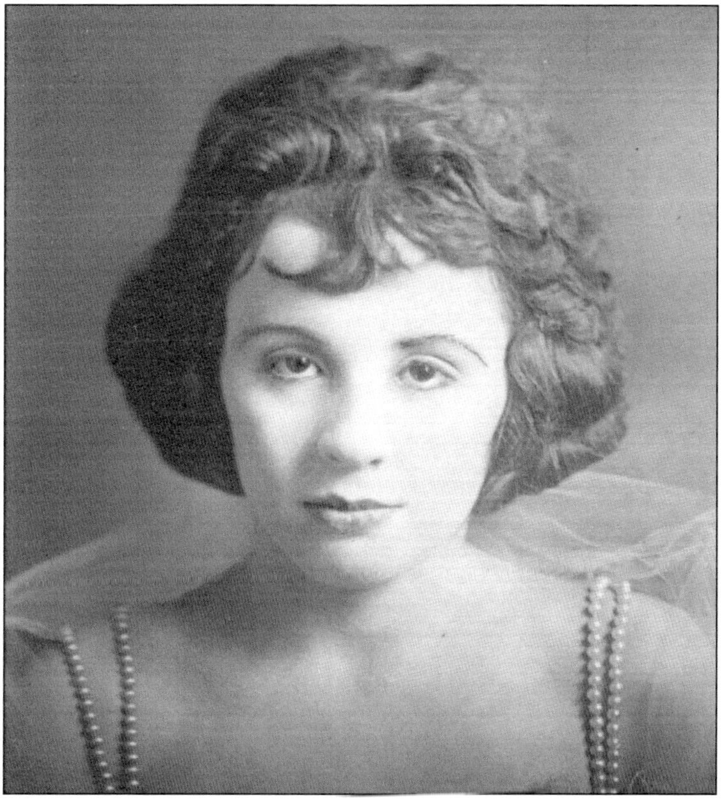

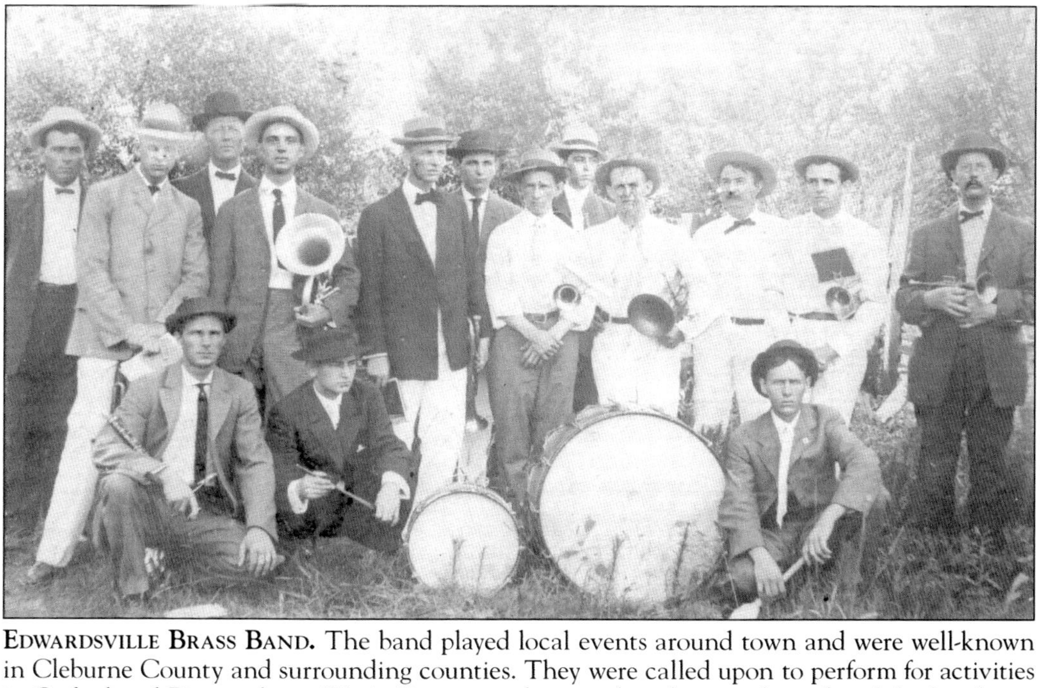

EDWARDSVILLE BRASS BAND. The band played local events around town and were well-known in Cleburne County and surrounding counties. They were called upon to perform for activities in Oxford and Birmingham. W. A. Burgess is the man kneeling to the right of the big drum. (Courtesy Charlotte Funderburk.)

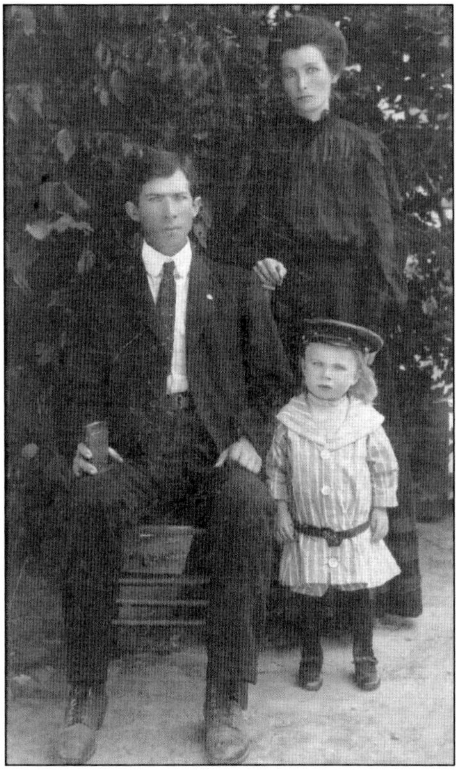

Brown Family. Alter Brown is seen here with his wife, Maggie, and an unidentified child. Brown operated a business in the 1920s and 1930s in Edwardsville and also became a Baptist preacher. He later changed denominations and attended the Church of God. (Courtesy Charlotte Funderburk.)

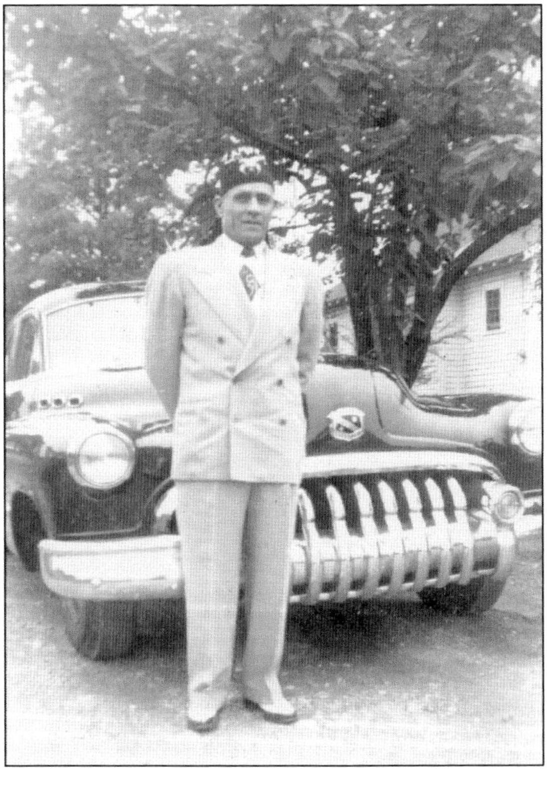

Burgess and His Buick. Edwardsville resident Burton Burgess posed in front of his Buick some time around 1950. Burgess worked at the Birmingham Iron Works in Birmingham, Alabama, and he was a Shriner, as can be seen from his Zamora hat. Burton was well known in the community. (Courtesy Charlotte Funderburk.)

Five

Ranburne
A Frontier Town

Ranburne is the oldest community in the county. As early as 1814, white settlers homesteaded the area, which was Creek Indian lands. The community was known as Lost Creek, and frontiersmen and Indian traders made up the first families and businesses there. The historic McIntosh Indian Trail came through the area from Georgia to Okfuskee, Alabama, and a small boy became lost from a wagon train. Both white and Native American settlers searched for the child, hence giving the name "Lost Creek" to the community. Lost Creek was situated between the Cherokees on the north and Creek Indians on the south and west. Due to tension and conflict between these two tribes, the white population of Lost Creek dwindled, but after 1830, as disputes were handled in a peaceful manner, the area once again began to grow.

Some of the earliest settlers were the Hansons, Alewines, Pirkles, Smiths, Mobleys, Merrills, Joneses, Durretts, Buchanans, Cooks, McLeods, Gibbses, Pollards, Lowerys, Turners, Richardsons, and Andersons. According to census records, many of these settlers were younger than the average Alabama residents. The percentage of females to males was very small, and there were few among them who were slave owners. Most of their agriculture efforts were toward a variety of crops, and the town later became a grazing and cattle center.

Daniel Alewine moved from South Carolina to Lost Creek before 1850 and donated land for a one-room school that was built in 1860. During the Civil War, Wilson's Raiders camped near Lost Creek and obtained supplies seized from local civilians. Ranburne received its name in 1894, when local merchant Emmett Thomason and his brother, Judge T. J. Thomason, decided that since the area of Lost Creek had been in Randolph County and was now in Cleburne County, they would combine the name of each county to come up with "Ranburne." A post office was established on January 8, 1899, and some of the first businesses included a gin, gristmill, store, blacksmith, and several churches. The town was incorporated on November 12, 1957, with Adrian Cook as mayor.

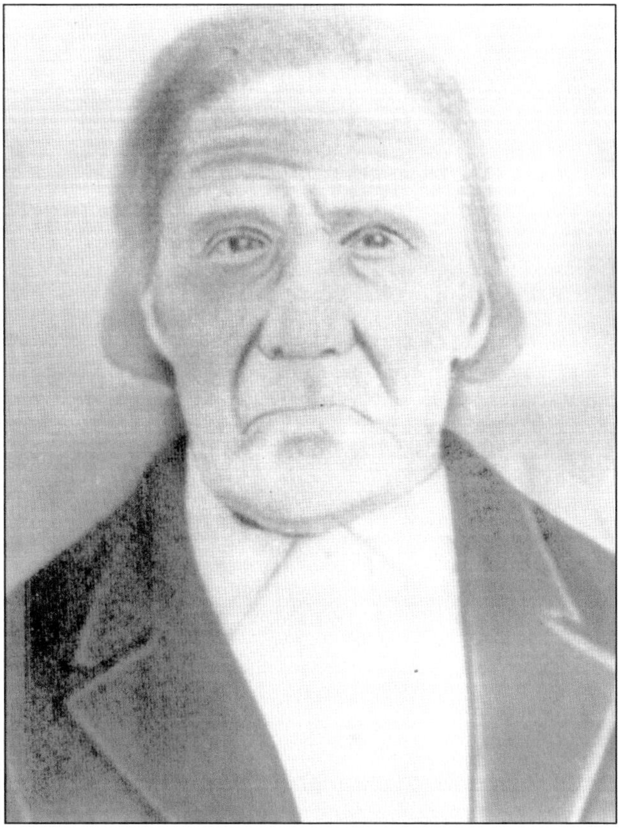

Founder of Ranburne. Daniel Alewine is considered the founder of Ranburne. He died on August 15, 1880, at the age of 87. He was born on February 10, 1793, in South Carolina and moved to Lost Creek in Cleburne County before 1850. He donated the land for Ranburne school and requested burial space for his family. The family plot is located near the Ranburne High School band building. (Courtesy Mike Pollard.)

Proud Owners. This Ranburne-area family posed for the photographer in front of their car some time in the late 1920s. Cars began to appear in Cleburne County around 1914 and in Heflin during the 1920s. Fords were sold at one dealership and Maxwells at a general merchandise store. Manufactured from about 1904 to 1925, the Maxwell was the forerunner to Chrysler. (Courtesy Christine Cantrell.)

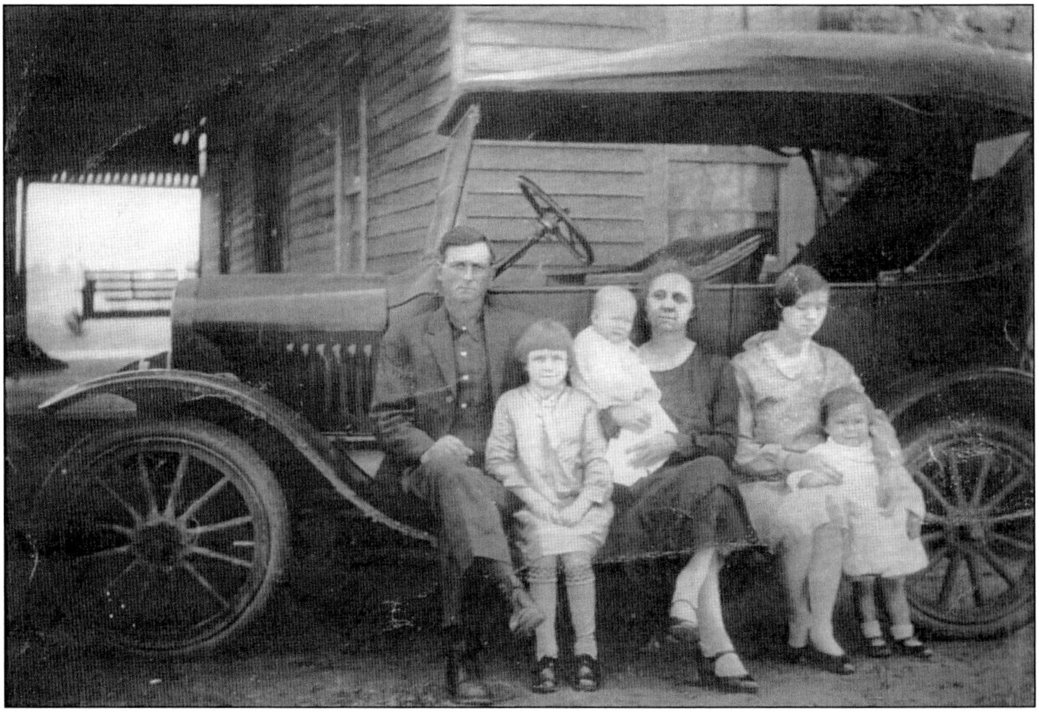

FIRST MAYOR. Adrian Cook was the first mayor of Ranburne. He is shown with his wife, Alice. Cook was elected February 14, 1958, and served until 1962. The town was incorporated November 12, 1957, though it already had a long, rich history. (Courtesy Mike Pollard.)

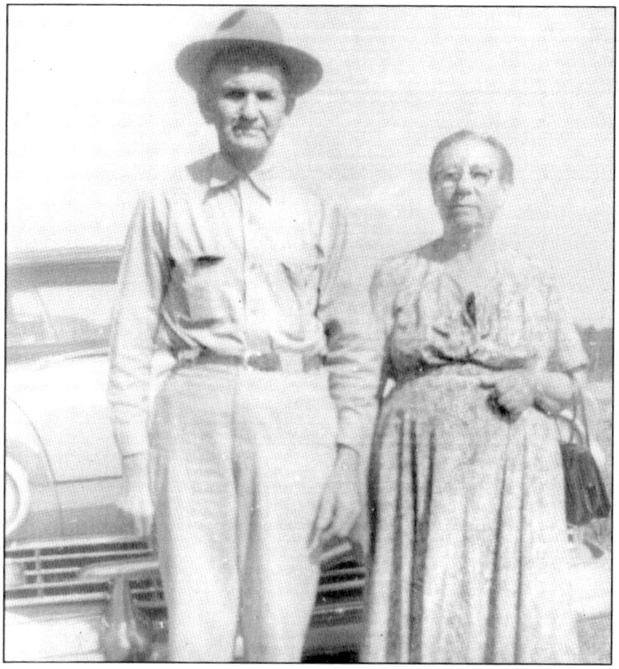

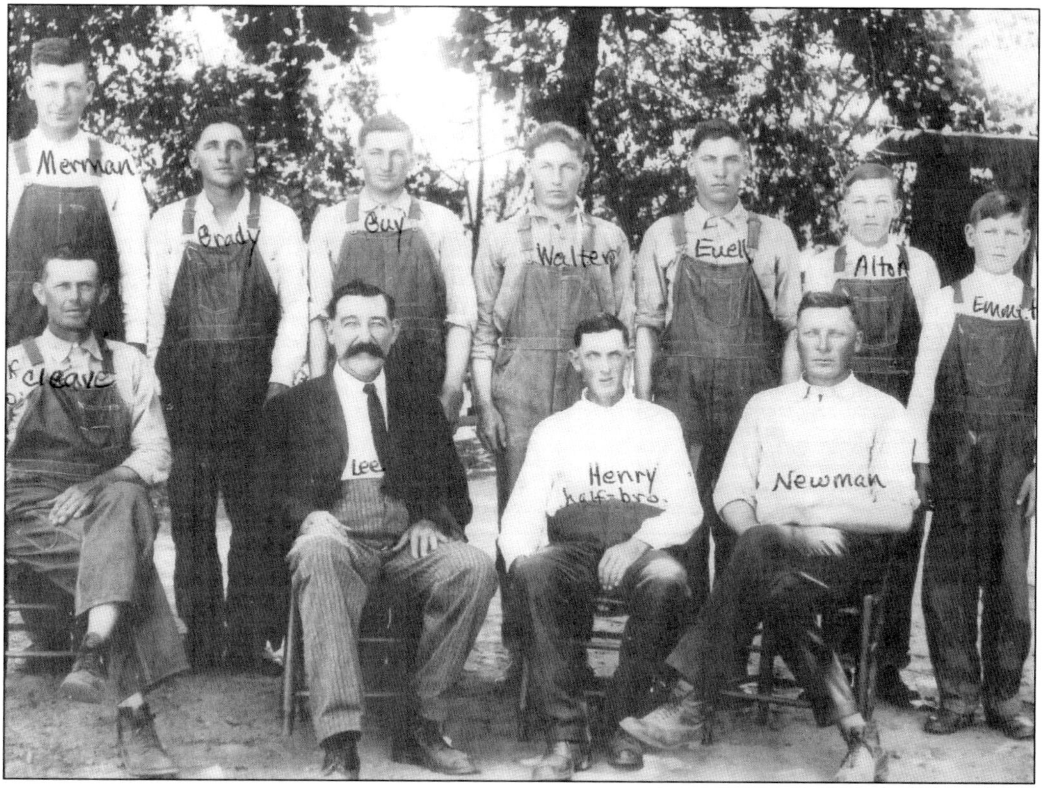

POLLARD BROTHERS. The Pollards were among early prominent families in Ranburne. Standing from left to right are brothers Merman, Brady, Guy, Walter, Euell, Alton, and Emmett Pollard. Seated are Cleave, Lee, Henry (a half-brother to Cleave) and Newman. (Courtesy Mike Pollard.)

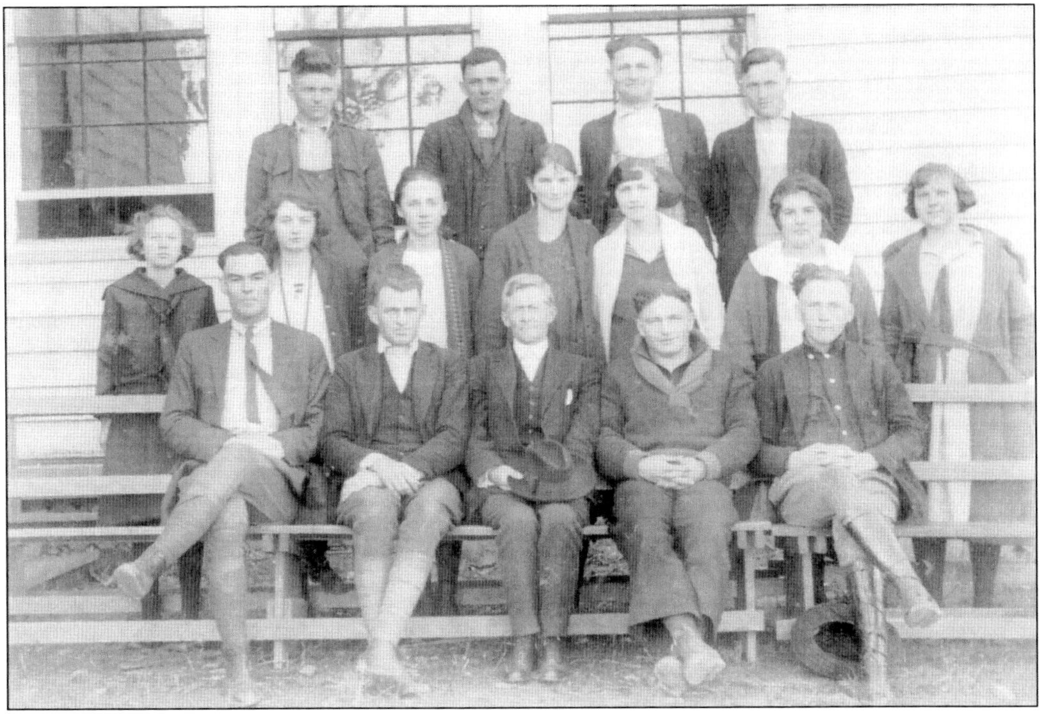

GOLDRIDGE STUDENTS. These *c.* 1920 students at Goldridge School are, from left to right, (first row) Paul Holliday, unidentified student, unidentified teacher, Ponder Kitchens, and James Smith; (second row) Bernice Sellers, unidentified student, Flora Whitman, Bird Farmer, two unidentified students, and Dessie Smith; (third row) Bige Overton, Frank Lowery (who went on to own a lot of property in Ranburne), Issac Truett, and unidentified student. (Courtesy Patsy Smith.)

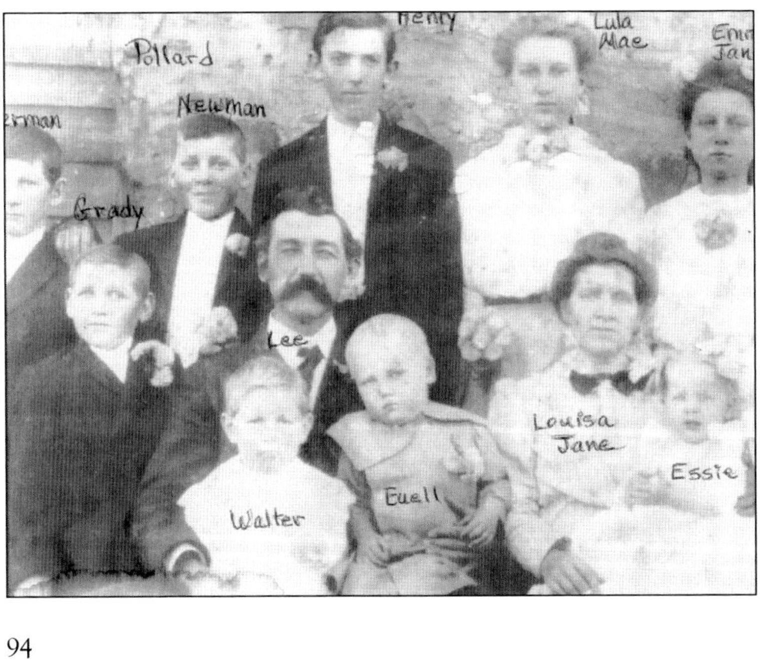

EARLY SETTLERS. The Pollards were among the first settlers in Ranburne. From left to right are (seated) Lee, Walter, Euell, Lee's wife Louisa Jane (who is pregnant), and Essie; (standing) Merman, Grady, Newman, Henry, Lula Mae, and Emma Jane. (Courtesy Mike Pollard.)

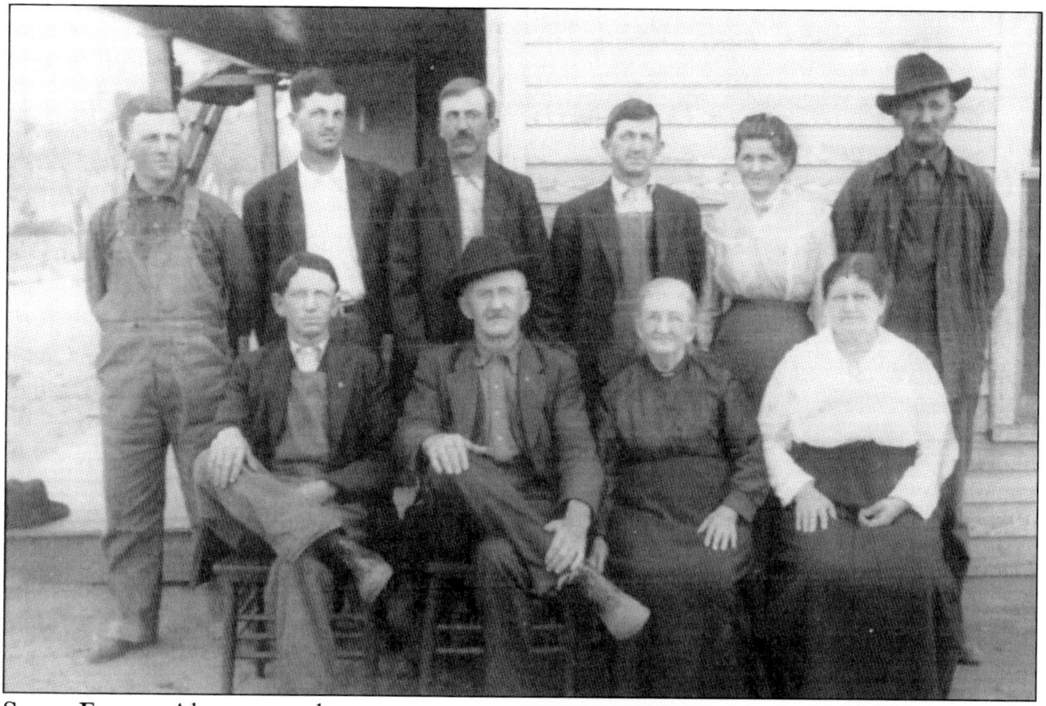

SMITH FAMILY. Also among the early settlers of Ranburne was the Smith family. From left to right, this photograph, taken at Melvin Smith's home on the road between Ranburne and Bowden, includes (first row) Willie, Melvin, Almelie, and Izora; (second row) Walter, Luther, Lewis, Melvin, Ida, and James. Before this photograph was taken, Melvin Smith owned and operated a large hotel at Hopewell. (Courtesy Patsy Smith.)

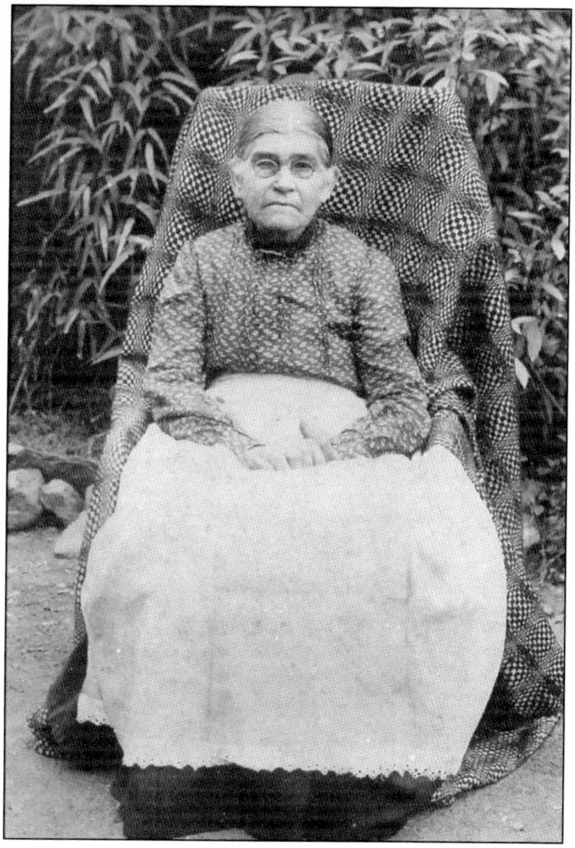

"BABB" HAND. Eliza "Babb" Hand came from Virginia and was part of one of the first families to settle the area that is now Ranburne. Former Cleburne County superintendent of education Noel Hand was Eliza's great-great nephew. She is buried in Corinth Cemetery. (Courtesy Patsy Smith.)

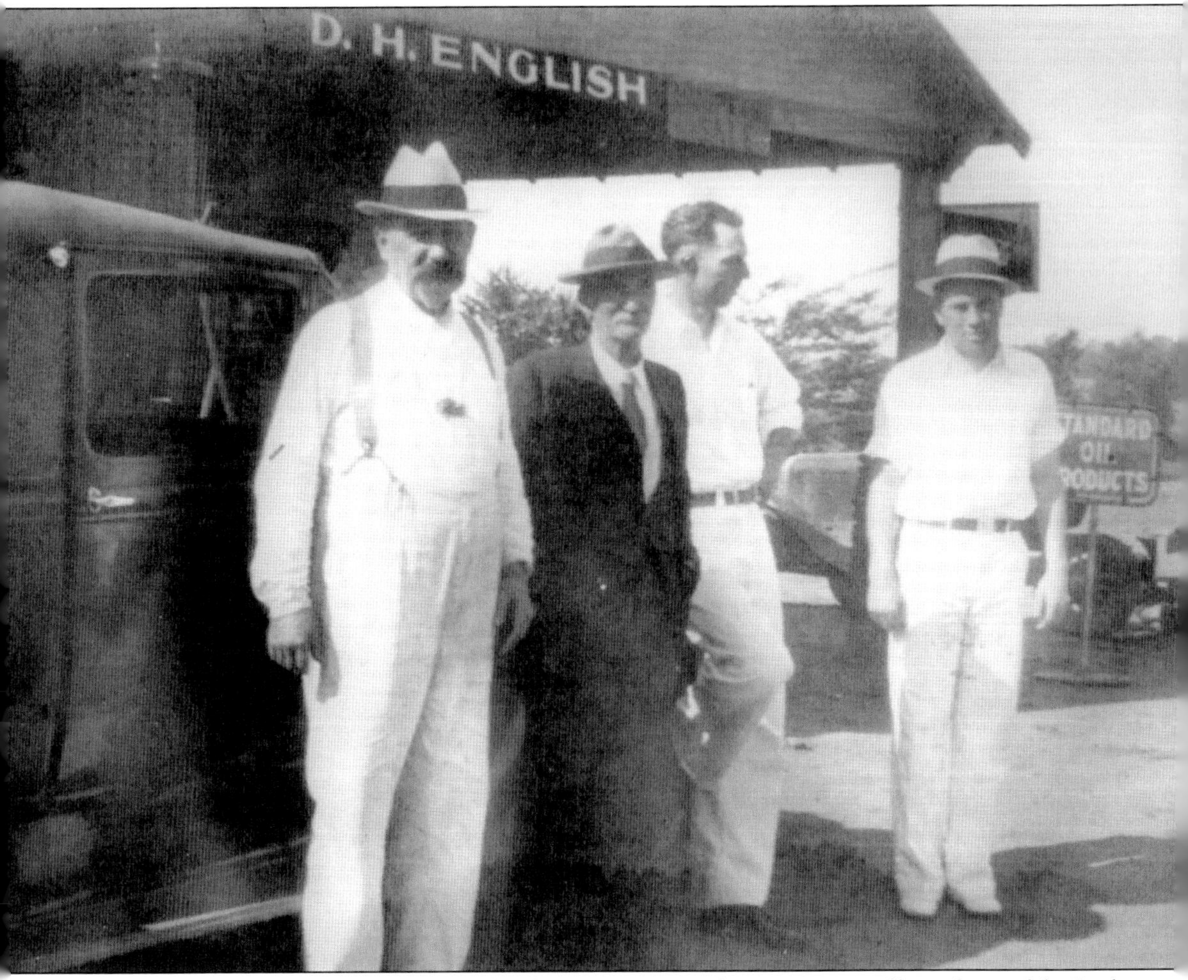

WATCHING TRAFFIC. From left to right, the men seen watching passing traffic in front of the Luther Baughn Store in Ranburne in the early 1930s are Lee Pollard, Dr. Jerry Lindsey, Doc English, and vocational agriculture teacher Waters. The men are standing in front of a 1933 Model A Ford. (Courtesy Mike Pollard.)

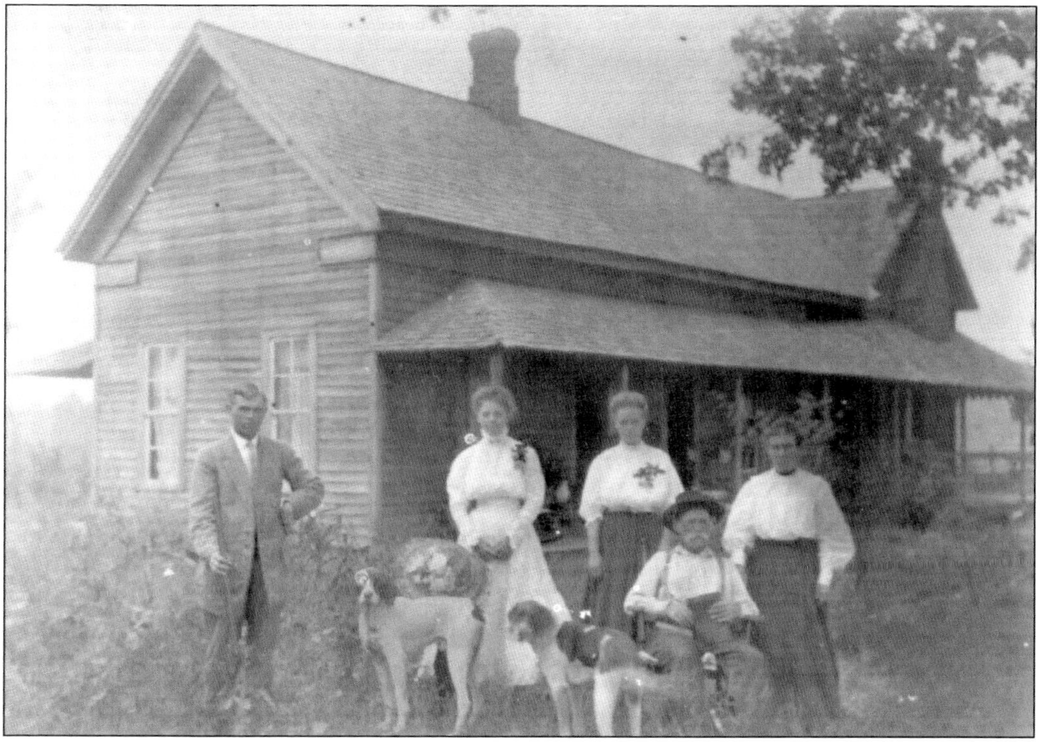

TYPICAL COUNTRY HOME. This is typical of many of the country homes around Ranburne in the late 1800s and early 1900s. (Courtesy Mike Pollard.)

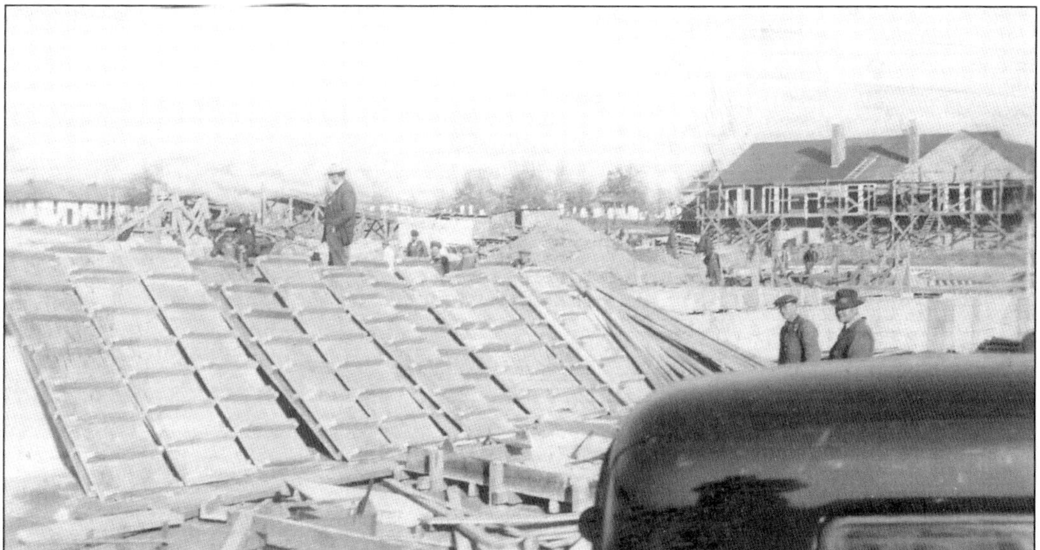

RANBURNE SCHOOL PROJECTS. This photograph shows construction at Ranburne, but since there were several schools built, it is difficult to date the photograph. A two-story building with four classrooms on the first floor, an auditorium, and two classrooms upstairs was built prior to 1933. Later a rock building was built on the site of the present school, and it burned in 1936. Another school, made of concrete, was built in 1940 with the aid of the National Youth Administration and Public Works Administration. (Courtesy Carolyn Parker.)

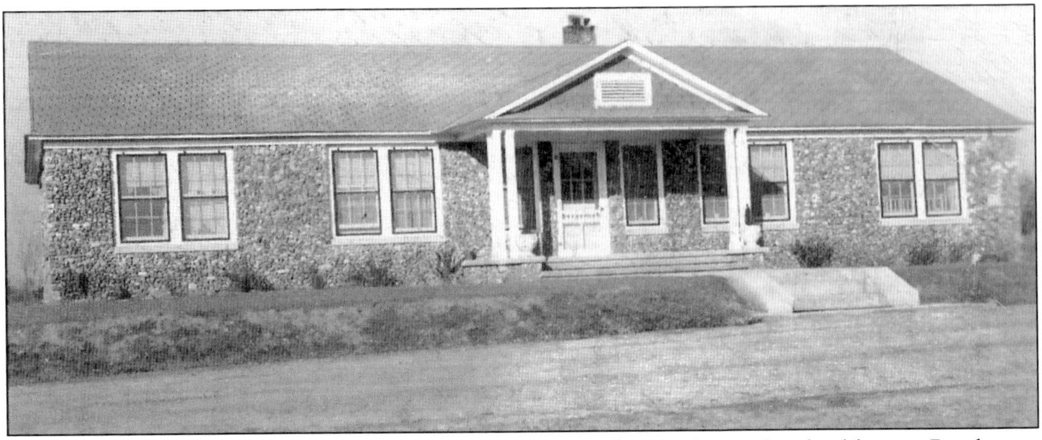

VOCATIONAL BUILDING. This is the home economics and agriculture class building at Ranburne High School. The structure is believed to have been built in the mid-1930s. Most of the time, female students met on one side of building and studied home economics while male students met on the other side and studied agriculture. (Courtesy Carolyn Parker.)

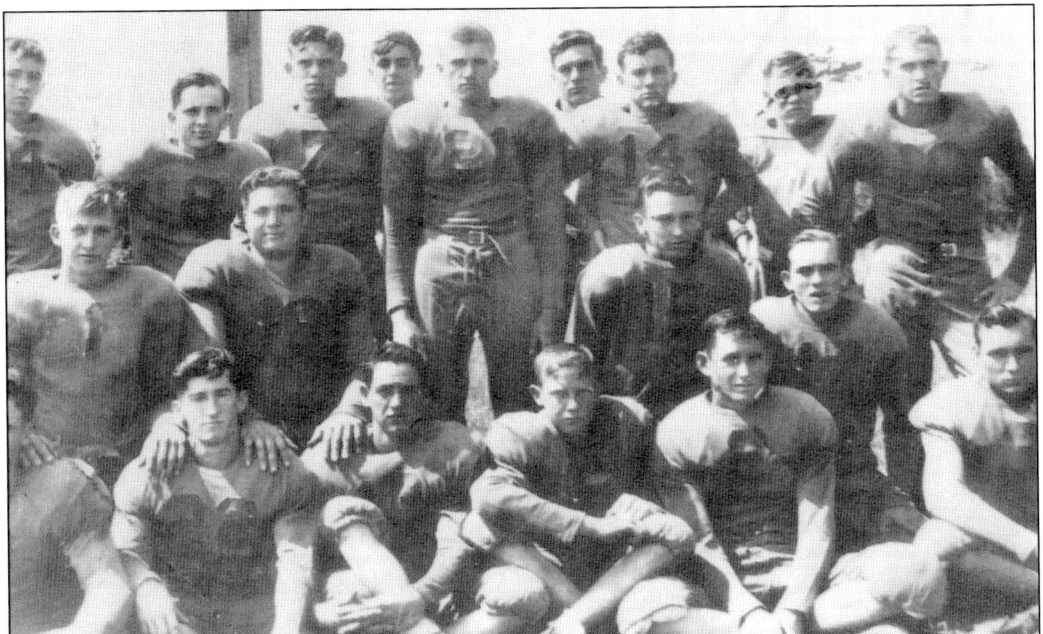

RANBURNE BULLDOGS. The Ranburne High School Bulldogs posed for this photograph in 1948. Ranburne High School had its first team in 1931. According to the Alabama High School Football Historical Society, the Bulldogs played five games in 1948. They lost 0-41 to Ohatchee on September 10, lost 0-41 to Piedmont on September 17, lost 0-32 to Woodland on October 15, fell 0-31 to the Anniston B Team on October 28, and suffered a 0-13 loss to Hokes Bluff on November 5. The Bulldogs ended the year with a 0-5 record and without scoring a single point. (Courtesy Mike Pollard.)

Six

Schools
Focused on the Three Rs

Prior to the 1900s, there were numerous small, one-room schools scattered across Cleburne County. In those days, some schools and churches were combined in the same building. Most students used a Noah Webster "Blue Back" speller and a small slate to write on. Students walked to school, and the distance could be several miles each way. Seats were hewn halves of logs cut to the right length and legs made of small poles driven into augured holes.

Early schools in Cleburne County stressed the "Three Rs" of "reading, 'riting, and 'rithmetic." Many had only one teacher. Since children were expected to help on family farms, the school sessions might only run for a few months in the winter and a few months in the summer. District schools flourished in Cleburne County between 1907 and 1917. In 1917, the number of district schools peaked at 65, and the Cleburne County Board of Education maintained those schools until 1921, when the ability to transport children from one district to another became feasible. With the passing of each year, the number of schools gradually decreased as more and more were consolidated.

Former school teachers Don Chandler and Frances Wright noted in *The Heritage of Cleburne County, Alabama*, "The old district schools served a great need in that they caused the citizens of the different settlements to become school-conscious. The county board, with the help of the state, would match any money raised by the citizens of the district. The citizens felt responsible for raising their share of the money, and this attitude caused them to have more interest in their school."

A typical school of the early 1900s consisted of one room, one teacher, and an average of 35 students who met three to seven months of the year. As consolidation continued and school buses could run routes, the number of schools in the county declined to the present two high schools, four elementary schools, and one middle school.

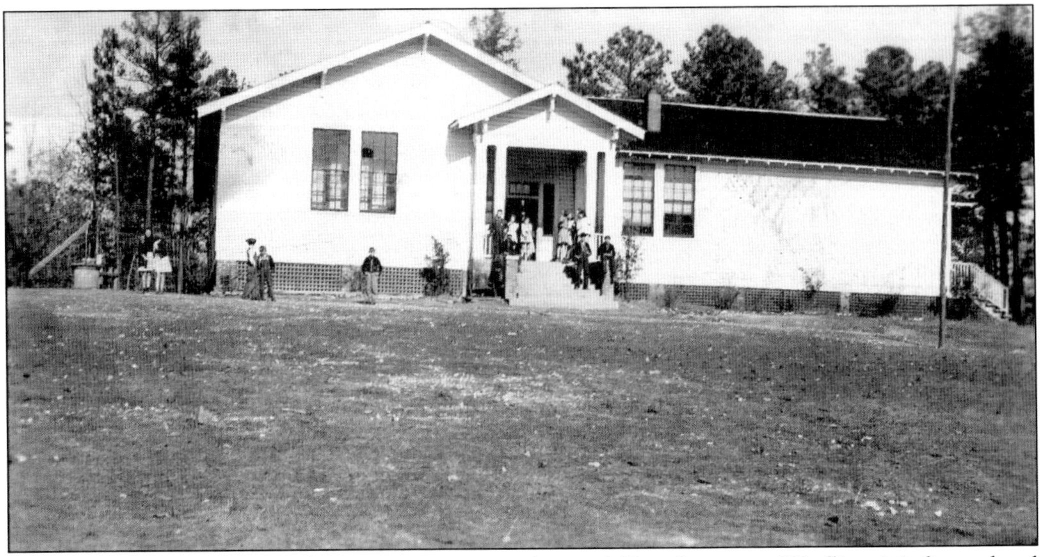

AI JUNIOR HIGH SCHOOL. The Ai community is located 10 miles east of Heflin. Ai's first school was built around 1900. In 1924, the state voted to build a junior high school but only furnished doors and windows and the money for carpentry. Timber for construction was donated by citizens, and a small sawmill was set up to prepare the lumber. The school burned in September 1948 due to defective wiring. (Courtesy Carolyn Parker.)

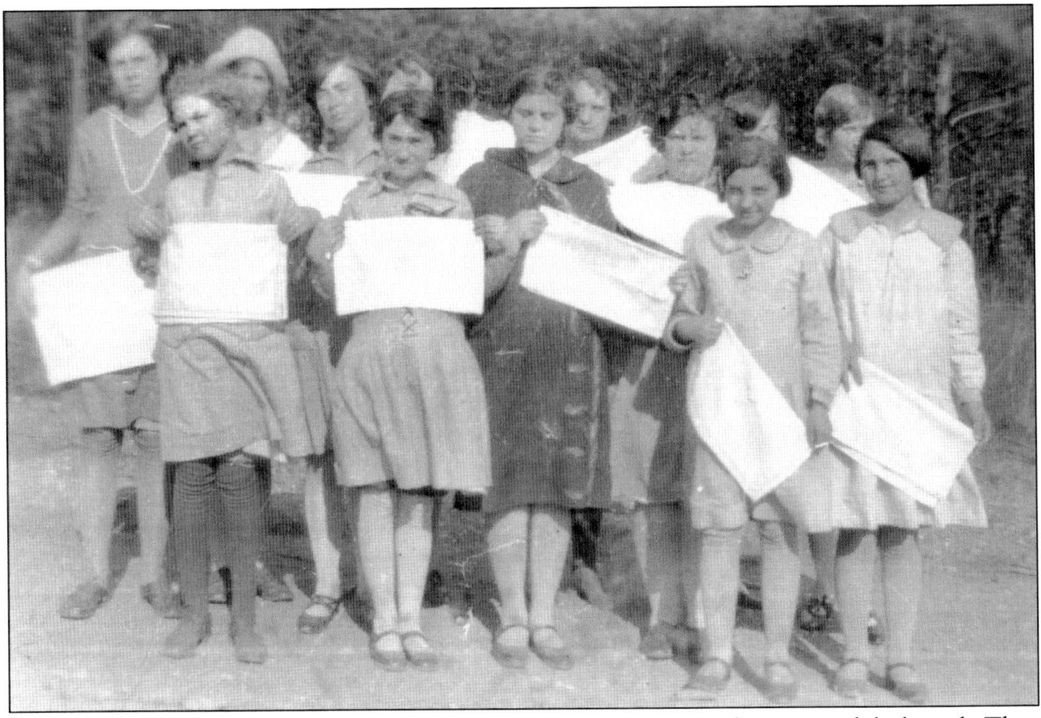

AI 4-H CLUB. These Ai Junior High School 4-H club girls show their first piece of cloth work. They each made an Italian hemmed dresser scarf with satin embroidery work. The boys also excelled at Ai, as their basketball team won a championship cup. The school was closed on September 14, 1956, due to decreased enrollment. (Courtesy Cleburne County Extension Office.)

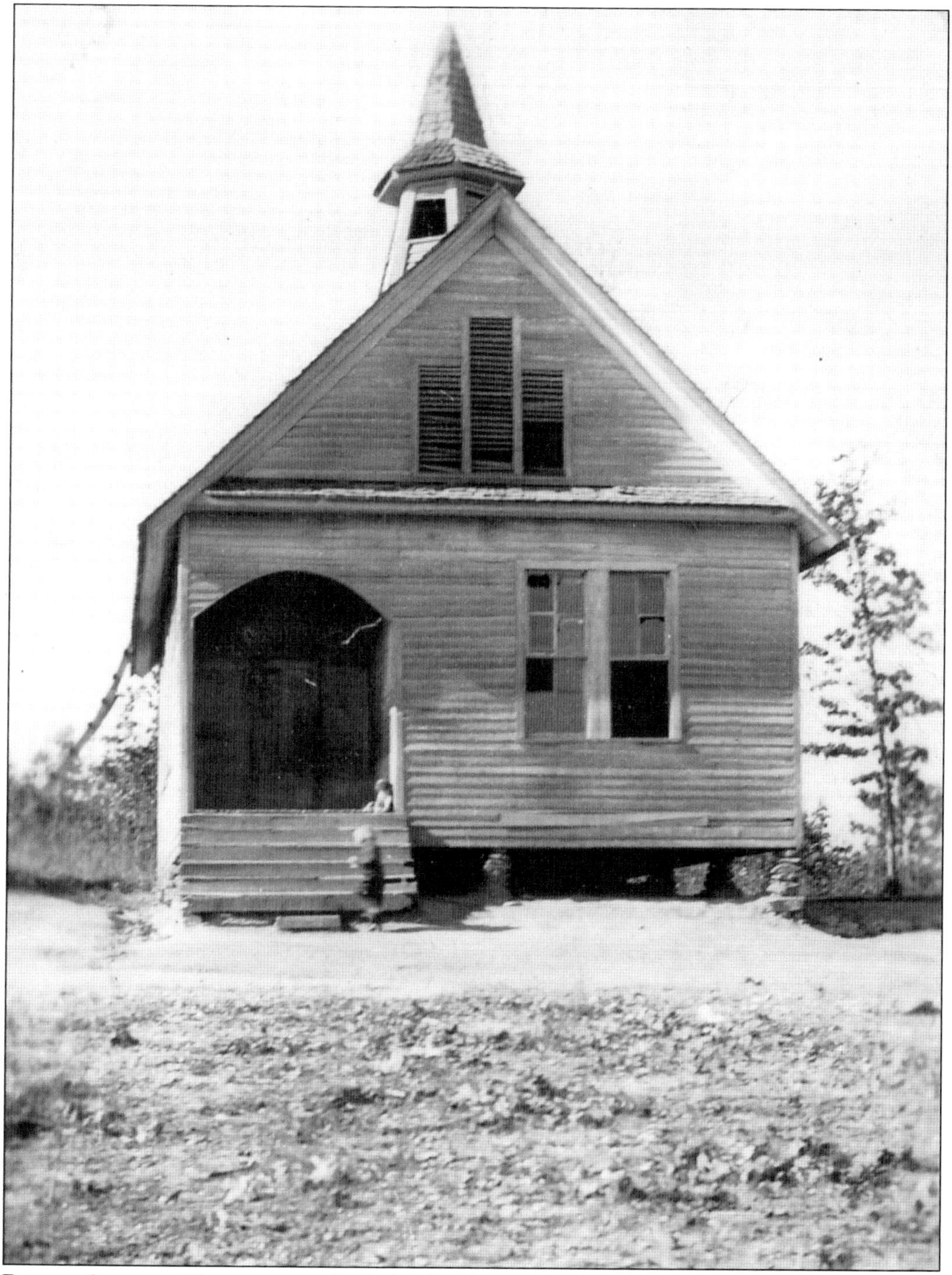

Bethel School. The one-room Bethel School near Muscadine was built about 1888 on land donated by the Thompson family. One teacher, Mary Lizzie Yates, had a habit of saying "Throw that in the stove." Student Melvin Laminack was chewing on an old shotgun shell and threw it into the old potbellied stove, and it exploded. The school hosted "box suppers" to raise money for a new stove. (Courtesy Carolyn Parker.)

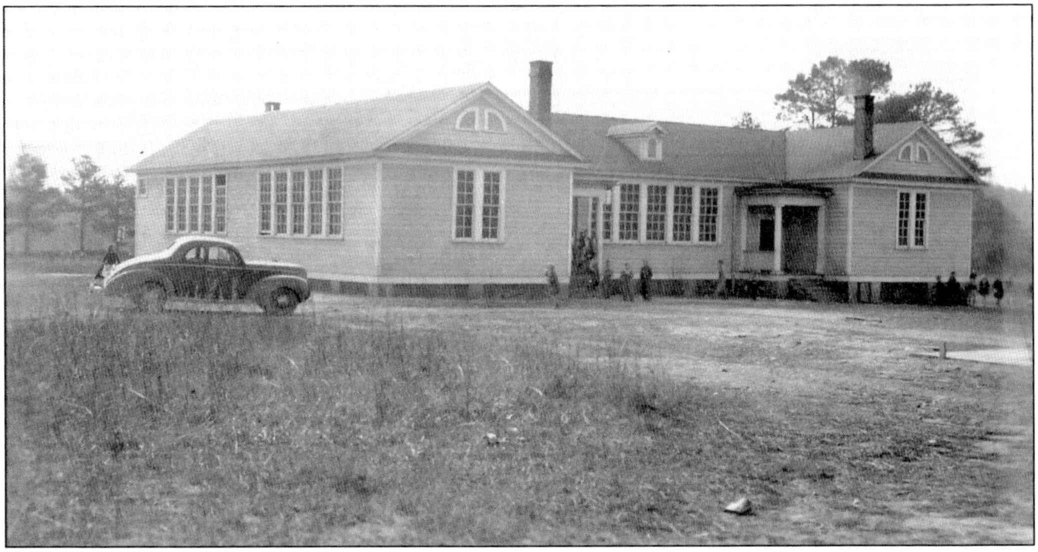

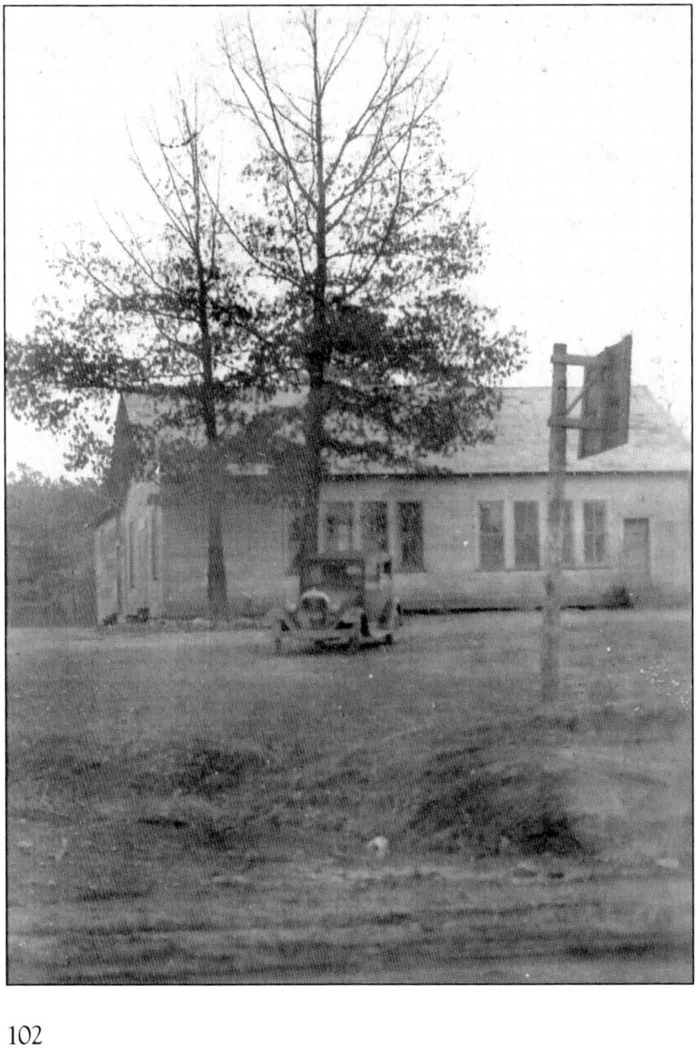

Borden Springs School. Located in north Cleburne County in the Borden Springs community, this school started with three teachers who taught grades one through eight. A high school was added about 1932, including grades 9 through 11. It was reported in 1925 that the school would have a basketball team, and players raised $7.20 for a ball by selling 144 pencils. (Courtesy Carolyn Parker.)

Cedar Creek School. Located on Highway 19 South, Cedar Creek School taught grades one through nine. It had three teachers. The school was built on land owned by an early pioneering family, the Tates. They donated land on which the church was constructed in 1845. The school was already operational. On September 18, 1937, a decision was made to consolidate the school with Heflin. (Courtesy Carolyn Parker.)

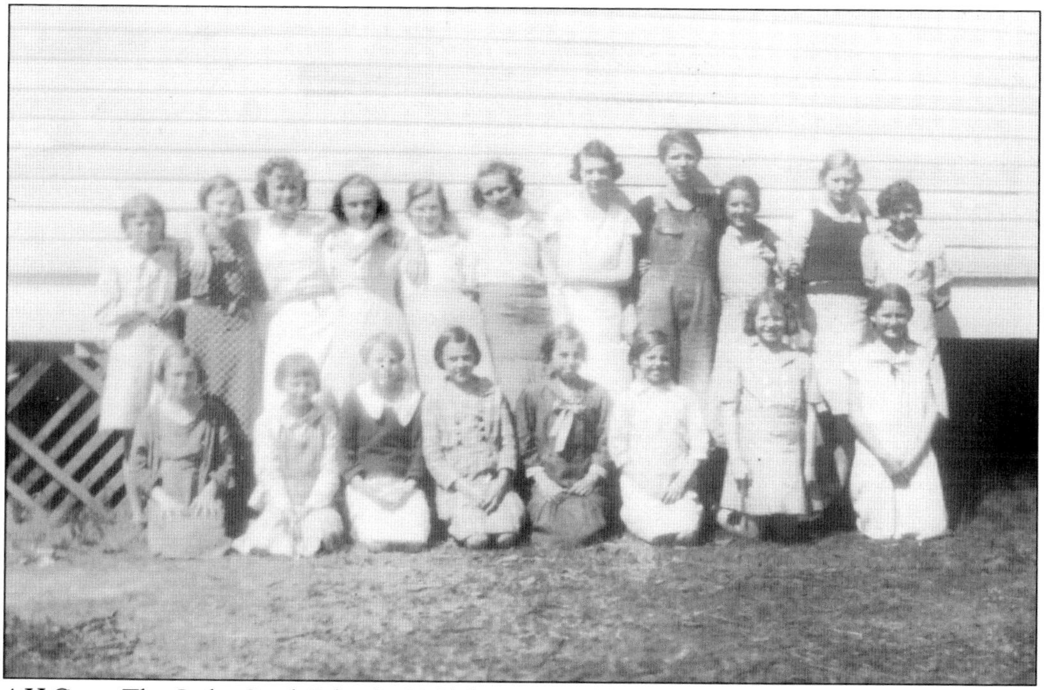

4-H CLUB. The Cedar Creek School 4-H Club was one of the smallest in Cleburne County; however, its members did some of the best work. (Courtesy Cleburne County Extension Office.)

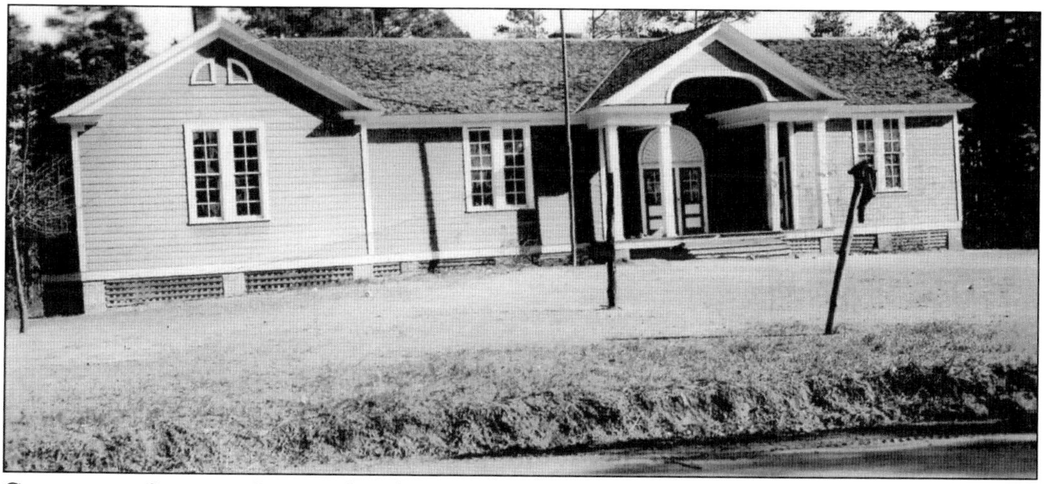

CROSSROADS SCHOOL. Crossroads School was located in the Crossroads community and probably built to consolidate the old Crossroads School and Campground School. The two-room school began classes in 1929. Charlie and Lissie Bennett donated land for the school in 1927. Nine grades were provided. After the first year, another room was added. The Crossroads girls won the county basketball tournament three consecutive years. (Courtesy Carolyn Parker.)

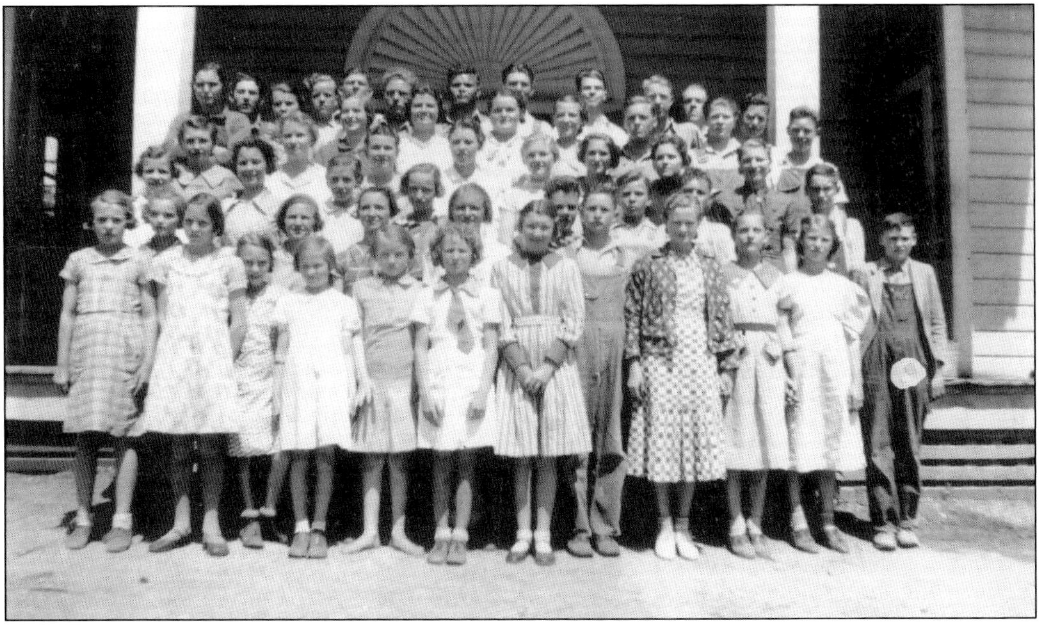

Crossroads 4-H Club. Crossroads 4-H girls and boys club members gathered outside the school for this photograph. Crossroads 4-H Club has 43 members and had the largest enrollment of any club in the county. Club members entered contests and learned leadership, citizenship, and communication skills. (Courtesy Cleburne County Extension Office.)

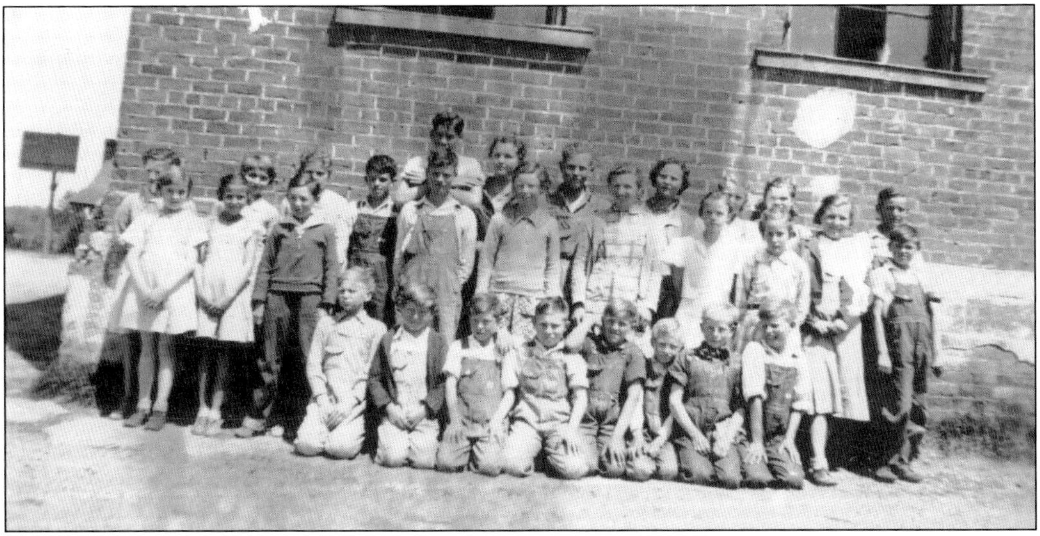

Edwardsville 4-H Club. Both girls and boys enjoyed participating in the 4-H club in Edwardsville. The first school was a two-room log building with two teachers. There were no grades, and each student was promoted by completion of a book. Slates were used for writing. In 1896, the Edwardsville Methodist Seminary was established. By 1899, enrollment was 80, and 5¢ tablets replaced slates. (Courtesy Cleburne County Extension Office.)

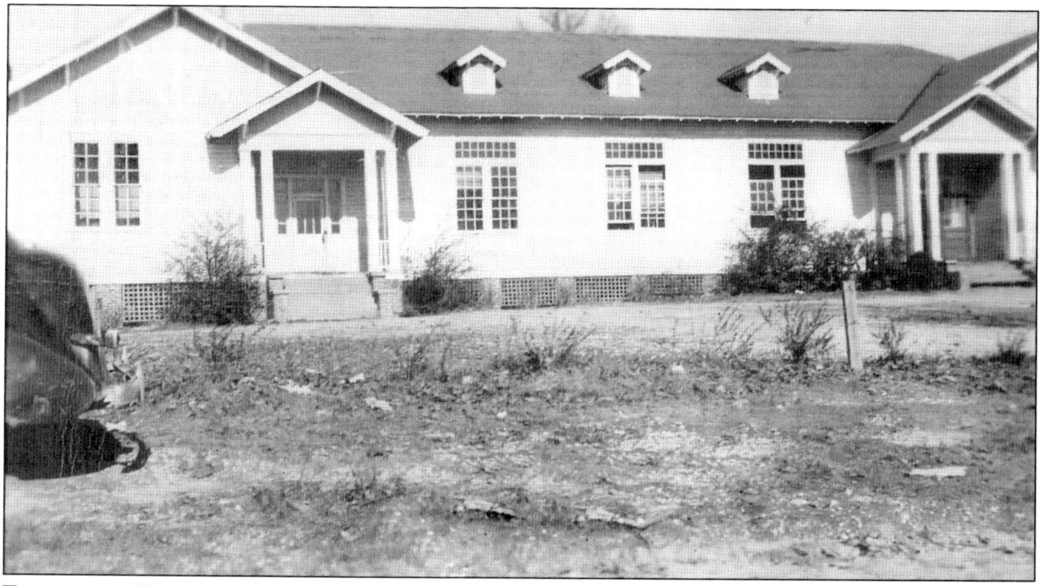

FRUITHURST SCHOOL. This school was originally a wood-frame structure built around the beginning of the 20th century. The building burned, and another wood structure was built and later replaced with block. The present building is a brick structure. Classes were offered for grades through 11. Students wishing to attend 12th grade went to Heflin. Classes were often large, with as many as 40 students. (Courtesy Carolyn Parker.)

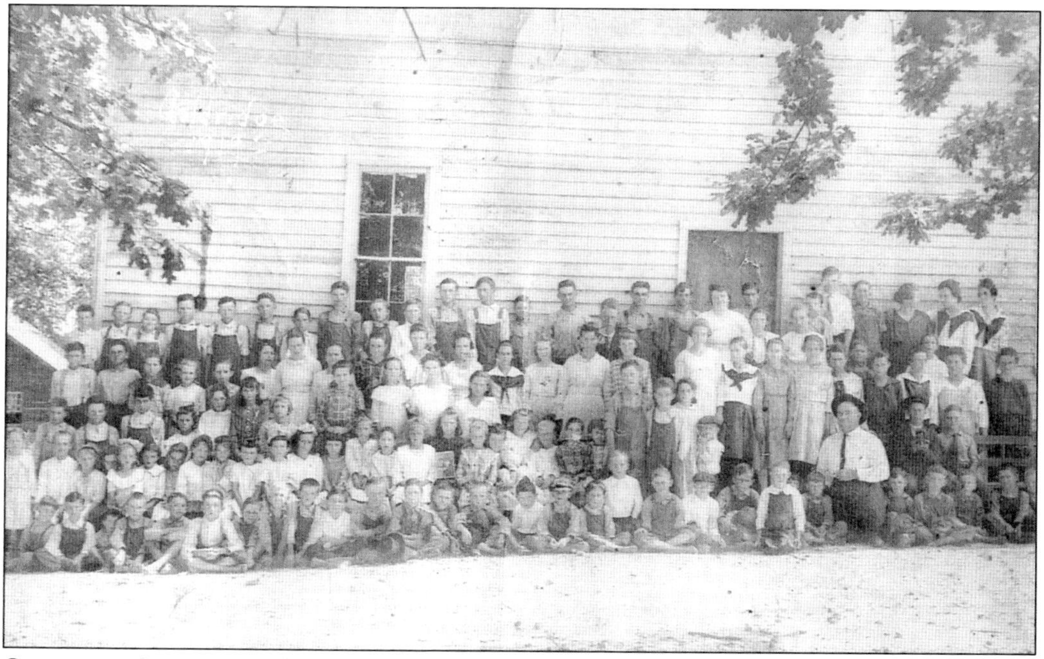

GOLDRIDGE SCHOOL. Students gathered outside for this 1919 photograph at Goldridge School. The teachers were Bunk Lee and Stella Dye. Some of the students attending that year included Gordon Gibbs, ParaLee Gibbs, Mamie Gibbs, Hazel Gibbs, Effee Yates, Howard Gibbs, Dorsia Gibbs, Ezelle Stephens, Garland Cooley, Annie Yates, Oscar Yates, and Barnie Gibbs. (Courtesy Mike Pollard.)

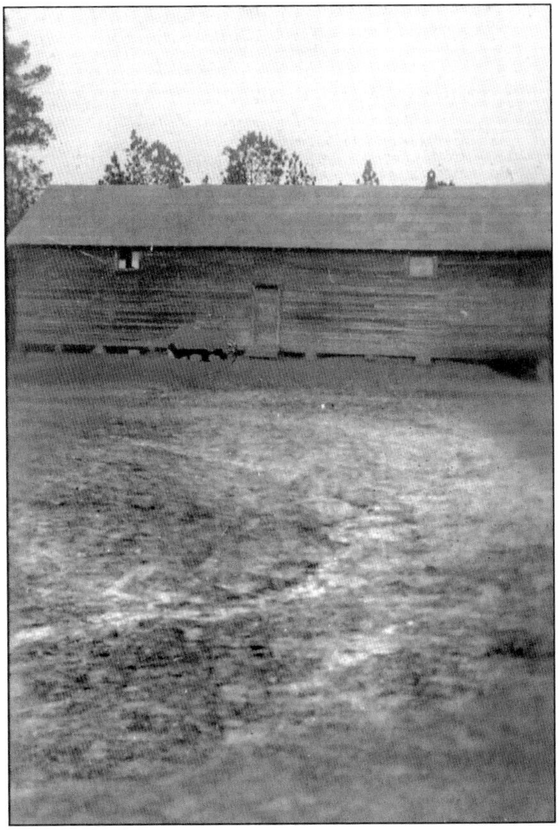

GREEN'S CHAPEL SCHOOL. Located on Cleburne County Road 19, Green's Chapel School was built on land given by Uriah Beason. The school was already established in 1904, and the church at the same location was established around 1869. The school burned, and on March 5, 1920, the community was instructed to build a new one. At the time, there were two schools, one for each race. (Courtesy Carolyn Parker.)

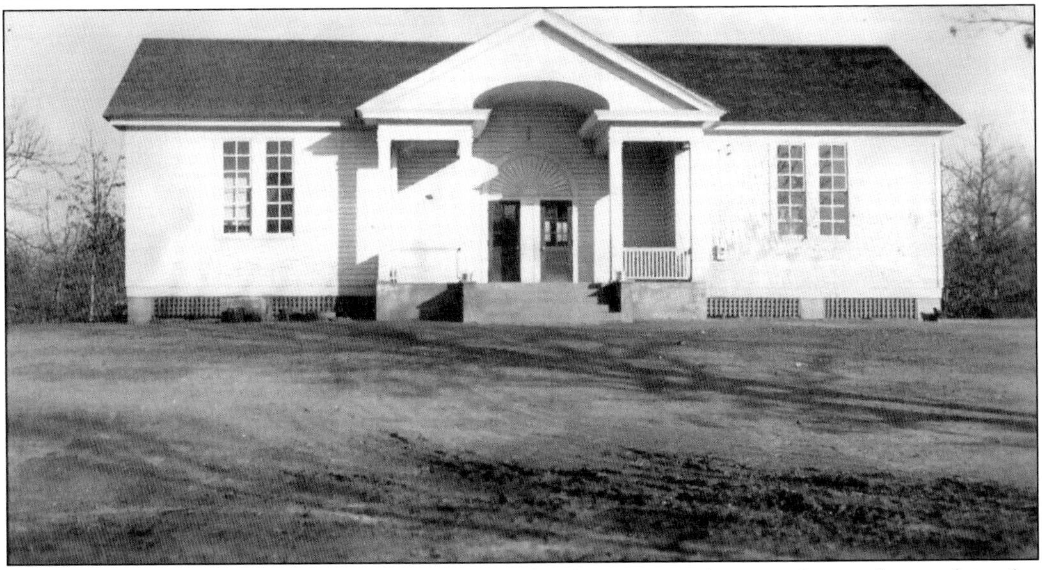

HIGHTOWER SCHOOL. This school offered grades five, six, and seven. It was located in the Hightower community as early as 1912. The school burned in 1933 or 1934. The school was rebuilt and continued to operate until the mid-1950s. The last teacher is believed to have been Susie Green, who taught grades one through five. The school was later consolidated with Ranburne. (Courtesy Carolyn Parker.)

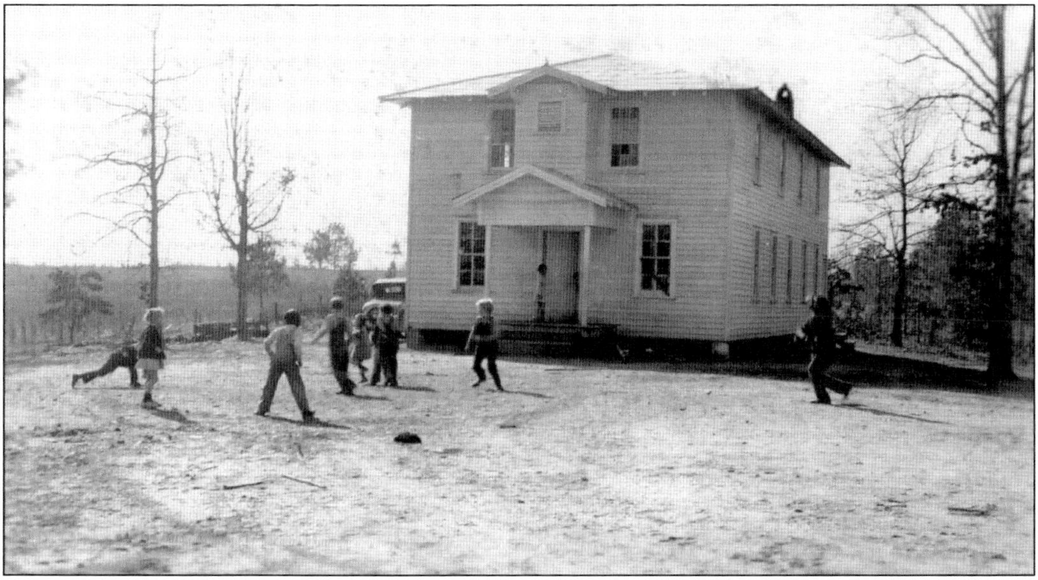

HOPEWELL SCHOOL. The Vanderbilt Railroad, which ran a line from the Hopewell community to Tallapoosa, Georgia, was instrumental in establishing a school at this location. Indications are that the school was in existence as early as 1904. In 1918, the school had 64 students in grades one through eight. The school was closed in the early 1940s. (Courtesy Carolyn Parker.)

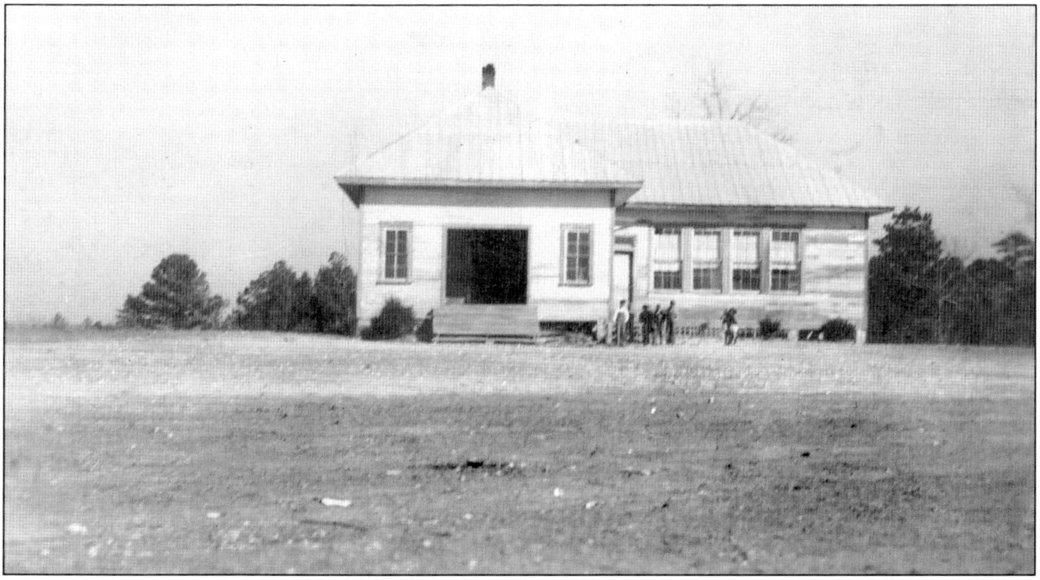

LEBANON SCHOOL. This school was located in the Lebanon community and contained grades one through eight. This school had two teachers and was established prior to 1904. Due to growth, school trustees applied to the board to have a junior high school established. The school board contracted on May 14, 1946, to dismantle the school and to use the material to build a four-room annex to Fruithurst School. (Courtesy Carolyn Parker.)

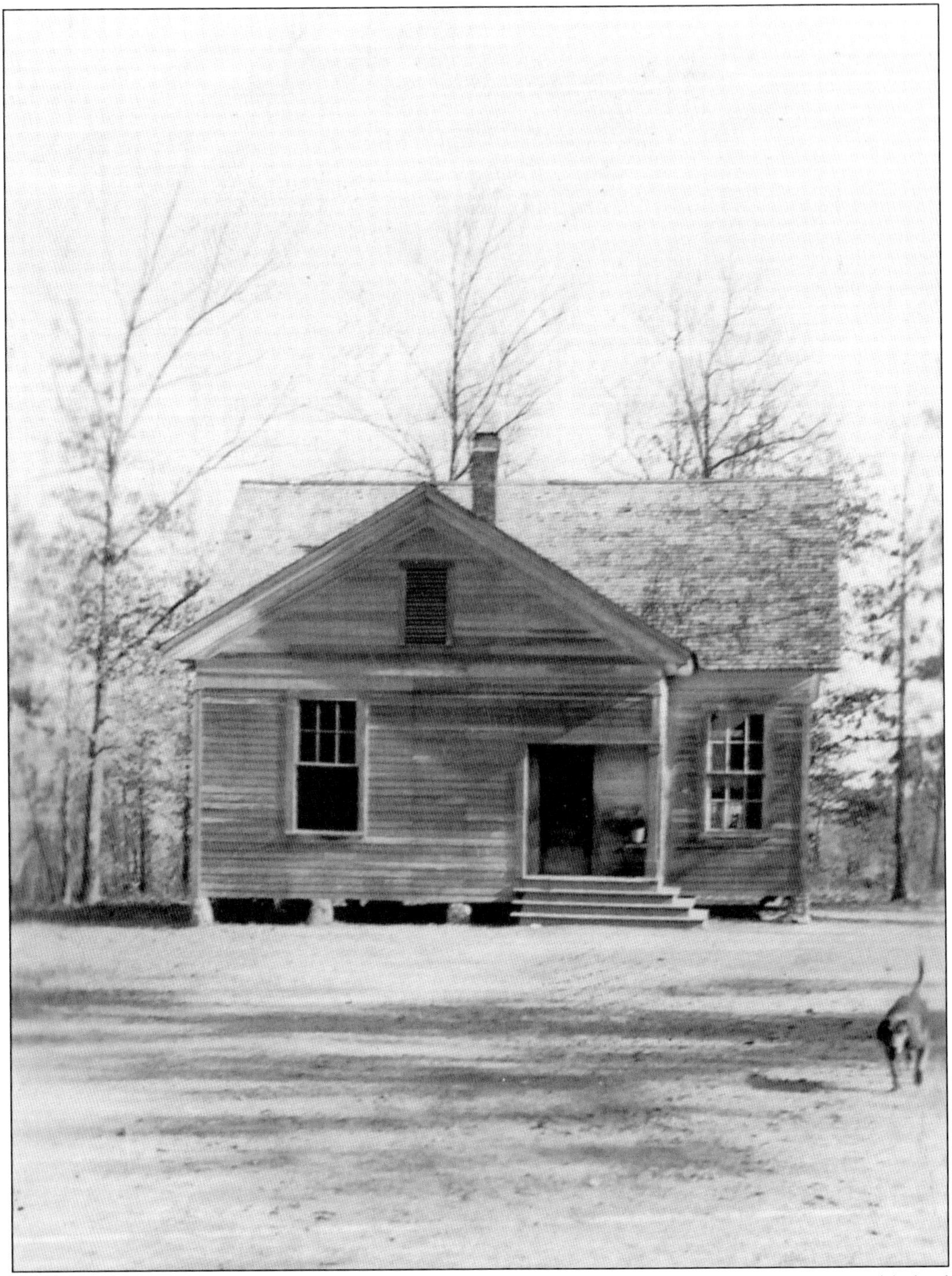

Lecta School. This school was located between Hopewell and Trickem and was established prior to 1904 with two teachers. Some of the teachers included Bela Fordham, Fay Lasseter, Lera Brown, Hobart Murphree, Louise Setzer, J. H. Hearn, Velma Hearn, J. A. McMahan, Paul Young, Mackie Smith, Fred Weir, Alma Stephens, Howard Cunningham, Beulah Mae Thrasher, Natye Watson, Jewell Brown, and William Gibbs. (Courtesy Carolyn Parker.)

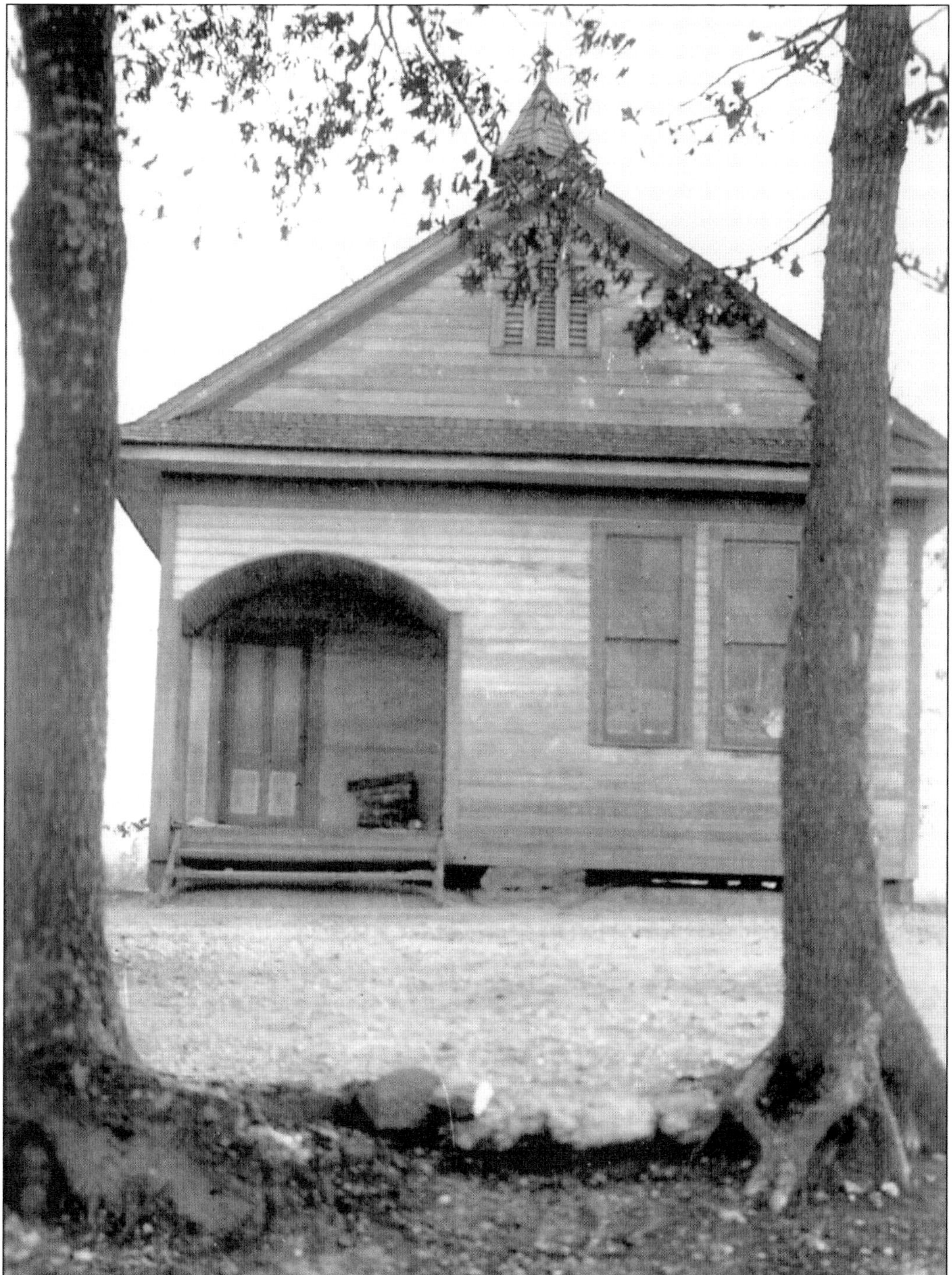

LIBERTY HILL SCHOOL. Located between Five Points and Chulafinnee on U.S. Highway 431, Liberty Hill School was established prior to 1904 and had grades one through eight. The school was sold at auction on October 19, 1942. W. J. Cole purchased the building for $180, and M. M. Rollins bought the land for $15. In 1918, Delia Morris was teaching 25 students. (Courtesy Carolyn Parker.)

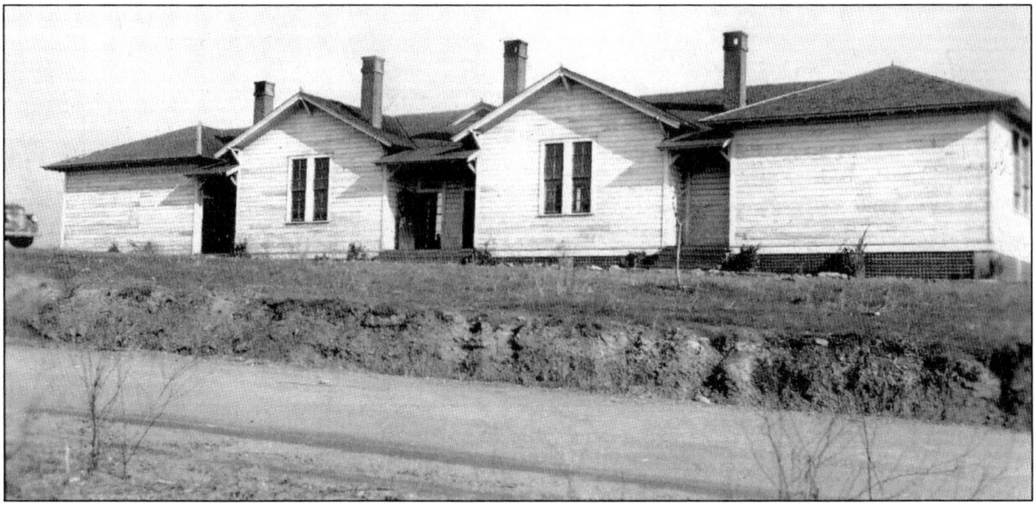

Muscadine School. Children in Muscadine had the opportunity to attend school at the one-room school near Muscadine Methodist Church. At one time, there were between 60 and 80 students in grades one through seven. Louise Jones Brown Allen was a teacher there. Students went on to Fruithurst when they finished the seventh grade. Later, Muscadine School dropped the seventh grade and taught grades one through six. (Courtesy Carolyn Parker.)

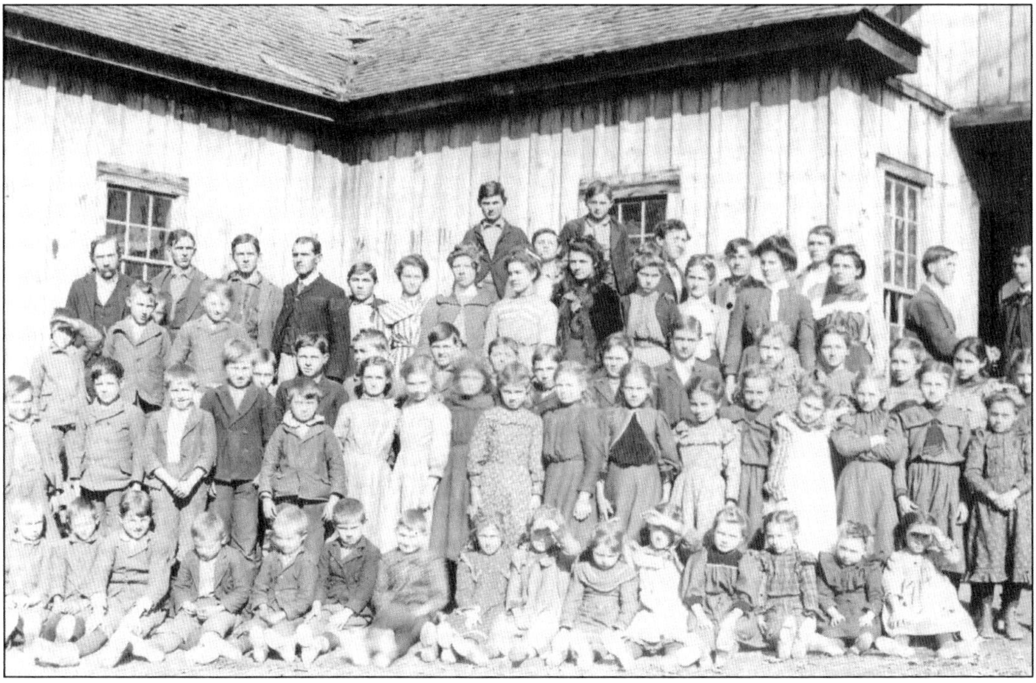

Oak Level School. This photograph of Oak Level School was taken in 1902. Francis Whited provided this photograph, and her father taught at the school. As early as 1860, there was a school known as Oak Level Academy. This 14-by-16-foot school was built prior to 1904 in northern Cleburne County. John Howell was the first teacher, and he taught children from four families, including his own. Over time, the school increased attendance, but in 1930, only grades one through six were taught, and junior high students were transported to Fruithurst. (Courtesy Francis Whited.)

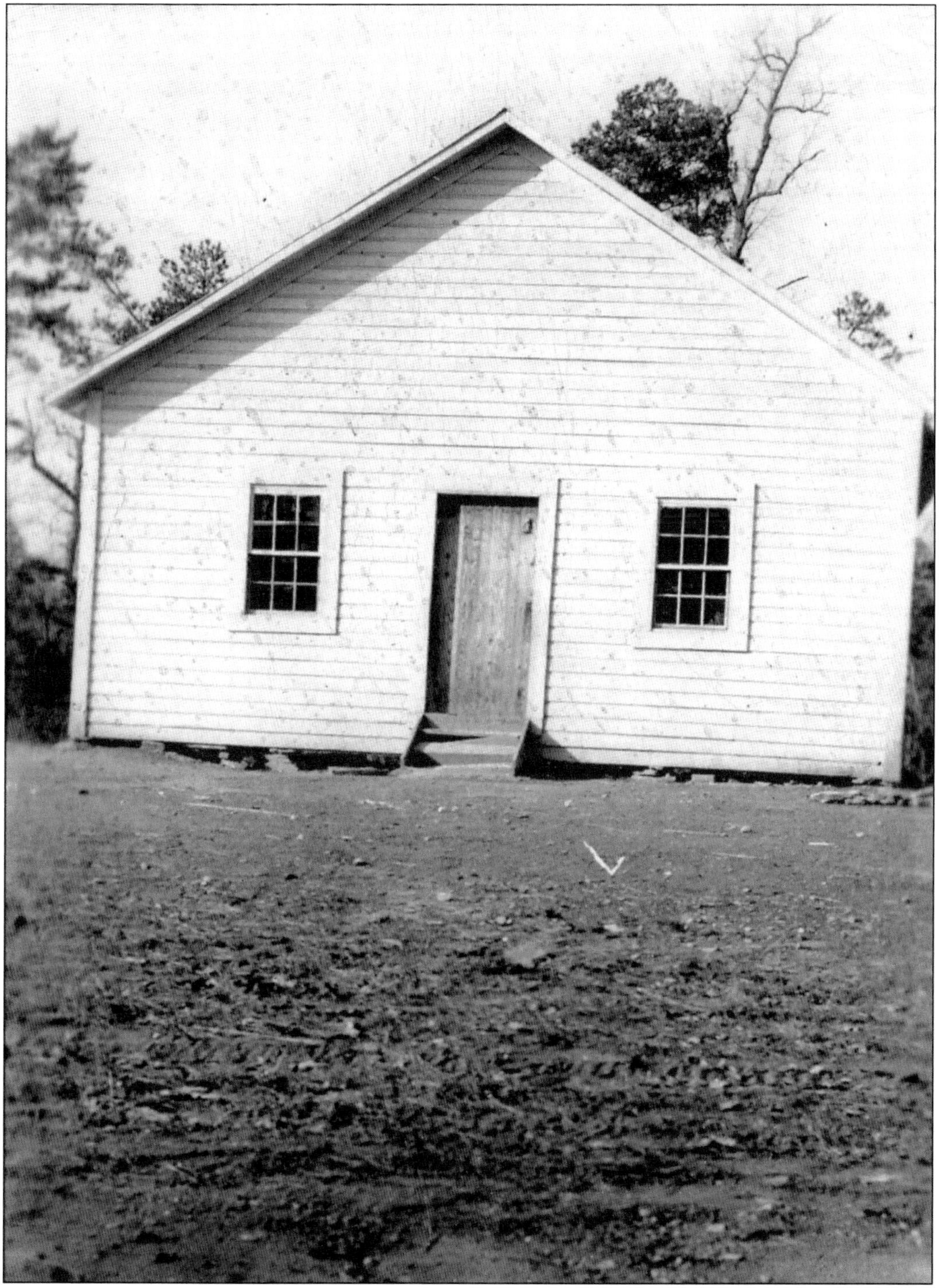

PILGRIM'S REST SCHOOL. This schoolhouse was built between 1904 and 1912 on Cleburne County Road 205 north of Oak Level. The school was closed on May 30, 1930, but because severe road conditions meant that students could not be transported easily, the school board voted to reopen it as a one-teacher school on July 22, 1933. It remained open until 1946. (Courtesy Carolyn Parker.)

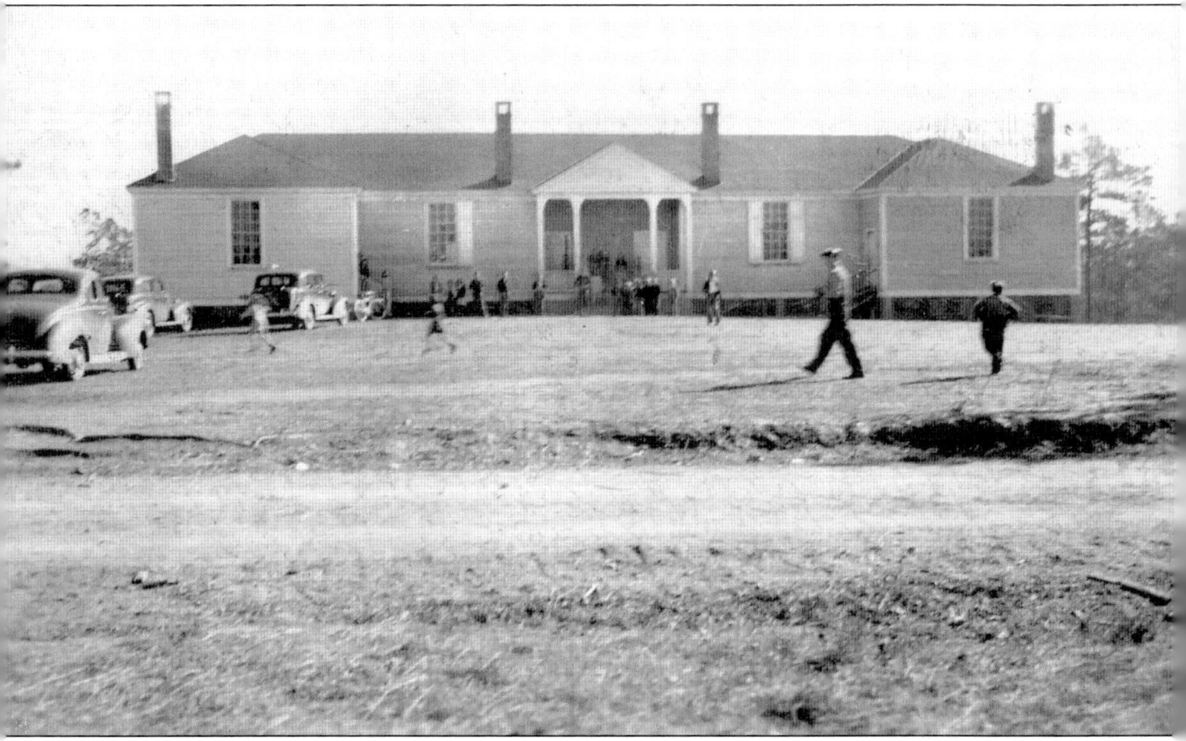

PINEY WOODS JUNIOR HIGH SCHOOL. Here is Piney Woods Junior High School as it appeared in the late 1940s. The original school was built in the Piney Woods community some time before 1912 and served grades one through six. Some of the early teachers were Genie Sanders, Ollie Cofield, Minnie Tweedell, Inez Millican, Clois Newell, Vivian Savage, Nettie Owen, Mildred Rhodes, and Iris Gardin. Between 1936 and 1938, Lovella Finnell taught primary classes, while Bennett Vaughn taught grades four through six. (Courtesy Carolyn Parker.)

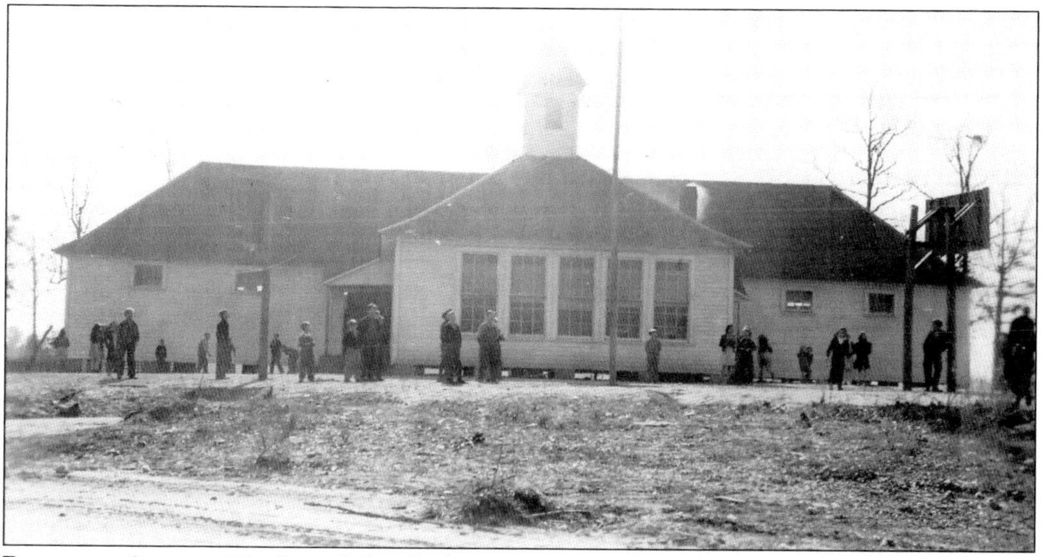

Plainview School. The Pounds family donated land for the first school, named Pounds School, and it served both as school and church until New Hope Church was built. In 1919, Pounds, Lebanon, and Abernathy schools were combined, and Vernor Harris was principal. In 1925, work began on a new school with three rooms, and a fourth was soon added. At that time, the name "Plainview" was chosen. (Courtesy Carolyn Parker.)

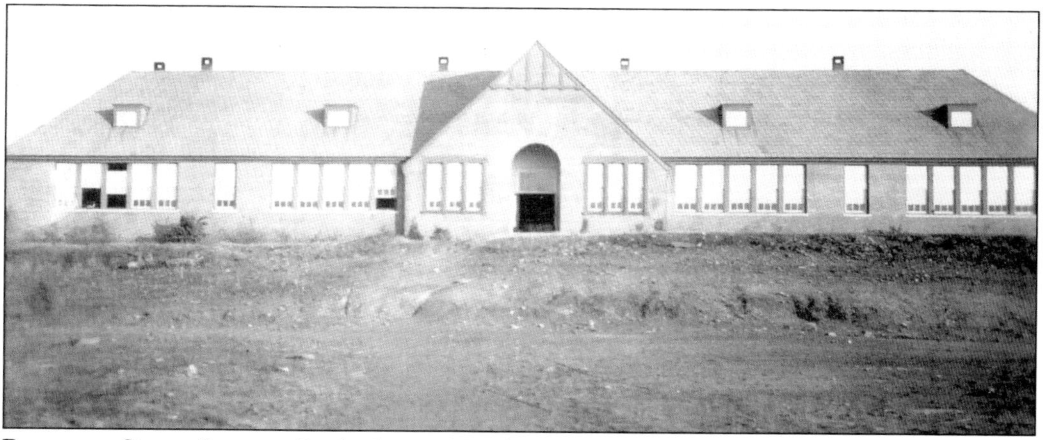

Pleasant Grove School. By the late 1800s, there were two one-room schools near Hollis—the Mulligan Chapel School and the Shady Grove School. In the early 1900s, the two schools merged, and a two-room school was built on the northwest corner of the intersection of U.S. Highway 431 and Alabama Highway 9. It was called Pleasant Grove School and was later moved to the northeast corner of the intersection. (Courtesy Carolyn Parker.)

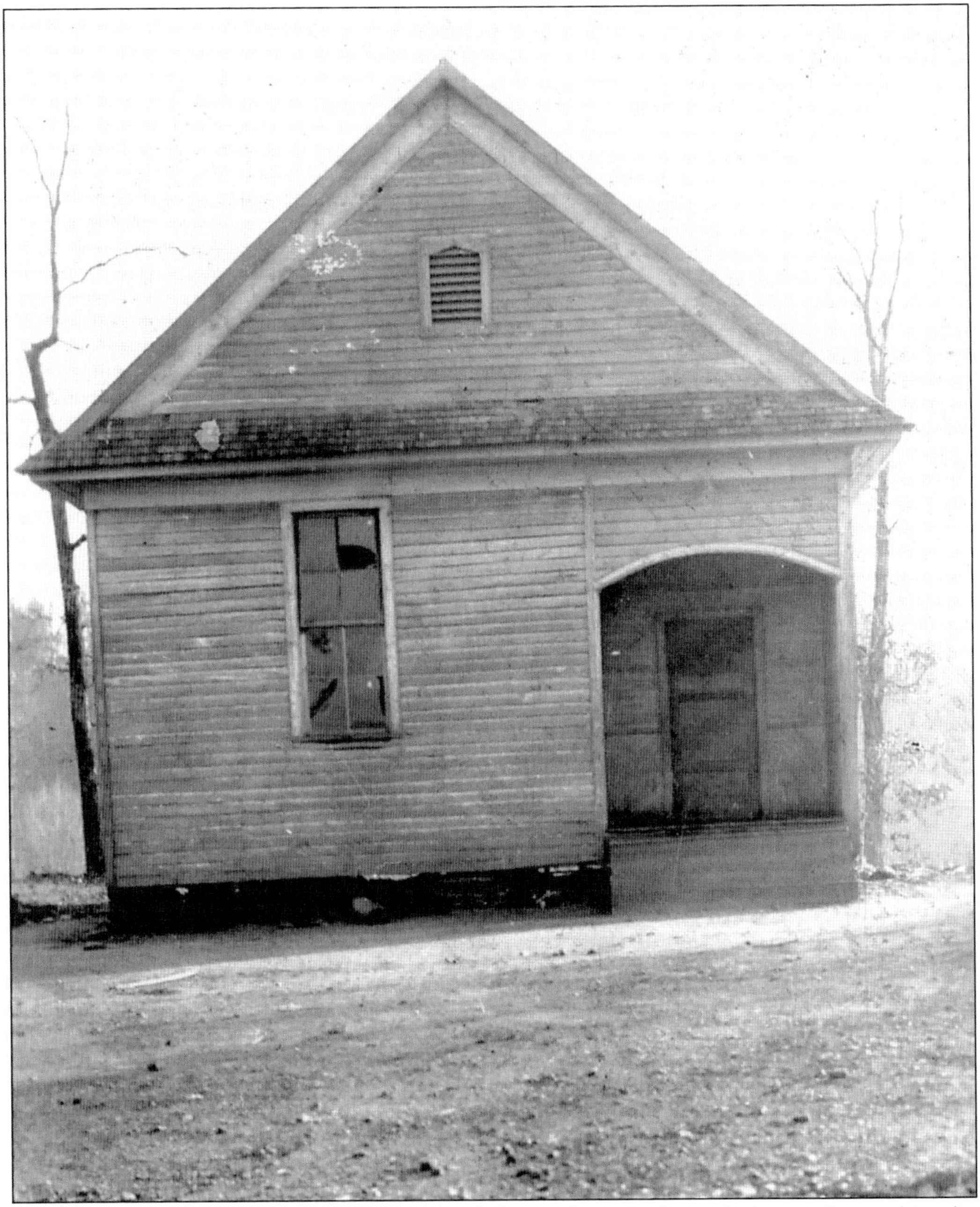

STONEHILL SCHOOL. This one-teacher school for grades one through six was located in the Redlands and Micaville area near the Cleburne/Randolph County line. Heflin resident A. J. Haley, age 80, wrote an article for the September 24, 1931, edition of the *Cleburne News* in which he recalled "In those days we had no schools, we had to work to make a living; all I learned was over a pine knot fire after a hard days work on the farm. In 1873, I entered what was then a high school. I spent seven months in that school. In 1874, I came to Wood's copper mines in Cleburne County. I worked at the mines until July 1, 1875, at 80¢ per day. I then took up an eight months' school at Stone Hill, and on October 14, 1875, I married the best woman in the world." (Courtesy Carolyn Parker.)

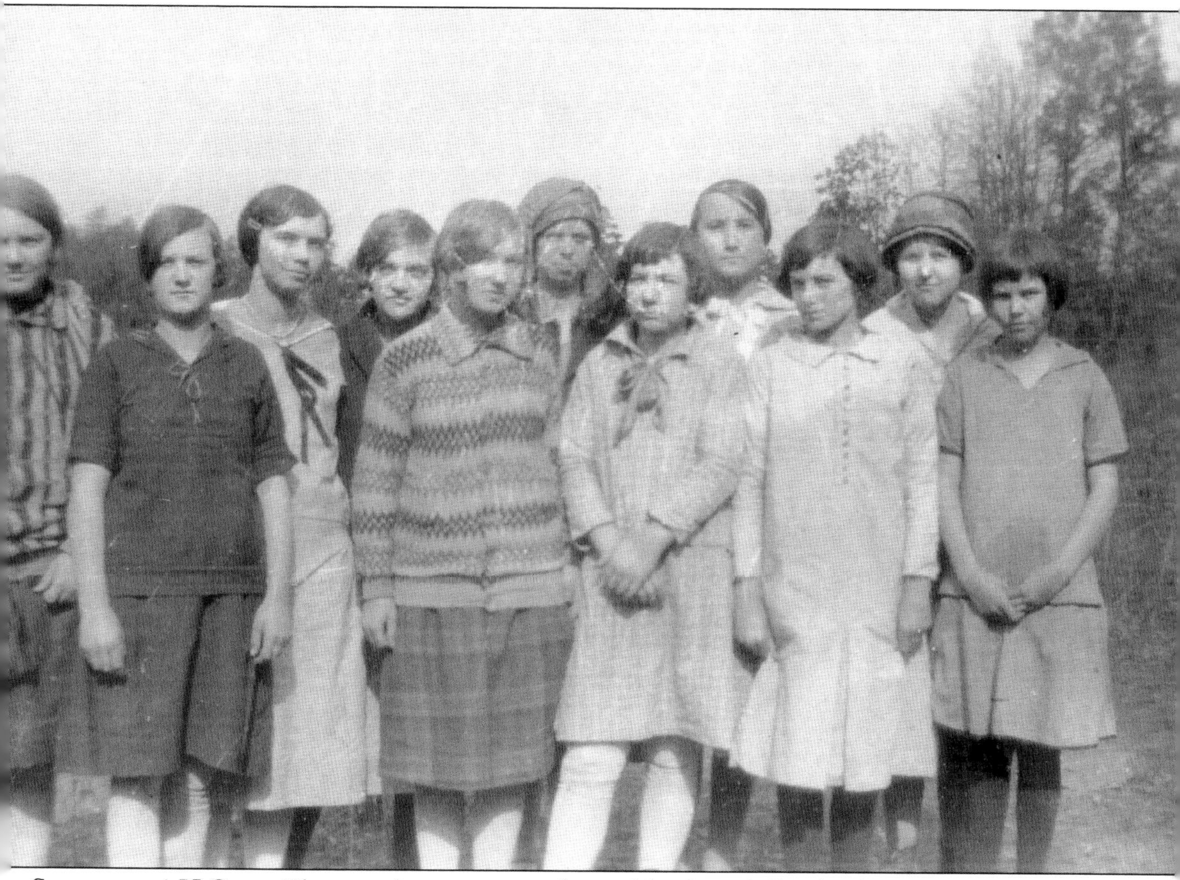

STONEHILL 4-H CLUB. These students were members of the Stonehill School 4-H Club. Among the teachers at Stonehill School were T. C. Holley, Delia Morris, Grace Brazeal, Velma Jones, Amos T. Williams, Ella Mae Warren, Gladys Kidd, Mackie Smith, Lucy Chase Williams, Lizzie Mae Merrill, I. V. Voss, and Mae Merrill Nelson. (Courtesy Cleburne County Extension Office.)

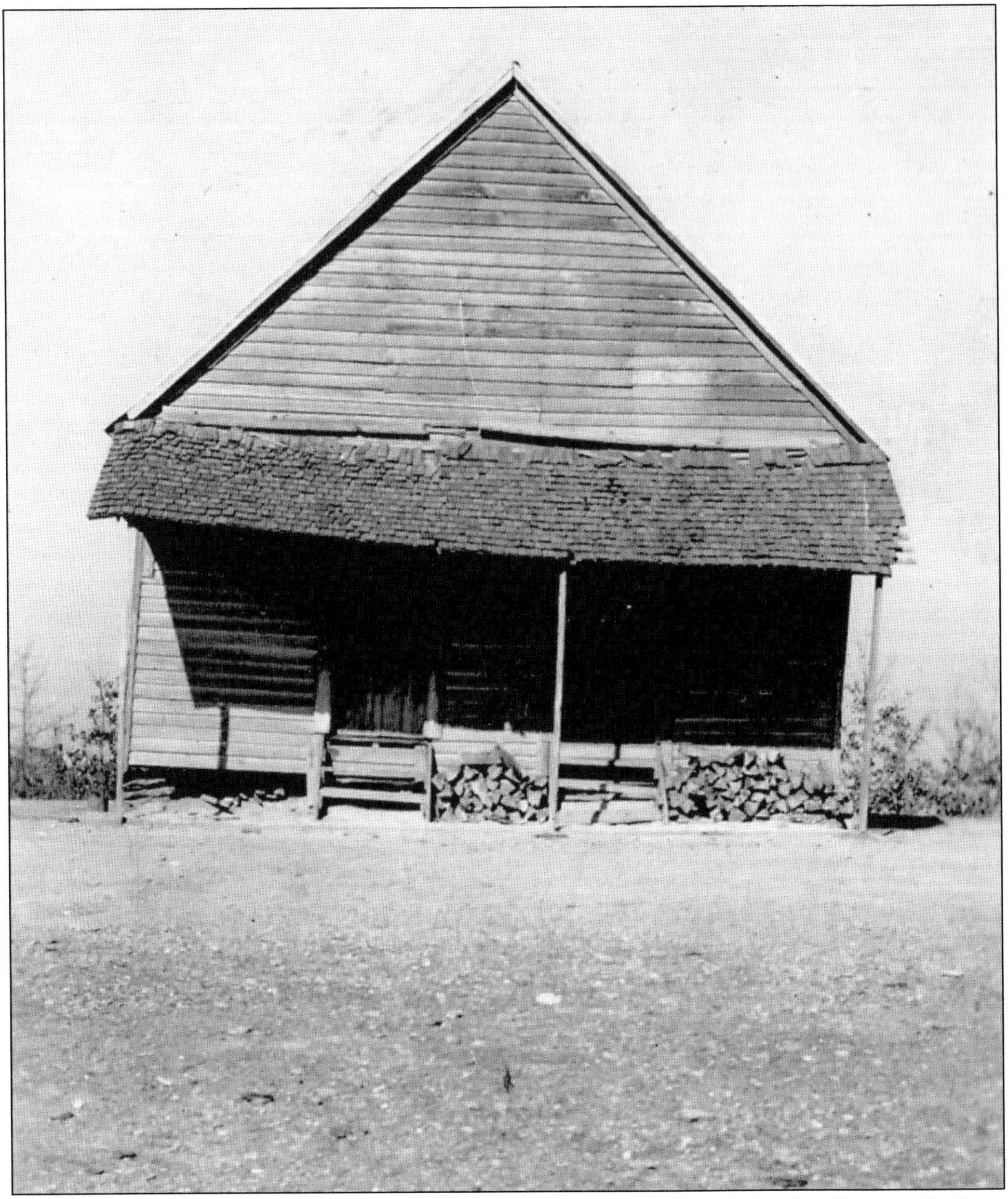

Trickem School. Trickem Valley had two schools—Upper Trickem School and Lower Trickem School. Teachers included Dessie Pounds, Albert Gibbs, ? Black, Elsie Stamps, and ? Heath. The classrooms were heated with a pot-bellied stove. The schools only went to the sixth and seventh grades. Students would then transfer to Ranburne School. (Courtesy Carolyn Parker.)

ARMSTRONG SCHOOL. Armstrong School was located in the Hightower community. Early teachers included Sam Young, Clara Vaughn, and Eva Riddle Bain. Like many schools in Cleburne County, Armstrong School was later closed, and the students were bused to larger schools in the county. Cleburne County now has two high schools, a middle school, and four elementary schools. (Courtesy Carolyn Parker.)

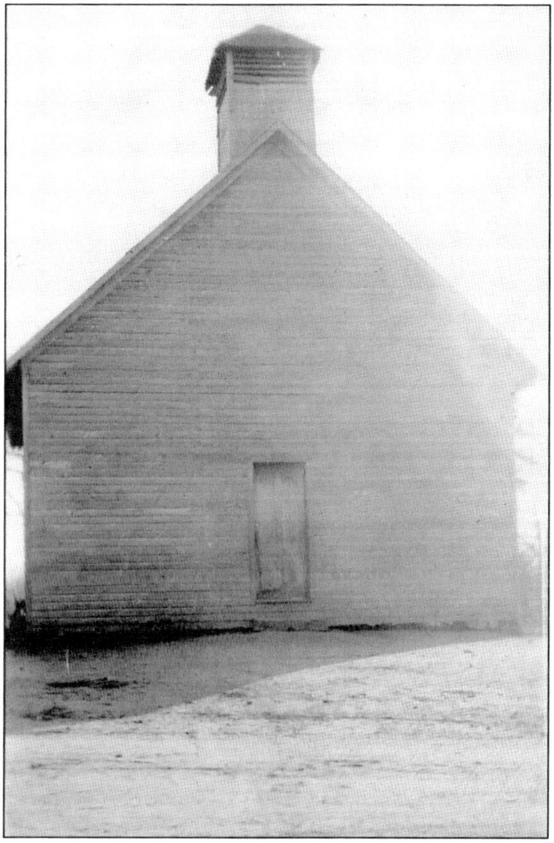

VICTORY SCHOOL. This one-room school was built after 1916 due to over-enrollment at Bell's Mill School. Irene Wood was hired in 1917 to teach grades one through nine. Children walked to and from school from 2 miles away. During the winter, parents donated wood for the heating stove, and the boys would arrive early to build the fire. The school was consolidated with Heflin Elementary School in 1935. (Courtesy Carolyn Parker.)

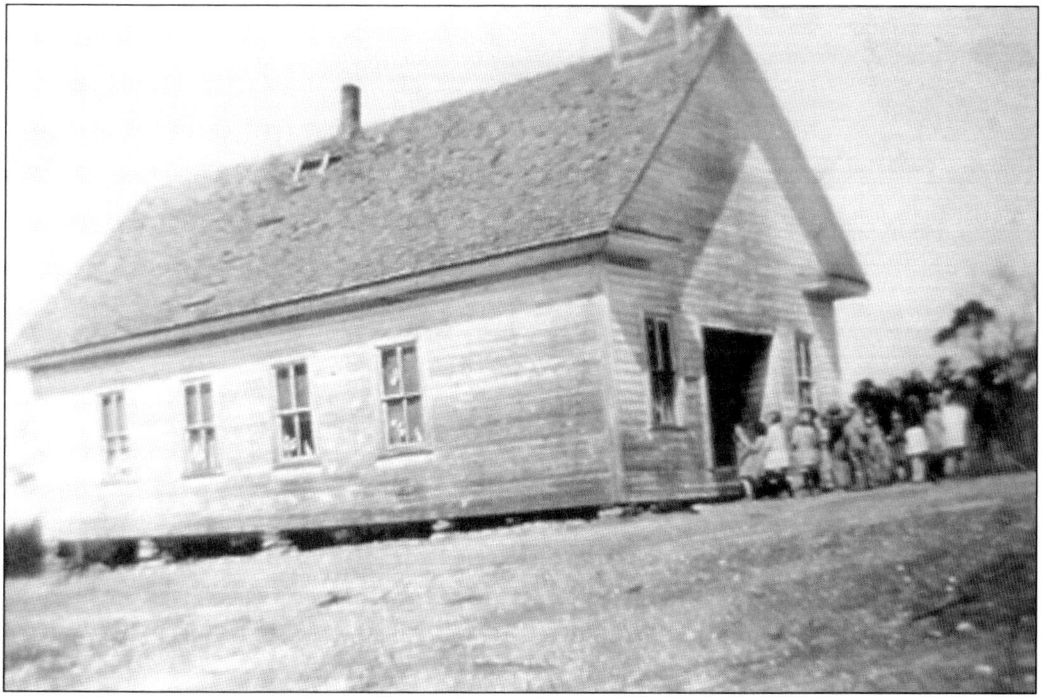

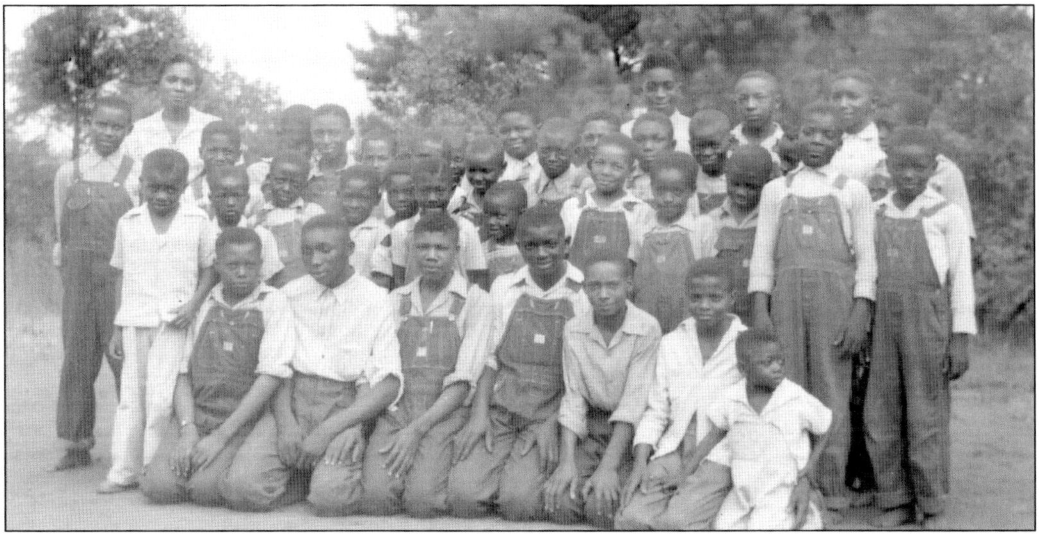

Young Future Farmers. This was a gathering of the Pleasant Grove School Future Farmers of America club around 1944. Those identified are: (kneeling) J. B. Akles (third from left), Elbert Cooley, Clifford Stephens, and Yulas Johnson (second from right); (standing) Rosetta Chatman (second from left) and Otis Cooley (third from right). (Courtesy Cleburne County Extension Office.)

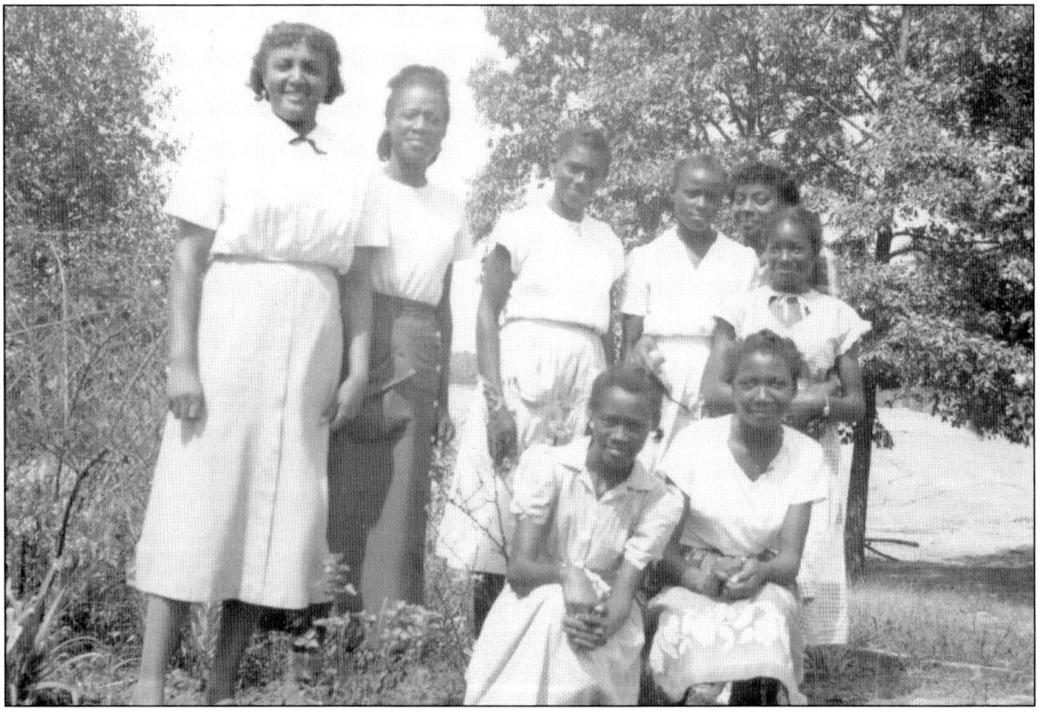

Practical Skills. These girls were students at the Heflin Training School around 1950 and participated in Future Homemakers of America. Seen here from left to right, they included (kneeling) Sarah Johnson and Bessie Lee Stockdale; (standing) teacher Francis Weatherly, unidentified, Constance Freeman (a 1952 graduate), Katie Edge, Annie Dobbins, and Bronzel Cooley. (Courtesy Cleburne County Extension Office.)

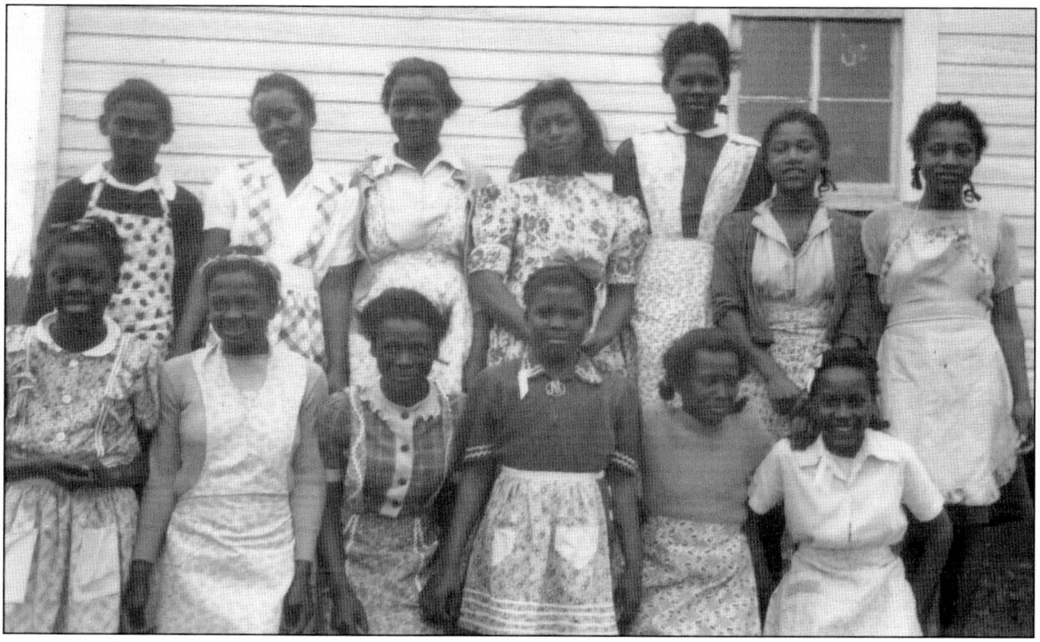

ATTEND TRAINING SCHOOL. These students attended the Heflin Training School some time in the 1940s. Seen here from left to right are (first row) three unidentified, Margie Townes, and two unidentified; (second row) Constance Freeman, two unidentified, Ester Phillips, and three unidentified. The school was located in the predominately black section of town. The facility has been renovated, and it is now a cultural arts center. (Courtesy Cleburne County Extension Office.)

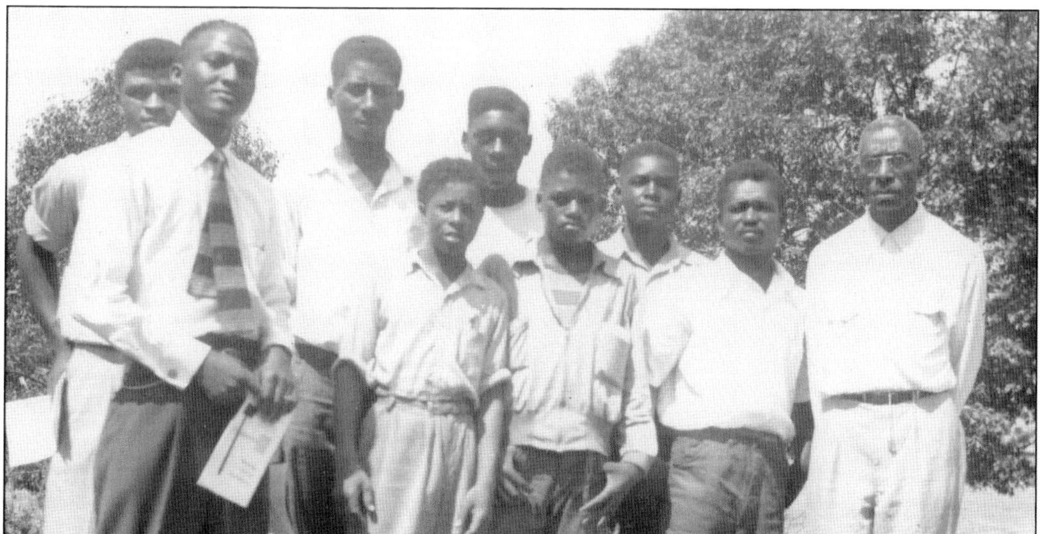

HEFLIN TRAINING SCHOOL STUDENTS. These young students attended the Heflin Training School around 1950. From left to right, they are Charles Freeman, Clarence Wilson, Claude Johnson, Gary Blalock, Bobby Hayes, Ray Ervin, Lee Drummond, J. B. Phillips, and professor and principal J. H. Gaines. When Cleburne County schools were integrated, students attending the Heflin Training School started going to Cleburne County High and Cleburne County Elementary. (Courtesy Cleburne County Extension Office.)

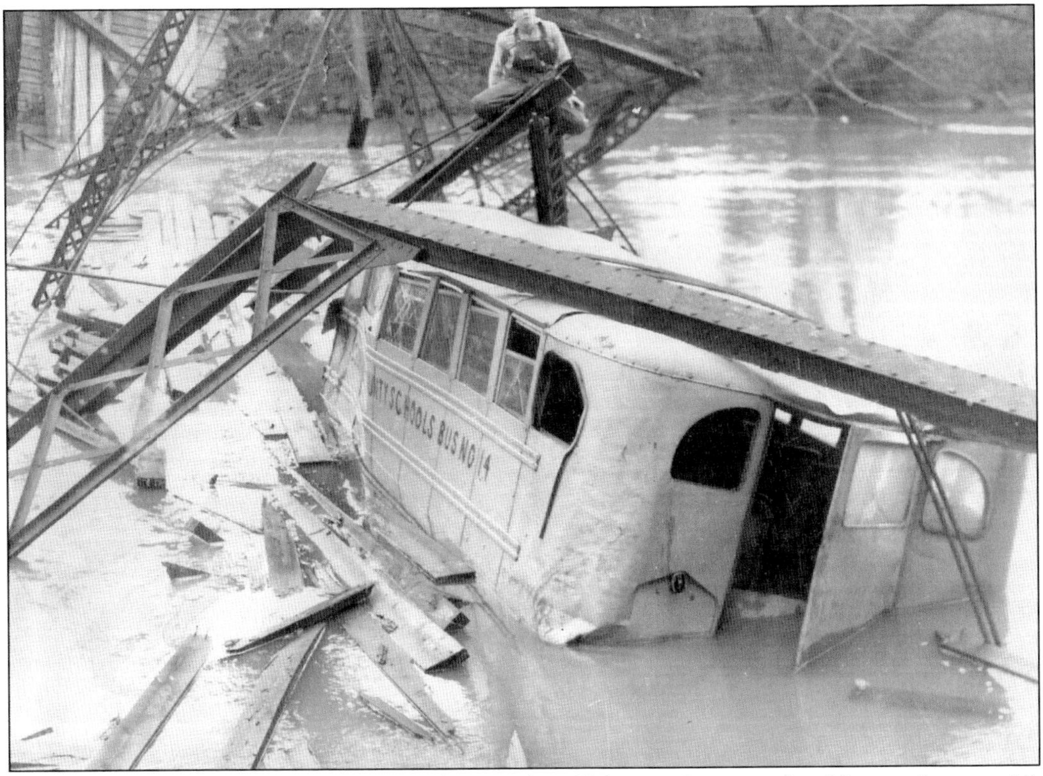

Bridge Collapse. Virgil Lumpkin was driving this Cleburne County school bus on January 16, 1950, when the bridge across the Tallapoosa River on Evans Bridge Road collapsed. There were 22 students on board, but no one was injured. Royce Benefield, seen sitting atop the bus, helped rescue the passengers. (Courtesy Johnny Laminack.)

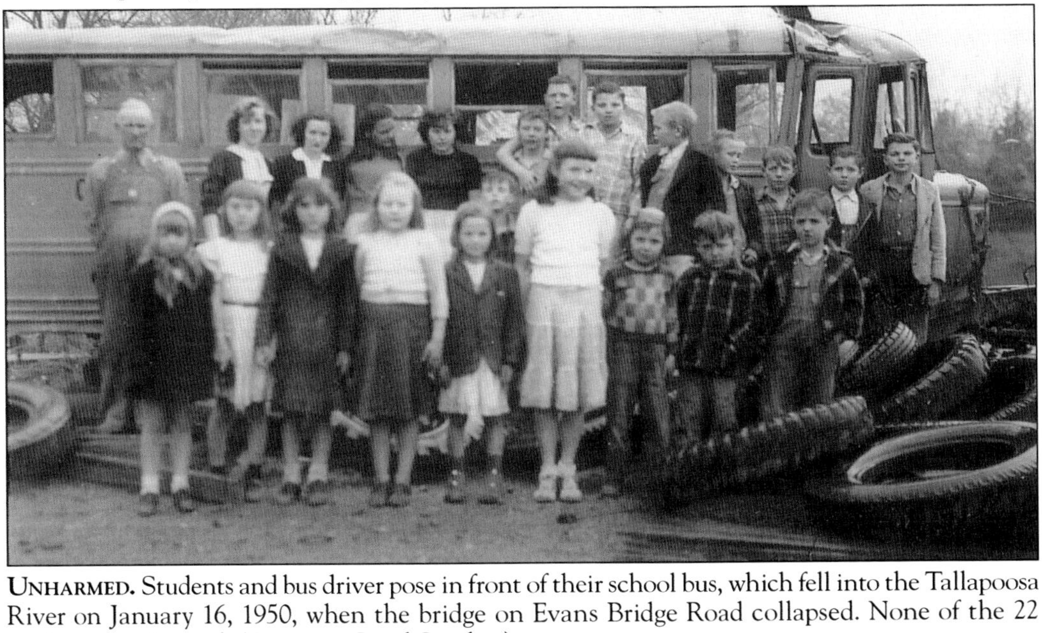

Unharmed. Students and bus driver pose in front of their school bus, which fell into the Tallapoosa River on January 16, 1950, when the bridge on Evans Bridge Road collapsed. None of the 22 students was injured. (Courtesy Carol Sanders)

Seven

CHURCHES
AN INTEGRAL PART OF COMMUNITIES

Ever since the first settlers arrived in what would become Cleburne County, churches have been an integral part of the lives of local residents. Many times, the church building would also serve as a community hall and became the physical center not only of people's spiritual lives but of their social lives as well. Some early churches also served as school buildings, giving the buildings a third purpose in the community. The first churches were simple, one-room structures, and many small congregations first met in members' homes, in schoolhouses, or under a brush arbor before they ever erected a church building. Brush arbors consisted mostly of limbs and brush scattered over a frame to create something like a roof for worshippers.

At one time, Cleburne County was home to as many as 75 churches. Many of these continue to serve county residents today: Cane Creek Primitive Baptist Church, Cherry Grove Church and School, Chulafinnee Baptist, Chulafinnee United Methodist, Church of the Messiah (Episcopal), Concord Baptist, Cedar Creek Baptist, Corinth Primitive Baptist, Crumley's Chapel Church of God, East Heflin Baptist, Edwardsville Baptist, Edwardsville United Methodist, Freedom Baptist, Fruithurst Missionary Baptist, Fruithurst United Methodist, Green's Chapel United Methodist, Happy Hill Missionary Baptist, Harmony Grove Baptist Church and Cemetery, Harmony Primitive Baptist, Heflin Baptist, Heflin Church of God, First United Methodist of Heflin, Hepsabah Baptist, Hillcrest Independent Mission, Hurricane Methodist Episcopal Church, the Lebanon Congregational Methodist Church and Lebanon School, Lecta United Methodist, Liberty Hill Congregational Methodist Church, Lighthouse Baptist, Macedonia Missionary Baptist, Mars Hill Primitive Baptist, Mount Carmel Methodist Episcopal Church South, Mount Olive Baptist, Mount Olive Church of God, Mount Paran Baptist, Mountain View Baptist, Muscadine Baptist, Camp Ground United Methodist Church, New Harmony Baptist, New Hope Methodist Episcopal Church South, New Hopewell Missionary Baptist, New Zion Baptist Church of Heflin, Oak Grove Baptist Church and School, Oak Level Methodist, Old Hopewell Baptist, Pilgrim's Rest Baptist Church No. 1, Pine Grove Baptist, Pinetucky Baptist, Pleasant Hill Baptist, First Baptist Church Ranburne, Rock Springs Baptist, St. Michael's Lutheran Church, Shoal Creek Church, State Line Primitive Baptist, Union Hill Baptist, Upper Cane Creek Southern Congregational Methodist Church, Verdon's Chapel Baptist, Vise Grove Baptist, Wise Chapel United Methodist, and the Born Again Apostolic Church.

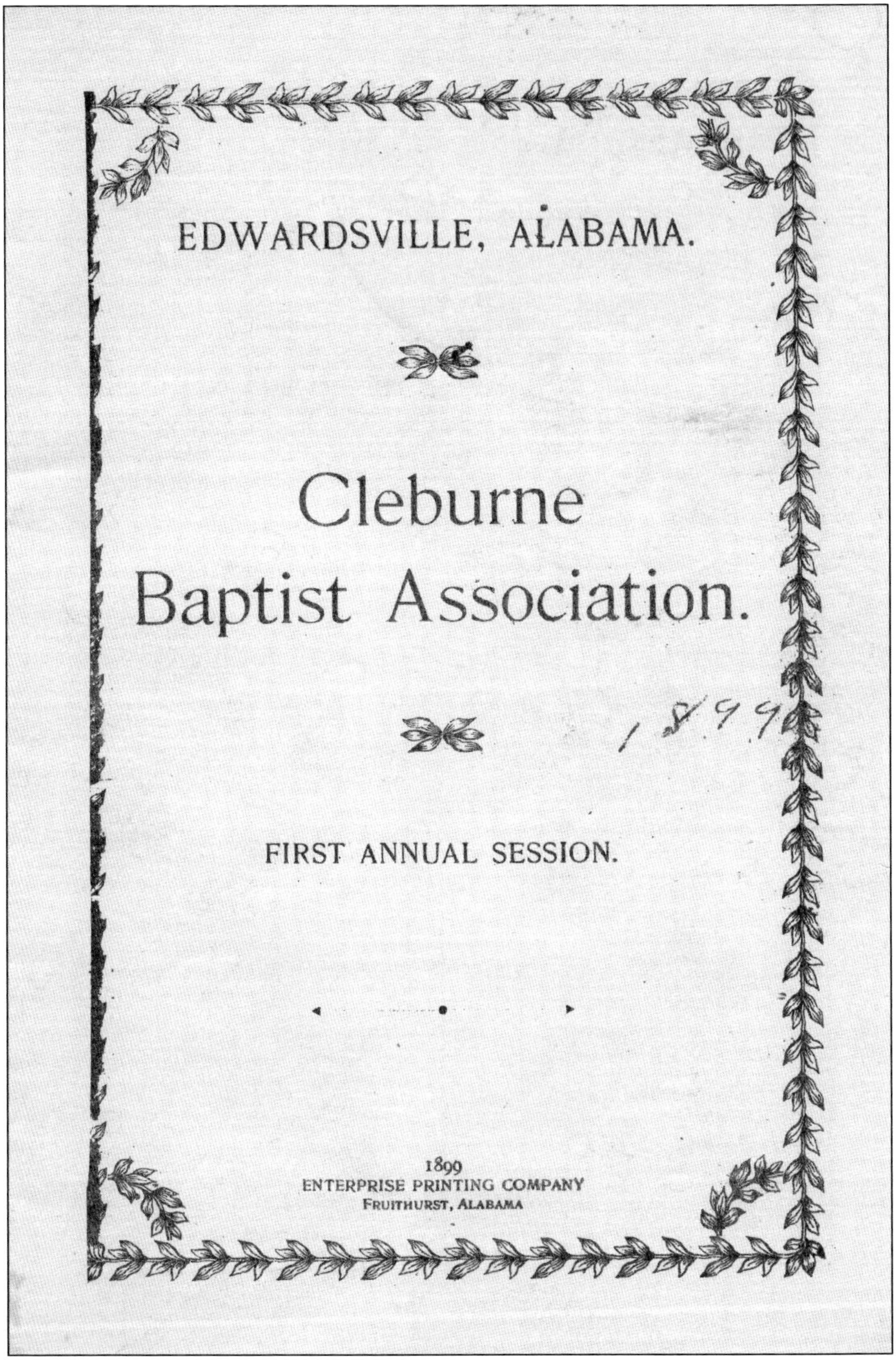

EDWARDSVILLE, ALABAMA.

Cleburne
Baptist Association.

FIRST ANNUAL SESSION.

1899
ENTERPRISE PRINTING COMPANY
FRUITHURST, ALABAMA

ASSOCIATION SESSION PROGRAM. The Cleburne Baptist Association held its first annual session in 1899 in Edwardsville. The Baptists used Enterprise Printing Company in Fruithurst to print their material. From this early beginning, the Cleburne Baptist Association now has 36 churches in the association, and its main office is located on Ross Street in downtown Heflin. (Courtesy Charlotte Funderburk.)

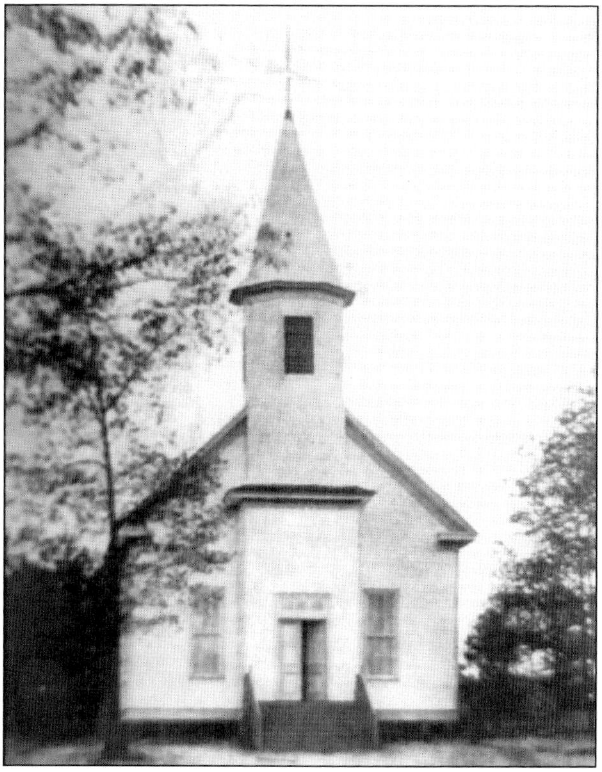

Baptist Rebuild. Following a fire in 1904, the Baptists rebuilt, and the two front doors were combined into one main entrance. (Courtesy Lucile Morgan Public Library.)

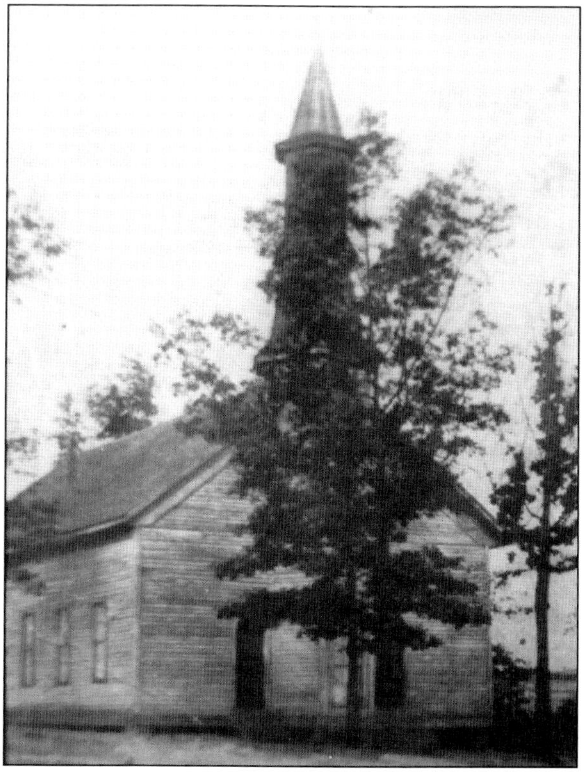

Heflin Baptist Church. This is believed to be an early photograph of the Heflin Baptist Church, built in 1882. The photograph was taken in 1916 and shows two doors, one for the men and the other for the women. (Courtesy Lucile Morgan Public Library.)

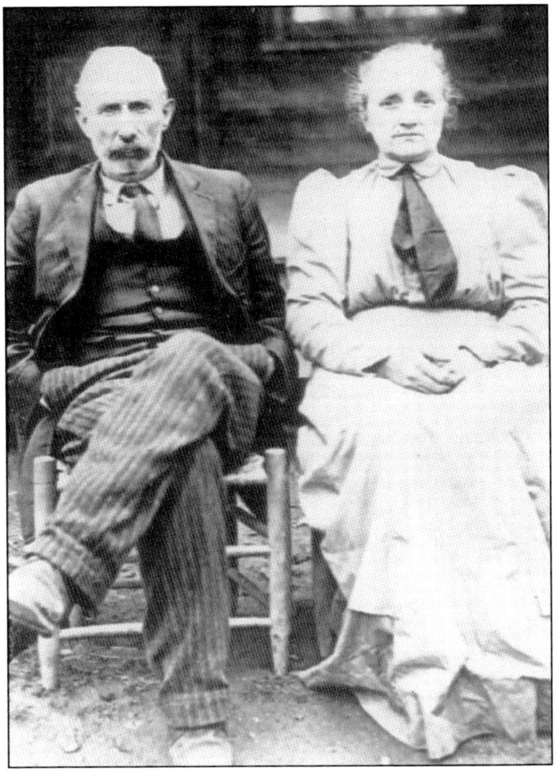

METHODIST DEACON. John Stephen Edwards (1859–1926) was the son of Josiah Edwards, an early settler of Cleburne County (known then as Benton County). Edwards was a farmer, Master Mason, and deacon at Upper Cane Creek Methodist Church. His wife, Sarah, died in 1954 at the age of 88. She left 137 direct descendants and worked on the family farm up until four years before her death. (Courtesy East Alabama History Museum.)

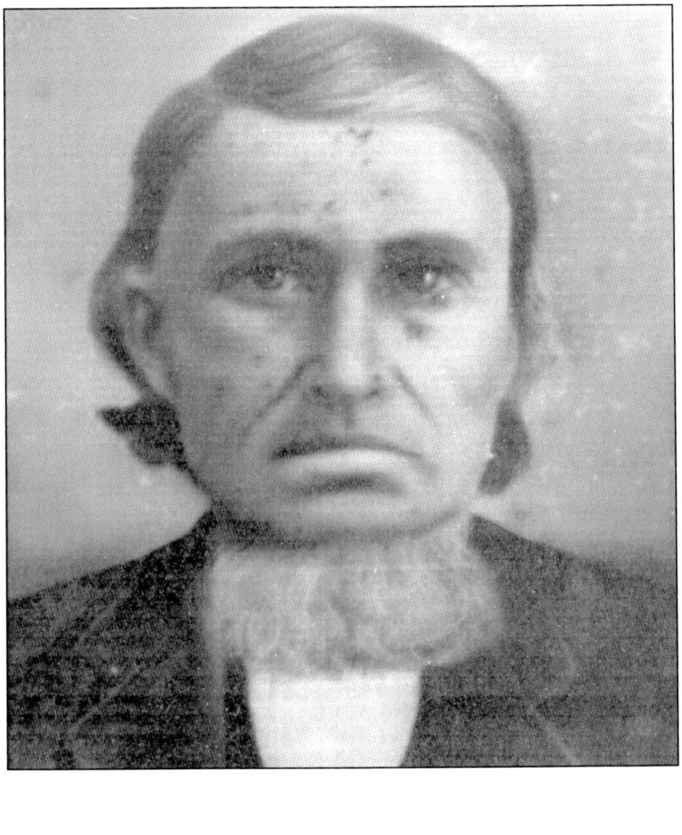

CIRCUIT RIDER. Richardson Chandler Jr. (1818–1905) was a Primitive Baptist circuit rider and one of the early residents of Benton County (later to become Cleburne). He ministered to congregations at Cane Creek Baptist and Harmony Baptist, and served other area churches in the mid- to late 1800s. His wife, Dicey, was a member of the family that helped found Edwardsville. (Courtesy East Alabama History Museum.)

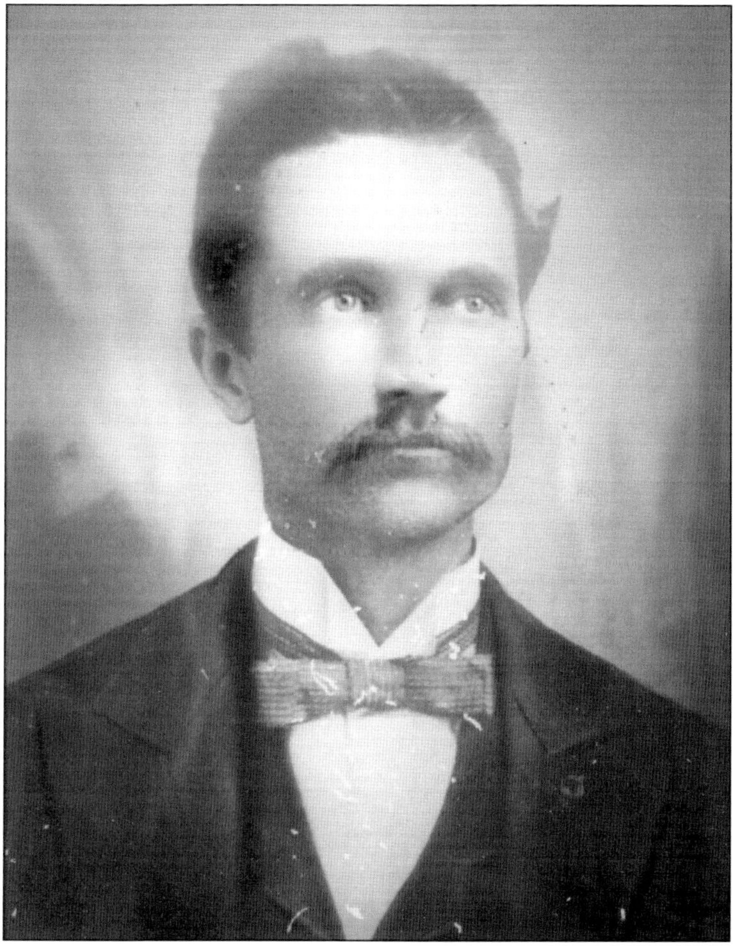

METHODIST PREACHER. William Riley Patty (1863–1913) was a well-known Methodist minister. He preached many sermons at Upper Cane Creek Church. Reverend Patty suffered from arthritis late in life and went to Hot Springs, Arkansas, for treatments. The hotel he was staying in caught fire, and he escaped but became ill with pneumonia. He died shortly thereafter. (Courtesy East Alabama History Museum.)

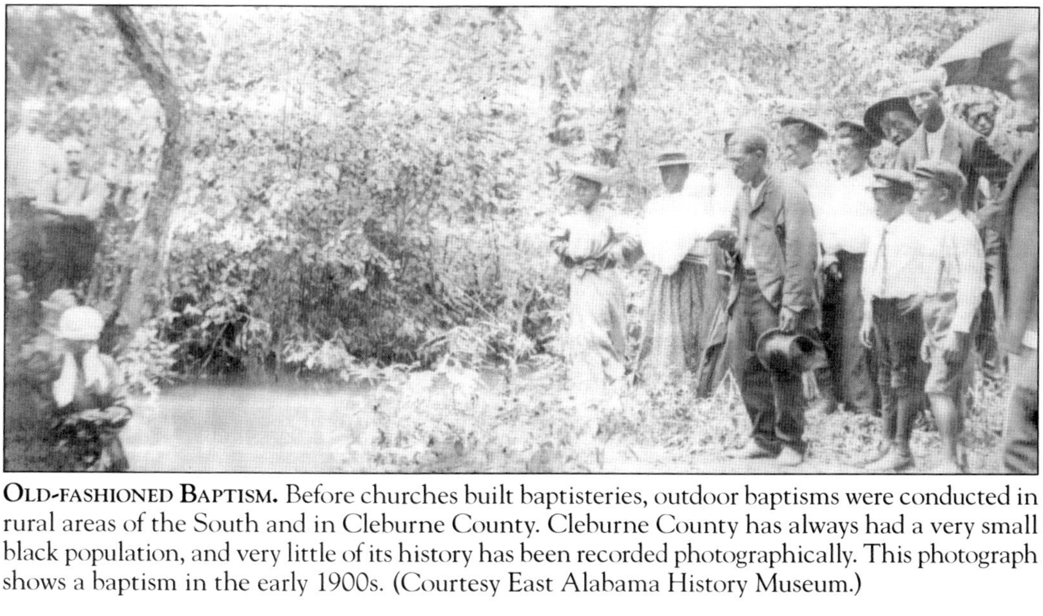

OLD-FASHIONED BAPTISM. Before churches built baptisteries, outdoor baptisms were conducted in rural areas of the South and in Cleburne County. Cleburne County has always had a very small black population, and very little of its history has been recorded photographically. This photograph shows a baptism in the early 1900s. (Courtesy East Alabama History Museum.)

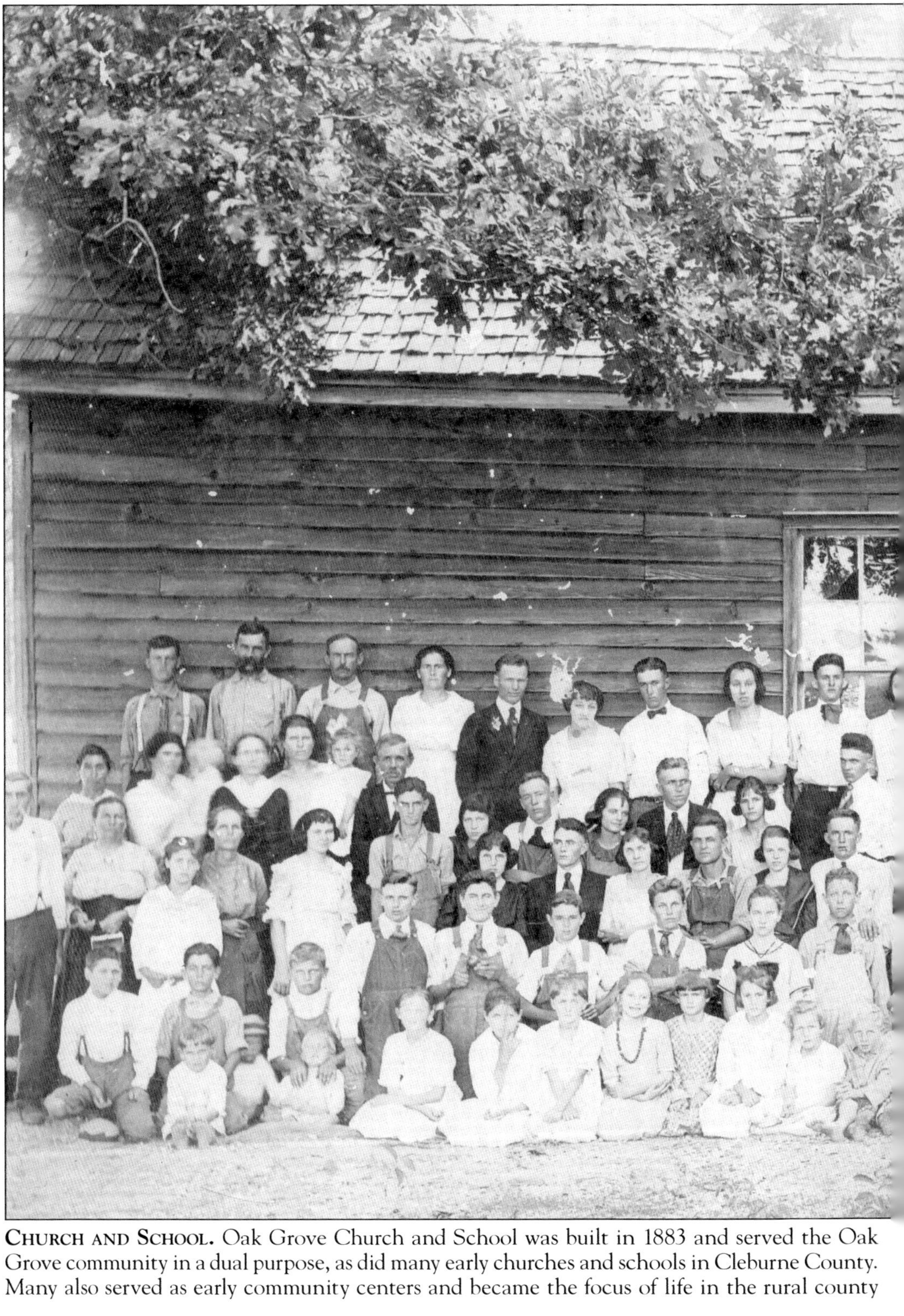

CHURCH AND SCHOOL. Oak Grove Church and School was built in 1883 and served the Oak Grove community in a dual purpose, as did many early churches and schools in Cleburne County. Many also served as early community centers and became the focus of life in the rural county

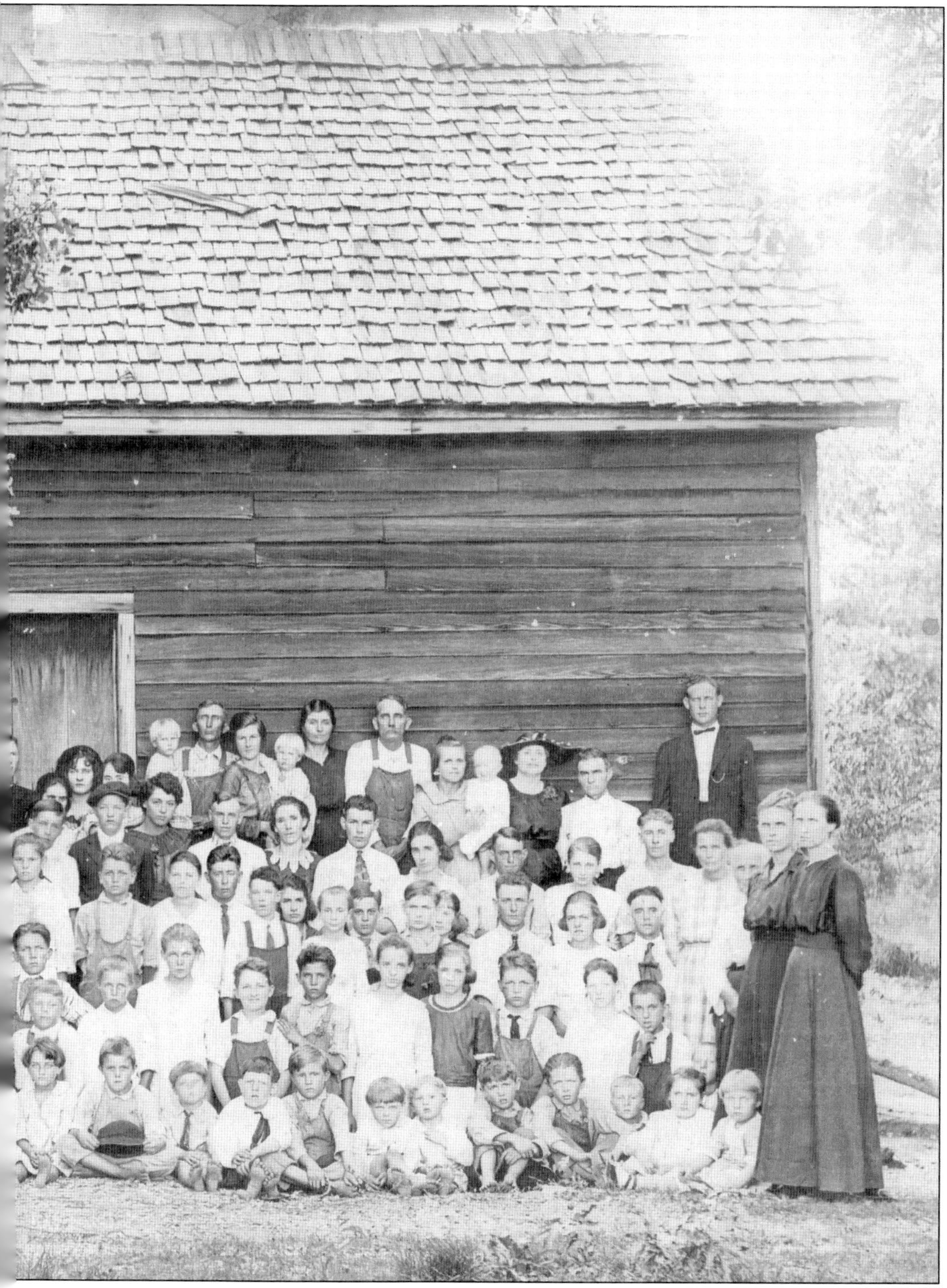

areas. As the county progressed, more schools were built. This photograph was taken in the late 1800s. (Courtesy Vertie Walker.)